BROCCOLI AND DESIRE

EDWARD F. FISCHER

PETER BENSON

Broccoli and Desire

*Global Connections and Maya Struggles
in Postwar Guatemala*

STANFORD UNIVERSITY PRESS

STANFORD, CALIFORNIA 2006

Stanford University Press
Stanford, California

Printed in the United States of America on acid-free,
archival-quality paper

Library of Congress Cataloging-in-Publication Data
Fischer, Edward F., 1966–
   Broccoli and desire : global connections and Maya
struggles in post-war Guatemala / Edward F. Fischer,
Peter Benson.
      p.   cm.
   Includes bibliographical references and index.
   ISBN-13: 978-0-8047-5404-0 (cloth : alk. paper)
   ISBN-10: 0-8047-5404-7 (cloth : alk. paper)
   ISBN-13: 978-0-8047-5484-2 (pbk. : alk. paper)
   ISBN-10: 0-8047-5484-5 (pbk. : alk. paper)
      1. Cakchikel Indians — Guatemala — Tecpán
Guatemala — Social conditions.   2. Cakchikel Indians —
Guatemala — Tecpán Guatemala — Economic conditions.
3. Cakchikel Indians — Wars — Guatemala — Tecpán
Guatemala.   4. Economic development — Guatemala —
Tecpán Guatemala.   5. Agricultural development
projects — Guatemala — Tecpán Guatemala.   6. Offshore
assembly industry — Guatemala — Tecpán Guatemala.
7. Political violence — Guatemala — Tecpán Guatemaal.
8. Tecpán Guatemala (Guatemala) — Social conditions.
9. Tecpán Guatemala (Guatemala) — Economic conditions.
10. Tecpán Guatemala (Guatemala) — Politics and
Government.   11. Guatemala — History — Civil War,
1960–1996.   I. Benson, Peter (Peter Blair).   II. Title.

F1465.2.C3F57   2006
972.81'6100497422 — dc22   2006005157

Typeset by BookMatters in 10/14 Janson

Wealth is not the accidental object of a morbid desire,
but the constant object of a legitimate one.
—JOHN RUSKIN, *Munera Pulveris*

What is desirable depends upon valuations that are not
universally accepted.
—FRANZ BOAS, *Anthropology and Modern Life*

Contents

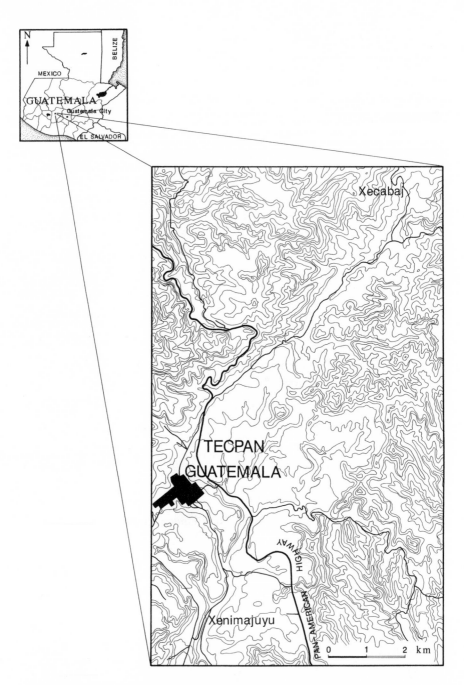

Map of Tecpán and Guatemala. Drawing by Luis Fernando Luin.

Guatemala Index

Guatemala's 2001 gross national product as a proportion of Bill Gates's net worth:
> 33 percent

Range of estimates of Guatemalans living below the poverty line:
44–80 percent

Range of estimates of the relative size of Guatemala's Maya population:
40–60 percent

Rank of Guatemala in the UNDP's Human Development Index,
out of 177 countries*:
121

Rank of Guatemala in Transparency International's
Global Corruption Barometer, out of 145 countries:
122

Exchange rate of Guatemalan quetzales to U.S. dollars in 1982:
1:1

Exchange rate of Guatemalan quetzales to U.S. dollars in 2002:
7.8:1

Guatemala's official top three exports:
coffee, sugar, bananas

Guatemala's probable top three foreign-currency earners:
foreign remittances, tourism, drug trafficking

---

*The Human Development Index (HDI) is used by the United Nation Development Pro-gramme to rank countries based on a combination of factors, including not only gross domestic product but also indicators of health and education. The figures here come from the 2004 report, available online at http://hdr.undp.org/reports/global/2004/.

Land area of Guatemala in proportion to the size of Tennessee:
99.8 percent

Size of Guatemala's population in relation to Tennessee's:
215 percent

Preferred academic term for Guatemala's
Spanish-speaking, non-Indian population:
ladino

Term of self-reference for Guatemala's ladino population:
Guatemalan

Ethnonyms preferred by Guatemala's Indian population:
Maya, indígena, natural[†]

Number of Mayan languages spoken in Guatemala:
22

Pronunciation of "x" in Kaqchikel Maya:
like an "sh" in English

How to pronounce the Maya glottal stop ('):
constrict your throat muscles to briefly close off all air

How to pronounce (q'):
try swallowing the back of your tongue and pronouncing an English "q" sound

Top suppliers of U.S. broccoli imports:
Mexico, Guatemala, Canada

Top recipients of U.S. broccoli exports:
Japan, Canada, Taiwan

[†]In this book we refer to Guatemala's native population as Maya, indigenous, or Indian. We use the term "Indian" as a salient English translation of *indígena* and not as a gloss of the pejorative *indio*.

BROCCOLI AND DESIRE

Introduction

Susan, a single, thirty-two-year-old nurse in Nashville, Tennessee, walks through the produce aisles of her neighborhood Kroger supermarket, examining the fruits and vegetables as she decides on her meals for the next few days. When she first enters the store, Susan breezes past the produce, picking up milk (low-fat, organic), cereal, and a few Lean Cuisine™ frozen dinners before returning for a more leisurely stroll through the rich colors and aromatic smells of what she considers to be the "real food." Susan is not a vegetarian, but she explains that she often cooks without meat. Along with carrots, bananas, and a couple of types of lettuce, Susan selects a large bundle of broccoli, still wet from the misters. She may make a stir-fry, or just have it steamed — she is not yet sure.

Pablo, a married, thirty-nine-year-old Kaqchikel Maya farmer in Tecpán, Guatemala, walks his fields early one morning, surveying the crops and making a mental note of where weeds are hiding. Pablo farms land that has been in his family for generations; unlike many of his neighbors, he is fortunate to have more than enough acreage to supply his family of five with maize and beans throughout the year. He has turned some of his surplus land to growing export crops — at first snow peas, then French beans, and now broccoli. The new crops are more labor intensive and risky, but Pablo has managed to make a good profit with the broccoli. He is now considering converting more of his subsistence cropland to broccoli production — he says he would like to make enough money to send his children to the Catholic school in town, to buy a truck, to expand his house.

The stories of Susan and Pablo call attention to the proliferation of hopes, desires, and aspirations that characterizes the current age of globalized commodity chains.[1] In the first case, we see the sort of late-capitalist consumption from which we may maintain a cynical distance even as we willingly and gladly participate in it.[2] Susan's shopping patterns are part of a life project formulated around certain desires: she wants to eat healthy and stay in shape; she wants to be ecologically conscientious, have a nice figure, and save time in the kitchen. These desires and valuations are shaped in relation to market forces, public discourses, and the changing structure of the global produce trade. Susan's life project is figured against a different set of opportunities than the life projects of the Maya farmers who grow broccoli in the Guatemalan Highlands. Yet, the year-round supply of fresh and frozen vegetables that is so important to Susan and other consumers in her broad demographic group is only possible because of the low returns and high risks that these farmers feel compelled to accept. Comforting images effectively hide the ugly truths of the commodity chains that bring Susan her food. Product packaging, for example, does not disclose that a large corporate dairy produces her organic milk or that poor Maya farmers grow her beautifully symmetric and vivid green broccoli. It turns out that the global broccoli trade is not only about material channels of production, distribution, and consumption; it also depends on the productive flow of images and ideals that condition and are conditioned by consumer desires.

If the desire to buy broccoli is in part shaped by market forces, it also, through Susan's purchases at the grocery store, folds back to reproduce the material worlds of production and distribution. This brings us to Pablo, whose walking and wishing is also driven by desire, if of a different sort than Susan's. Given the risks, we may see Pablo's desire as more of a gamble, with much more at stake. Some would be inclined to characterize Pablo as acting according to "need" rather than "desire," because of the impoverished conditions in which he lives. But this situates need and desire in a hierarchy laden with moral and cultural assumptions about what is good, or better, about how and why people want (Soper 1981, 1993; cf. Doyal and Gough 1991). It privileges a presumptively more basic "need" as righteous, justified, and neutral, as compared to ephemeral and fickle desire. Even taking into account his relatively meager material and symbolic resources, Pablo's situation is not reducible to need alone. Although his circumstances are humble by North American standards, he has enough land to supply his basic subsistence needs and produce a surplus. He wants to get ahead (*superarse*), to achieve *algo más* ("something more," or "something better"), with all the multiple meanings and attenuated risks that implies[3] — goals he prefers to communicate in Spanish rather than in his native Kaqchikel. He has a stake in his heritage as a farmer and feels an obligation to carry on certain cultural traditions. But he also envisions a better future for himself and his children, a modern future that is not ironic or cynical. This future is projected with all the anticipation and anxiety that "not yet" entails (that the hoped-for "something better" has not yet arrived), even as it remains compellingly close, close enough that he has decided to take up the risky business of export agriculture in order to realize his project. Pablo's vision of the future is built around the immediate and practical desire for economic well-being as well as the more diffuse and existential desire to participate in and belong to the global ecumene.[4]

Let us be clear: these are poor farmers, struggling every day to make ends meet and, perhaps, earn a little extra cash. Pablo characterizes his situation as *luchando por la vida*, fighting to survive. Compared to the Northern consumers who eat the fruits and vegetables of their labors, Maya export farmers in Guatemala are at a great economic and political disadvantage. The outcome of this trade (a cheap supply of produce in the United States versus a little extra cash and a whole lot of risk for Maya farmers) is not evenly shared. For farmers like Pablo, surviving, meeting the basic needs of human existence, is always present as an imperative that must be met and satiated. But there is something else at work here: emergent aspirations and affects that go beyond the daily task of putting food on the table. Export agriculture is compelling for farmers like Pablo not because it is the only way they can survive but because it plays into the desire for "something more," or "something better," a diffuse desire with which the average American broccoli consumer would also be familiar even if the particular desiderata differ.

Admitting that poor people might have a desire to make some extra cash is not to divorce those wants from the realities of surviving and struggling. Rather, it is to emphasize that the basic struggle to survive ("need") often clings to desire and that desiring can not only coexist with but also feed on feelings of desperation. Sometimes the social production of desire plays into structures of power and inequality; sometimes it threatens them. Our ethnographic examination of the desires and struggles of Maya farmers might not contain the kind of resistance narrative about exploitation and inequality that we initially set out to uncover. Yet we have been pushed to more honestly and humbly consider how broccoli production becomes desirable, if also dangerous. Broccoli production is compelling for farmers because it responds to conditions of poverty, violence, and social suffering; in this way the global promise of "something more" feeds on desperate conditions.

Both Susan and Pablo are pursuing their desires against cultural and moral backgrounds that are not entirely of their own design. In this book, we trace the often opaque channels of desire that bind together Maya farmers like Pablo and supermarket shoppers like Susan. Maya farmers in Tecpán are venturing into nontraditional export agriculture as a moral project that acquires meaning in relation to the past, present, and future — the compelling sense and expectation of *algo más*. Their desires to engage in this project emerge from the dense cultural intersection of their memories of violence, their hard feelings about being shortchanged in Guatemala's postwar political economy, and from new, globally framed modes of consumerism, imagination, and self-fashioning. But such projects — usually discussed in terms of making more money, getting ahead, raising children with certain core values, holding onto land, building community — must reconcile the generalized desire and narrative encoded in global political-economic flows with the moral values, practical imperatives, and existential demands of the local setting.

Clearly, Pablo and Susan live in worlds far removed from one another. But instead of telling a story of divergent interests and fundamentally different existences, we highlight the confluence of desires that connects producers and consumers. Globalization is a relational process that takes shape as people make and move things (and ideas) about the world, creating connections full of tensions, frictions, contradictions, and hostilities, as well as sometimes fantastic rewards (Tsing 2005). We envision the global broccoli trade not simply as a material infrastructure (the commodity chain) consisting of points of production, exchange, and consumption, but also as a corresponding flow of affects and effects, with personal and collective desires manufactured along the way. Such a "global assemblage" links technologies of production with emergent forms of social life, political identities, and ethical or moral orientations (Collier and Ong 2005; M. Fischer 2003). Thus, this mode of production is also a mode of global connection within which people become subjects with certain kinds of desires — in cool Highland fields and air-conditioned grocery stores where acts of growing and eating broccoli are embedded in life projects and visions of the future. The broccoli trade actualizes a "commodity chain" linking sites from the point of origin to the point of consumption. But tracing the global is more than a matter of connecting the dots on a map, for beyond the refrigerated containers, shipping yards, and airplanes are social and existential dimensions that far exceed those material bases. In the movement of things around the world, people are already more than just abstract producers and consumers. They produce and consume for certain reasons, with certain expectations, and they depend on each other, whether they know it (or like it) or not.

We (social scientists, humans) tend to think about the world in terms of how it is divided up: there are different cultures or ways of life; there are national divisions and international alliances; there are "identities" to which we belong, selves defined in relation to Others. The global seems to be a patchwork of identities, realities, and worlds. Yet, connections inevitably outstrip all the breaks in the "global stream of humanity," meaning that there is always at least a modicum of ambivalence, some relation to the Other (Tsing 2005, 1). Broccoli consumers do not identify with and may not even care about poor Maya farmers in Guatemala, but without their efforts — and for very little reward — the evening meal would not be the same. It is no wonder that many consumers remain ignorant, perhaps willfully so, about where their food comes from. Global food chains often depend on relations of economic exploitation and political domination. Even where consumers are unaware of the lives of producers in the Global South, they nonetheless express a silent trust in the commodity chain as a whole, not needing to reflect on how it works in order to take advantage of it (see Bestor 2001; Shapiro and Alker 1995; Friedburg 2004).

We prefer to think about the broccoli trade in terms of a confluence of desires, a global assemblage that allows us to foreground moral and political questions and move beyond the language of need so often invoked to understand the economic lives of poor people in the Global South. Need speaks to the realities of utility and subsistence that define a basic register of human experience. Need converges with the economistic language of "interests" insofar as both terms are assumed to be value neutral, a priori features of human existence that can be used to analyze economic behavior in terms of individual intentions, rational calculations, and sovereign choices (see Mitchell 2005; Ruskin 1862b; Sayer 2004).

Our key concept is desire, or rather the process of desiring. In our ethnographic and pragmatic approach, desiring refers to how and what people want; simply put, desiring indexes what is important and meaningful for individuals. Desires are socially shaped, inflected with cultural meanings and logics. Yet, desiring is different from "interests," in that it is a collective process, and it is different from "needs," in that it is historically and culturally contingent. Desiring also differs from "agency" in that it emphasizes the production of wants and not just the practices needed to achieve a desired end; thus, we focus not only on *what* Maya farmers want but *how* they want (and are left wanting). The material dimension of "economic well-being" (Goldin and Asturias de Barrios 2001) must be understood within the broader dimension of social experience and existential well-being that cannot be reduced to "need" or "interest." Thus, we show how broccoli producers and consumers are connected within a common process of desiring, even though there are contradictions between these two ends of the commodity chain. There are ethical and political stakes in this framing and it is vital to acknowledge that there is more than an opaque financial trail surfacing in invoices and bills of lading that link broccoli consumers and producers. There is also a relationship that goes beyond the basic organizing factors of the broccoli trade and makes distant worlds interdependent and mutually constitutive. It is our hope that in recognizing such a connection consumers of produce in the affluent North will come to see themselves as economically *and* socially connected to Maya farmers. Consumers' desire for cheap but perfect food might then be transformed into a desire to pay for the cost of more mutually beneficial and equitable global connections.

The Task at Hand

This project began in conversations with Kaqchikel Maya farmers in Guatemala about the rise of export broccoli production and their views on market dependency. To some extent, we found what we expected: subtle resistance and overt denunciation, cynicism and skepticism, fear and loathing. But these sentiments were intertwined with stories of hope, desire, and aspiration, belying any easy moral judgment.

This project also began in conversations with anthropologists and economists who are attempting to understand the various processes of what is conveniently, and now mundanely, termed "globalization." Ethnographic sensibilities tend to privilege the local over the global, often assuming a broad backdrop of globalization as either hegemonic imposition into a local world (a globalized locality) or local resistance against distant market forces (a localized globality). For their part, economists — at least of the mainstream, neoclassically minded sort — tend to look at globalization from the theoretical remove of mathematical utility functions, which possess the virtue of parsimony but at the expense of considering cultural norms and collective moralities that cannot be reduced to tidy variables. In the final analysis, it is often assumed, the pursuit of one's own self-interest works toward a greater good through the invisible hand's transubstantiation of personal greed into public benefit.

In both perspectives what is actually going on out there in the various human dimensions of global processes — why producers and consumers do what they do — too often gets left out. The specific and multifaceted ways that individuals and groups negotiate and participate in global processes are subsumed to larger cultural narratives and the abstracted ethical deliberations of researchers and observers. The practical linkages of scholarship to social, political, and moral problems is what makes research worth doing, and yet we must avoid letting our agendas and assumptions overshadow what is most important for the people we study. This admonition is not in the interest of greater objectivity or neutrality. Rather, it emphasizes a concern with the changing moral conditions and basic quotidian structures of social experience upon which viable political alliances, policies, and workable futures are built.[5] As Don Kalb (2005, 197) argues, "our pasts, ethnic or religious, are becoming our future now because categorical values, beliefs and loyalties, buried deeply in the imagined roots of our cultures, are taking the place of the universalist modernisms gone awry." In its finer moments, ethnography attends to the competing forms that desire takes at the intersection of local worlds and global flows. The existential commitment of fieldwork points us toward changing and competing moral orientations, the ongoing dialectic between perceived predicaments and pragmatic responses, and opens anthropology to what Carrithers (2005, 437) calls "a moral science of possibilities."

What Maya farmers have to say about globalization is often at odds with both utopian paradigms of neoliberal economics and celebratory models of resistance and solidarity. They acknowledge the power of global cultures and economies to erode traditions, create new opportunities, and make life more complicated or more efficient. For them, the business of export agriculture remains compelling despite economic hardships because it is precisely at the everyday level of desiring that global processes are engaged, not at the purely cognitive level of rational economic decision making. In the chapters that follow, we offer a critique of the totalizing discourses and practices of free-market globalization, while also showing how related neoliberal reforms can have the effect of encouraging indigenous agency in certain contexts. Highland Maya broccoli farmers are better positioned than many other agriculturalists around the world to benefit from global food chains because they can hold onto their small plots, retain their means of production, and fill a gap in the global production schedule (cf. Freidberg 2004). But there are also consequences and shortchanges, the risks and letdowns that make this global connection inherently complicated and give it meaning and force. From the perspective of the Guatemalan Highlands, there are multiple effects, some beneficial and some detrimental, such that there is no absolute ground from which to make ethical pronouncements about whether the global broccoli trade is a "good thing" or a "bad thing." We prefer to delve into the social and moral world of the farmers themselves, to learn why they find the trade compelling, despite the hardships, and how they envision the future.

Global Connections

We offer broccoli (*Brassica oleracea*), that humble and often maligned member of the mustard family, as an unlikely entrée for a study of the entangled global connections between power and desire. At first blush, broccoli may seem far too mundane a commodity to invoke the passion and intrigue that power and desire entail. But we need not look to the genre of vegetable erotica (Garber 2002) to find all sorts of desires and symbiotic relations — some dangerous, others beneficial — in the increasingly global traffic in broccoli and the human labor it embodies.

We had originally planned to write a straightforward commodity chain ethnography of Mayan export agriculture. But the closer we got to the production of broccoli, snow peas, and other nontraditional crops in the area around Tecpán, Guatemala, the more the story shifted outward to the global trade and inward to local forms of violence and resistance in the Highlands. If we originally wanted to uncover exploitation at the hither side of the commodity chain, we found that the story could not be encapsulated in a simple narrative about exploitation. Rather, we found that we had to account for competing models of development and progress, multiple expressions of modernity, and convergent and divergent senses of what "better" means across locations. In this light, the global broccoli trade appears more as a rough patchwork of competing moral obligations and desires than a seamless weaving of material supplies and demands.

Complex webs of desire connect consumers in Nashville, Tennessee, to Maya farmers in Guatemala. The desire to eat healthy foods at cheap prices intersects with the desire to get ahead and make a bit of money. In the first part of this book, we trace a material infrastructure that links witting and unwitting American consumers of healthy foods, supermarkets seeking to sell premium produce, importers determined to expand their markets, and Maya farmers wanting a better life. We show how these desires converge and diverge along the way, creating contradictions and practical dilemmas for those involved. We look at the forms of discipline and training that are crucial to reproducing the aspiration for "something more" among both farmers and broccoli eaters. Maya broccoli farmers need to adopt production methods that involve new forms of education and training in order to meet the arguably excessive quality standards of American consumers. By presenting ethnographic data on both production and consumption, we show the ways that individual lives are mutually constituted by the global broccoli trade. We want to emphasize how the desires of Nashville consumers for cheap and perfect produce — linked to advertising, ideas of beauty, and health instructions in their affluent world — affect, and even exploit, the desires of Maya farmers to improve their living conditions. But our approach counters the portrayal of Southern producers that assigns blame for their condition on structural inequalities in a manner that robs them of their agency. Broccoli growers will tell you about their desire to make some extra money, maybe build up some savings, increase the life chances of the family, or contribute to community and political organizing. Some want to take control of their means of production and avoid having to migrate to coffee plantations, while others speak simply of a desire to grow something different for a change. In the Guatemalan Highlands we find individuals and families who are drawn together by the basic need to survive, more than by any need to placate the consumers who will buy their products. Yet their everyday lives and plans for the future are determined not by simple neediness but by desires shaped locally and from afar.

Maya engagement with nontraditional agriculture cannot be understood apart from postwar conditions in Guatemala and memories of the violence that have shaped social experience in the Highlands. Many of the farmers with whom we spoke participated in the June 10, 2002, anti-tax protest in Tecpán, during which thousands of farmers rallied in the town square and youths burned the mayor's house and car and ran the police out of town. Pablo was there that day. He distrusted the mayor and believed that the tax monies in question would simply fuel the corruption in the town government. He was also motivated by proximate self-interest, as the tax would have cut into his already thin margin from selling broccoli. Anxious to express his discontent and eager to exercise his right to protest for the first time, Pablo went to the demonstration exhilarated. Yet he left demoralized, repulsed by the violence that broke out and deeply suspicious of his fellow protestors' motives. He had arrived at the protest cautiously optimistic about the new possibilities of the public sphere but not fully trusting in the promise of dialogue that has been the banner of postwar reconciliation efforts, but he left with a bitter taste.

Still, Pablo remains hopeful. He believes that what happened at the protest and in the meetings that followed does not so much indict the democratic system as it highlights specific problems related to how democracy has taken shape in Tecpán. The mayor was the problem, he says, not the government. He still believes that things will change in Tecpán and, interestingly, that nontraditional agriculture will be an important part of those potential changes. Because the financial returns on sales of broccoli and snow peas have not been as expected, he has come to realize that changes will likely fall short, the work will remain compromising, and the process will be frustrating and risky. But he affirms that growing export crops is a way for Tecpanecos to take control of the means of production, establish family-oriented agricultural enterprises, and create a local cash flow that could shape municipal politics. The economic dimension of broccoli farming cannot be separated out from these social dimensions. In figuring out why growers participate in this risky business that leaves them perennially shortchanged, we must consider not simply the financial rewards and material risks but also the moral values and social experiences that have emerged out of Guatemala's particular historical context and its place in the global ecumene.

Desiring and Desire

The word "desire" has been utilized in scholarship (as in real life) as a way to think about sexuality, affective states, and consumption practices.[6] The diverse approaches of Deleuze and Guattari (1983, 1987), Lacan (1977), and Levinas (1969) all converge on the idea that "desire" comprises a basic dimension of human existence that cannot be reduced to simple "need." Need can be requited: one can eat to satiate hunger, and one can drink to satiate thirst. But desiring is eternal — an ongoing, future-oriented process, what Deleuze and Guattari (1983) term the "production of production." At this basic level, desiring is not the production of something in particular, such as broccoli, but the general process of continuously making collective existence, something in which all humans share, even though it does not connote belonging and, in fact, often involves violence, exclusion, and domination. This general process plays out in concrete and specific contexts, in which desiring becomes "desire." Broccoli farming is "compelling" for the Maya farmers we write about: it congeals various particular desires and touches on desiring in general. Not entirely immediate, the goals it embodies cannot be requited and are aimed at filling out the future, making the world new and different, attaining "something better." To say that something is compelled is to say that "it is 'driven by desire' rather than by need or utility" (Massumi 2002, 108).

Our concept of desire pushes us to connect rather than individuate the desires of producers, distributors, and consumers. Whereas economic conceptions of "preferences" or "interests" are loaded with assumptions about human nature, the determinants of desire are socially, historically, and culturally specific.[7] What people want, what matters to them, is not natural or neutral. The pull of desiring moves individuals, usually in ways that remain opaque or unquestioned, to take up stakes in activities and projects that are compelling because they embody moral, economic, or symbolic values (Grossberg 1992). Controlling processes and political-economic structures combine to condition the transition from desiring in general to specific desires. In the case of the broccoli trade, political-economic forces shape collective desires for something better, and vice versa: at this level, desiring is general, simply a matter of making something new or more. But, of course, no one just "grows broccoli." Along the broccoli trail, we do not find disinterested actors. People grow broccoli for certain reasons, in specific situations, and with something to gain or lose. Here, desiring becomes grounded; it is no longer a process of social production in general but rather an interested kind of production. Yet, viewing such personalized and particular desires against the backdrop of desiring in general forces us to admit that the wants expressed in broccoli farming are connected to global flows, that they belie other possibilities, and that they are never resolved, even when more land is obtained, production is expanded, and extra cash is earned.

We can connect desire and power if we think about the latter as we have been thinking about the former, as a collective process and not an individual affair. If power is the collective "process which, through ceaseless struggles and confrontations, transforms, strengthens, or reverses [force relations]" (Foucault 1978, 26), then it follows that the shift from desiring to desire — from collective becoming to subjective being, from the production of the social world in general to the historical production of particular forms of social organization — is shot through with power. Desire thus encompasses a vast field of potentials and possibilities — ways of organizing the world, making a living, establishing community, and so on — while the projects through which particular desires are imagined, pursued, and realized are often socially narrow and politically inflexible. The general human orientation of desire is always actualized in a concrete locale, with clear and specific desiderata. This involves the concentration of meanings and values on particular orientations at the expense of alternatives.

At the ethnographic level, mapping desire is about getting at what matters most to people. This is different from the sociological mapping of preference or taste, the economic mapping of rational choice, or the psychological mapping of perception. It is an existential approach in which people themselves relate what is important for them. Desire thus reflects personal moral values and orientations. At the same time, our project also seeks to examine what people say within broader considerations of global cultures and economies, collective processes, and ethics. Desire thus emerges as a contingent and consequential process for people who are caught up in larger flows.

This conception of desire allows us to view export agriculture in the Guatemalan Highlands as neither a mechanistic behavior enacted according to structural determinations, nor as a rational calculation made apart from the social world. We see desire as arising in lockstep with social production, in which desire takes shape at the interface between local commitments and global flows, never fully belonging to one or the other. We try to convey a sense of Maya farmers' agency within a system driven by local supply and distant demand. We discuss how neoliberal reforms and nontraditional agriculture strengthen certain community values and renewed forms of solidarity even as they foster new forms of violence. By asking not just *what* Maya broccoli farmers want (e.g., a little extra cash) but *how* these desires have taken shape, we shift from a presumptively determinant past toward emerging practices and commitments guided by competing visions of *algo más*.

Focusing on what matters to people (personally and collectively), our view of desire overlaps with Arthur Kleinman's (1999a) concept of "moral experience." For Kleinman, moral experience refers to what matters most to people in their local world. Local worlds, in turn, are defined as social spaces in which something (such as status, worth, esteem, relationships, chances, security) is at stake. In our scheme, desiring refers to the process by which things come to matter deeply, certain goals become compelling, and anticipated futures are thought to be up for grabs. Alasdair MacIntyre (1981) likewise sees moral stakes as emergent in and intimately bound to the practical activities of everyday life that become organized into projects for the purpose of achieving goals or goods. In this view, practical activities take shape within "some large-scale project of the individual, a project itself intelligible only against the background of some equally large or even larger scheme of beliefs" (1981, 28).

This is thus not "morality" in the sense of codes or guidelines for how one should live. Rather, it is an existential concern with what seems important, vital, and desirable. Desire is productive of what we call "moral projects" (individual or collective, large or small), which orient people's active involvement in the world. It is in relation to the things that matter most — to what people desire in their lives and in connection to those around them — that people come to take an active stake in their activities (Kleinman 2006). It is in this way that desiring becomes desire, that the human task of making the world becomes a concrete project in a local world. Even though we can imagine multiple reasons to grow broccoli and various ways of organizing this production, in fact only certain reasons are actualized. The translation from "desiring" (production in general) to "desire" (the mode of production) involves the concentration of meanings and values on particular orientations at the expense of alternatives.

The Limits of Desire

Limiting alternatives takes place through what we term "limit points." Limit points limit the possibilities for social change by satiating desires and channeling energies toward what is practical and obtainable. As objects and goals around which desires are consolidated and moral projects constructed, limit points are effective because they allow individuals to retain a sense of self-determination by making available possibilities for change and action. It is this positive and productive rechanneling (rather than repressing) of desire that gives limit points their durability vis-à-vis changes that seem impractical, unpopular, or irrational.

Limit points are often identifiable through discursive "stopping points" in talking about how things should be. The archetype of such limit points are "at least" statements: "At least things are not as bad as they are there," "At least we did not lose more," etc. Such statements connect to conceptions of morality and ethics because they provide a seemingly commonsensical resting place between what "is" and what "ought to be." In this way, limit points are different from more familiar concepts, such as "structure," that deal with constraints and determinations.

Desire is often invoked in a romanticized view of resistance. Yet, we contend, hegemonic processes — such as the struggle to define "something better" and the way that definition is used to justify global food production — are paradoxically sustained where they provide at least some return, where they do indeed deliver, although not fully, on the desires and convictions that they promise to satisfy. The global food system gives American consumers cheap and cosmetically attractive food and, in the case of broccoli, delivers some extra cash to poor farmers. Global assemblages become hegemonic — even if always aspiring, never finally accomplished — where a consensus develops regarding their legitimacy and where they actually deliver on their foreshortened promises: freedom, a vote, extra cash, self-esteem, a sense of security or stability, belonging, and community. As such, hegemonic assemblages are powerful and durable because they partly satiate and always attenuate collective desires. Through strategies of appeasement, hegemonic processes produce limit points to which desire and power adhere — and the closer this relationship, the more limit points appear as unquestionable and unchangeable limits on common sense, the more effective an aspiring hegemonic formation. Yet history shows that this relationship is never so solid. It is not simply that desire always outstrips power and that power always gets ahead of itself. Through the social production of desire, universal aspirations find a grip in everyday life and global assemblages find at least some regularity and durability. But, we argue, it is precisely this grounding in everyday life, in collective processes of desiring, that makes the hegemonic process an ambivalent, open-ended, never fully enclosed field of struggle. With reference to the global broccoli trade, we show how broccoli farming does and does not extend the dominance of the West and of Empire. In gaining a foothold in the Highlands, this system of production and its ideological supports — namely, the values and moral orientations linked to the global promise of "something better" — are also rendered ambivalent, as competing definitions of what "better" means across the broccoli trail make consensus impossible and contradiction inherent.

The Places

The data for this study come from ethnographic fieldwork conducted in the area around Tecpán, Guatemala (1993–2004), and in a Nashville, Tennessee, supermarket (2002–2003).[8] Tecpán, a town of about ten thousand located eighty kilometers west of Guatemala City, has a reputation in the region as a progressive and affluent place. In the city proper, about 70 percent of the residents are Kaqchikel Maya, although a Spanish-speaking, non-Indian, ladino minority has historically exerted disproportionate control over local government and commercial institutions, buttressed by racist ideologies and colonialist inequalities. At the same time, Tecpán is home to an exceptionally strong indigenous bourgeois class that has long supported ethnic consciousness, the value of education, and economic experimentation.[9] In the late 1980s and 1990s, this group became increasingly assertive in local as well as national politics.

In this book, we delve into the life projects that Tecpanecos undertake, the resistance that they encounter in the world, the commitments by which they ground and justify their activities, and the potent sense of courage, anxiety, and hope that defines local social life. Our concern with the connection between collective desire, political economy, and social experience drew us to examine the varied spheres of Tecpaneco life, from crime, gangs, and the drug trade to political protest, cultural activism, and discourse about victimization. We found that an understanding of the growth of the export broccoli trade — why some growers have switched from traditional subsistence crops to take up the riskier business of exporting — was impossible without a consideration of how the trade articulates, often in concealed and surprising ways, with the larger formation of "desire," in the Highlands and in the world at large.

In the globally bullish years of the late 1990s, Tecpán experienced its own economic boom: two relatively large supermarket-style stores opened; the town went from having fewer than a dozen telephone lines to having several thousand (as well as new and inexpensive cell-phone service); an Internet café opened (a notable portion of whose clientele are teenage boys who surf the Web for pornography); a sizable percentage of households have tapped into the local, makeshift cable operator's lines; and there are now a handful of video rental stores in town. Tecpaneco kids are more enthralled by Pokémon and Buffy the Vampire Slayer than by the rigors (and rewards) of traditional agriculture or the observances of the ritual calendar. Many older Tecpanecos lament what they see as a "lack of respect" on the part of the younger generation, as well as the corrupting influence of foreign popular culture.

The sympathetic foreign observer, finding support in such grumbling for his own masochistically indulgent critique of Western cultural hegemony, meant to exorcise collective guilt for "our" position in the global scheme of things, might well side with the Maya elders. Such moral projects are based on implicit judgments about what is right and wrong, about what motivates individuals to strive for (to "desire") things that bring ethical or spiritual gratification as much as economic returns. Often, moral discourse becomes a way of mediating the contradictions within the spheres of economic production and consumption, a strategy that we identify at various points throughout the book. Moral projects are not just something that our informants have. Research is driven by moral projects, too. The kinds of places we go and the questions we ask are motivated by moral orientations, as they should be.[10]

But moral models can come to dominate anthropological research. The concerns of researchers can overshadow quotidian structures of life experience and the pressing concerns upon which ethnographic understanding is established. For example, the world of globalization studies and punditry is divided into two polarized ways of seeing things, each corresponding to an underlying moral position. From one perspective, the consumption of films, cartoons, toys, and other global fare in Tecpán is seen as a classic example of the imperialist and corrupting expansion of capitalism through cultural forms. From another angle, Tecpaneco youths are seen not as dupes of global marketing but as appropriating cultural forms and unleashing their affective desires by amassing resistance to local, gerontocratic authority. What gets missed in both perspectives are all the blindspots and gray areas in which power and desire run together in complicated, often contradictory, ways. The effects of production and consumption cannot be reduced to either power on the one hand or desire on the other. Hegemonic aspirations run together with resistant attitudes and practices that, from another perspective, are linked up with other kinds of hegemonic aspirations. Hegemonic aspirations are multiple and ongoing, residual or emergent, productive of resistance, skepticism, alternative formations, and attitudes at the same time as they are productive of spontaneous belief, confirmation, and acceptance (Williams 1977; see also Hall 1985).

It is crucial to recognize that competing views on globalization are moral projects, just as we recognize that producing export crops, eating healthily, and consuming popular culture are activities infused through and through with moral values. Across thousands of pages of ethnographic analysis concerned with the cultural meanings and moral commitments of the activities of others, ethnography as a moral project gets naturalized, abstracted, and sometimes sterilized. Scholarly and public debates about globalization and exploitation may be more urgent and less provincial than family feuds about television and demoralized youth — but only from a certain perspective, one that already starts at a remove. For the old Kaqchikel man who sees his world overwhelmed by products and images that were not here just a few years ago, there may be nothing more consequential and urgent. For the Tecpaneco youth smitten by television shows and derivative toys, it might seem that nothing could ever matter more. For ordinary folk in the United States, as they cruise the aisles of their grocery stores, there may be nothing more difficult than the temptation between choosing broccoli and brownies — and the decision that is made, perhaps unknowingly, will affect life projects near and far.

The Chapters

This is a work of ethnography, born of the dialectic of fieldwork and presented as a narrative that brings diverging moral projects into conversation and argument. The aim is not to produce a synthesis or to highlight relative strengths and weaknesses. By bringing into relief how material desires, affective states and senses, and aspirations interface in local settings and amid global flows, ethnography can highlight the cultural and social rather than remain just the study of an individual event or decision. But ethnography is not simply about describing realities. In identifying what matters most — why folks get up and do what they do each day — ethnography becomes a pragmatic tool for addressing social problems. To develop political strategies without taking into account what people care about is, to put it bluntly, impractical, since what matters to people usually turns out to be different from what matters to researchers or advocates.

This book is divided into two parts. Part One focuses on broccoli and other nontraditional export production in and around Tecpán. In Chapter 1 we trace the commodity chain of broccoli from the supermarkets of Nashville, Tennessee, to the Maya farmers in Highland Guatemala. We argue that the global broccoli trade is shot through with desire — the desire of Western consumers to eat healthy foods, as well as the desire of Maya farmers to get ahead economically. In Chapter 2, we compare the discourses of development of farmers, cooperative leaders, and government officials, showing how nontraditional production and neoliberal reforms are differently interpreted and acted upon by various actors. Chapter 3 offers a more explicit theorization of how desire (individual and collective) channels and is channeled through neoliberal economic relations. Showing how limit points operate, we move "beyond hegemony," not by rejecting it as a category but by expanding its usefulness for the current phase of global capitalism. This involves examining how desires are produced across global flows like the broccoli trade and how *certain kinds of desires* come to seem natural and normal, not contingent possibilities among many others but the way it is "supposed to be."

In Part Two we turn our attention to the broader context of social experience in which broccoli farming is emerging as a compelling pursuit. Chapters 4 and 5 look at the legacy of state terrorism in Tecpán and emergent forms of daily violence in the postwar period. We describe the "tragedy of June 10," an anti-tax demonstration that began peacefully but turned violent when local gang members tried to assassinate the mayor. We argue that the use of the term "postwar" in Guatemala implies a false dichotomy. Rather, in between the distinctions — success or failure, violence or nonviolence, war or postwar — we find a collective desire for a better future that runs together with persistent forms of discrimination, with the composite and ambivalent experiences of progress and failure. In Chapter 6, we attempt to move beyond "victimization," arguing that the concept is usually called upon to justify rhetorical and political empowerment while negating the very agentive potential it ostensibly seeks to ignite. We examine Maya efforts in Guatemala and in Chiapas, Mexico, to revalue their cultural heritage and to create a new space for themselves within regional, national, and global systems of political economy. We describe a war of representation and control over representation, but one with real-world consequences that bring to the fore the inherent contradictions of theories of literary deconstruction as applied to ethnographic representation. Reducing the Maya to victimhood situates blame for their situation in structural conditions. This is well, good, and necessary: Maya peoples clearly suffer from structural iniquities within Guatemalan society. But pan-Mayanist leaders are promoting creative and concrete alternatives to the present system, and here they are not mere victims but protagonists in the creation of their own future.

The hard-fought struggles among Maya leaders, activists, and broccoli farmers has produced a sense of community that is neither reducible to, nor neglectful of, a traumatic past. In our representation, the future looms as both a project and a projection, a horizon within which individuals may take up meaningful and compelling projects refracted along the lines of historically, politically, and culturally conditioned desires.

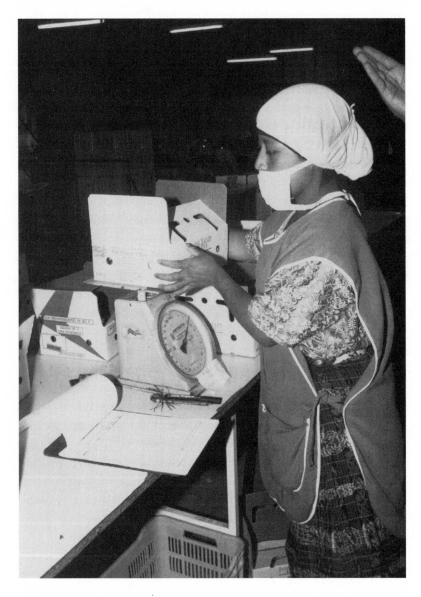

Packing vegetables for export at the Aj Ticonel cooperative. Note the boxes already labeled for U.S. distribution and the Kaqchikel workers' preferred style of wearing their sanitary masks.

PART ONE

How the Maya Want

ONE

Something Better

On days when he works in his fields of maize, beans, and broccoli, Felipe Xul wakes up before dawn, washes off with water cold from the night air, and wolfs down a fried egg or a leftover piece of meat along with a plate of black beans and a tall stack of tortillas. While he eats, his wife packs a lunch of maize dumplings in a large, handwoven napkin, which he will carry along with his machete and the other tools he needs that day (a hoe, perhaps, or a fertilizer pump). Along the three-kilometer walk to his fields, Xul occasionally greets other farmers headed to their plots, but mostly he keeps to himself, planning out the day's tasks. He also spends time thinking about the future. He farms not simply to survive, he tells us, although the basic need to put food on the table is essential to his life and work.

Xul lives with his wife and six children in a small Maya hamlet precariously carved out of a mountainside overlooking one of Highland Guatemala's fecund valleys. The several-room cinder-block house is larger than average for the area, evidence of the little extra cash he has secured through export agriculture. More than simply a roof over his head, the house is a spot of repose that reflects the closeness of living in a place for decades, the close-ness that makes a shelter into a home and a fuel source into a hearth. In the same way, his fields are more than a site of basic survival — they embody a host of legacies from the past and possibilities for the future, some good and some bad. Xul speaks of his land in loving, anthropomorphic terms, and, in the abstract, he finds his work deeply meaningful.

Hearing Xul speak in his native Kaqchikel of the fertile Rajawal ("Spirit of the Earth") and his symbiotic relationship with Mother Nature, it would be easy to romanticize the life of a Maya farmer. But let us not forget that Xul's work is backbreaking labor. Xul is only forty-one, but his callus-covered hands and feet could belong to an eighty-year-old. He walks with the stoop of a much older man, a legacy of years of hauling bushels of maize back from his fields. His poor posture also comes, he explains with a wry smile, from keeping his head down during the violence and terrorism of the 1980s.

Xul's sons help in the fields after school, and he frequently reminds them that this land will one day be theirs. He consciously tries to instill in his chil-dren a love and respect for the land and a view that working it is part of a larger social context of meaning and planning. He tells them that working the land is important for the future. Part of the reason that he took up broc-coli production is because he realizes that growing only milpa (subsistence plots of maize and bean) will not, in the future, afford the standard of living that he desires for his family. He wishes for greater worldly success for him-self and for his children, and so he seeks fuller participation in a project of global capitalism that risks social alienation for the *algo más* of consumptive dreams.

At times, these various desires converge, as with Xul's venture in non-traditional agriculture. At other points, they diverge, leaving Xul feeling both shortchanged about the less-than-ideal returns on the export crops and anxious about whether his children will indeed want to take up farming. The horizon of fecundity that motivates Xul to not simply work milpa but to grow export crops threatens as well as inspires, embodying all of the contra-dictions involved in anticipating, even desiring, a changing form of life. He grows broccoli because he wants something better for his children. And yet, he realizes, it is exactly by encouraging his children to pursue broader hori-zons and goals that he also risks pushing them away from the land on which he wants them to stay and prosper.

In growing broccoli, Xul's general desire for *algo más*, his desire to take advantage of opportunities in the global marketplace, converges with the reality of local struggles, ambivalent outcomes, and transforming streams of social experience and collective identity. We might characterize such global connections as eroding local norms, threatening the very culture of Highland Guatemala. Yet, it is precisely because such practices become so deeply embedded in local forms of living that they are compelling, durable, and, for farmers like Xul, worth doing despite the many obstacles and risks.

The Commodity Chain

Broccoli is a cole crop (the same species as brussels sprouts, cauliflower, and cabbage) that was probably domesticated in the last centuries BCE in the cooler regions of northern Greece and Italy. Broccoli was reportedly first grown in the United States in Brooklyn in the 1890s, planted in backyard gardens by Italian immigrants and enmeshed in schemes of desire enjoining frugality and subsistence (the same historical juncture that conditioned the production of spaghetti, pasta e fagioli, and other "typically Italian" food items). By the 1920s, broccoli was being grown commercially in California and shipped back on trains to the large urban markets of Chicago and New York. However, it is only recently that broccoli has become a true staple in the American diet. California farming operations still supply the lion's share of the market during their "in" season, from May to October.[1] But supermarkets stock broccoli year-round, and in the winter months an increasing portion of their supply comes from Guatemala. In 2000, Guatemala exported about 60 million pounds of cut broccoli to the United States, up more than 900 percent over the previous twenty years, and most of this was grown by smallholding Maya farmers in the region around Tecpán.[2]

The production cycle for nontraditional crops grown around Tecpán is short — in the case of broccoli, less than ninety days from planting to harvest. At harvest, farmers, their families, and hired hands cut the broccoli stalks in the late morning and early afternoon, packing them into bushel-sized nylon bags or plastic boxes that look like milk crates. Packing plants and cooperatives send trucks to pick up broccoli produced under contract, but small farmers without contracts find themselves at the mercy of predatory intermediaries ("coyotes") who buy produce at a discount on the side of the road. One farmer complained: "Sometimes we don't get paid. This has happened a lot. Coyotes take the product and disappear, and we are left with a big debt. That's how the farmer loses. . . . It is work for nothing. We lose time, money, everything." Because produce such as broccoli spoils so quickly, and because it has virtually no value in the local subsistence market, farmers are compelled to sell their crop, giving buyers a clear advantage. Intermediaries play on the vulnerabilities of farmers, using their privileged access to market information and the farmers' need to sell to establish prices in a field of power where the rationality of choices always touches upon the anxiety of not really being able to choose.[3]

Like Adam Smith's (1976) "forestallers" and "engrossers" of grain who were often the subject of witchcraft-like accusations, coyotes occupy a morally ambiguous position in Tecpán. Most farmers view them as pariahs, making money not through hard work but through the rather arbitrary good fortune of owning a pickup truck: "If you own a truck, you can make more money," one farmer said. "But it does not mean that you work more." This negative view is largely shared by development workers encouraging nontraditional production; one explained that "the problem is that intermediaries are the ones who earn the most. The producer takes on the risks but does not share equitably in the earnings."

In Tecpán, the nefarious means that individuals can employ to get rich quickly — Faustian pacts with extra-worldly demons — is a common subject of gossip. Such stories are told about coyotes and their dealings. These stories speak to the sense that nontraditional agriculture is something of an anxious pursuit, linked as much to emergent dangers and uncertainties as to the optimism of new opportunities. It is also clear that these anxieties are not just about broccoli: the production of nontraditional produce articulates, at least in such stories, with the licit and illicit production of other products.[4] One man in Tecpán, a chronically underpaid schoolteacher who does not grow nontraditional crops, narrated a story he had heard about a friend of a friend, Marcos. "Some coyotes, acquaintances of Marcos," were hauling a load of bagged produce in their truck when they saw a police car down the road. They pulled in at Marcos's house and asked if they could leave their bags of broccoli until the morning. He agreed. At dawn the coyotes returned to retrieve their bags, giving Marcos 100 Quetzales [about $13]. He protested this was far too much money, but the coyotes urged him to just keep it, to not worry about the exchange, and they left." Looking at our clearly puzzled faces, our friend connected the dots: "It must have been marijuana. There are lots of drug dealers passing as vegetable traders. They fill their pickups with produce, but below that they put drugs, or sometimes they hollow out broccoli stems and hide the drugs inside. Because of this, they only do their business at night, when the police aren't around, and since they are posing as broccoli merchants the police don't suspect anything."

Whether such stories are "factual" or not is beyond the point, although it should be noted that in the late 1980s and early 1990s the Cali cartel shipped tons of cocaine through Guatemalan produce exporters in what the DEA dubbed "the broccoli routes."[5] More important for us, however, these stories fold together not only the terror signified by economic exploitation and the threat of losing traditional culture but also the imaginings of translocal flows of opportunity and potential excess, where making "far too much money" is possible but consequential, risky, and morally ambiguous. Such stories reveal the persistence of a moral economy based on fairness, on corporate labor over individual gains, and on modesty (for more on this, see the results of Ultimatum Game, reported in Chapter 3). Such a perspective makes clear that the economic well-being of producers is affected not just by changing political economies, but by changing streams of social experience and moral understandings. In this case, the allure of economic well-being draws producers close to cultural anxieties and illicit behaviors that reflect on the character of those involved, even if they are innocent.[6] This moral model intensifies at the margins of the global economy as local producers are brought into tense relations with the global marketplace, where they are not benefiting — as they are well aware — when compared to distributors and packers.

Once it reaches the export packing plants that line the Pan-American Highway between Guatemala City and Tecpán, the broccoli is weighed and classified according to size and aesthetic quality. Sanitized in warm chlorinated baths and rinsed in cool water for preservation, the produce is then packed in cartons already stamped with a U.S. distributor's brand logo. The packing plants truck boxes of broccoli to cool storage facilities at Guatemala City's international airport, where they arrive between 7 and 10 o'clock at night. Loaded onto early-morning cargo flights, the produce arrives in Miami before 6 a.m. and, if all goes smoothly, will clear customs within a few hours to be shipped to grocery distributors throughout North America. All in all, the produce usually arrives on supermarket shelves within forty-eight to seventy-two hours of the time it was cut in Guatemala. Broccoli can then last another fifteen or twenty days on the shelf and in the consumer's refrigerator.

Sipping coffee and eating apple strudel at Guatemala City's upscale Café Wein, exporter Tom Heffron extols the virtues of globalization and explains Guatemala's logistical advantages: "Any point in Guatemala is closer to Washington or New York than any point in California, so Guatemala has an advantage in the Eastern Seaboard market. Going to Miami with product is still closer than it would be from Salinas or other points in California." Heffron passionately advocates free trade, arguing that open markets for broccoli benefit everyone involved, not only Guatemalan producers and U.S. consumers but the California competition as well:

> The production we are doing [in Guatemala] is not competing with the
> U.S. There is a complementary relationship because most of the California
> production occurs from May to October. At that point, California bows
> out of the market, their weather not permitting year-round cultivation.
> Guatemala production begins at the end of October and bows out in May,
> at the onset of the rainy season. So we are sharing the same consumer in
> New York with our friends in California: they need us in the winter months
> to keep the product in front of the consumer's eyes, and we need them in
> the summer months to do the same thing. Hopefully, then, we are making
> sure that the same consumer is fed all year-round.

Heffron is not simply deploying an ideology of neoliberalism to cover over the crude self-interest of a businessman. He comes across as sincere, separating, at least in his own mind, the bad aspects of globalization from what he sees as its genuine benefits.

The reality is not so rosy, and the good and the bad are not so easily divided out. Packing and shipping plants in Guatemala work in close association with distributors and big retailers in the United States to predict demand and ensure the supply of broccoli. They then contract out most of the production to smallholding Maya farmers, buying the remainder of the produce needed to fill demand on the open market (which allows some leeway in the event that demand drops or in case more supply is needed). This is a crude but effective strategy: prices are minimized by strategically contracting for less than the anticipated demand, with the remainder purchased only as needed and at bottom-of-the-barrel prices. Farmers have little choice in this matter. They can sell whatever crops they have left over after the contract is fulfilled at prices set by the packing plants, or they can leave the leftover crop in the fields to rot (the latter option is not a culturally viable alternative, however). There are no local markets for the leftover supply since broccoli is not part of the local diet and is distasteful to the Tecpaneco palate — and so once they have entered into export production farmers must play the global food game as it is structured from afar. Thus, Tecpaneco farmers are vulnerable to market fluctuations predicated on consumer events in the United States and Europe about which they have little information. As production has dramatically expanded in the last twenty years, and as demand has begun to flatten, packing plants have lowered prices while raising quality standards. In this way, the strategies packers use to insure themselves against oversupply transfers risk to smallholding farmers who are financially ill-prepared to bear it.

Increased quality standards have brought a related set of concerns to bear on Highland growers. Because broccoli and other export crops are destined for U.S. consumers — with their socially produced desires for visually attractive vegetables — cosmetic quality is of paramount importance. Broccoli stems must be of a uniform length with no bruising or other deformities, and packing plants go to great lengths to ensure that each piece of produce lives up to these demands. This also means that the contracts that Maya farmers have to ensure them a market are not firm contracts at all since their produce can easily be rejected at the packing plant with the vague explanation that it does not live up to quality standards. And the difference between a perfect broccoli grade and an inferior, unacceptable one is slim. Danis Romero, a government development specialist in Guatemala, reports that packing plants "reject about 15 percent of broccoli based on appearance. The color has to be green or blue-green, and if it's yellow it will likely be discarded, even if the taste and quality are the same. If there are holes in the stem, they reject it. And it has to be completely compact, including the flower."[7]

Obsessive cosmetic concerns do not mesh with Kaqchikel Maya farmers' culinary standards. For them, wasting food is taboo (*xajan*), a cultural norm borne of necessity and instilled in children from an early age. They find it not only odd but immoral for packing plants to let produce rot just because the color is off or the stalks are out of shape. This local moral model intersects with the fluctuations in the marketplace in interesting ways. Farmers do not want to waste good food and yet they do not have a taste for the broccoli and other export crops they grow. One Tecpán farmer had a fair amount of leftover produce when we came to interview him in 2001. His wife prepared a Chinese-style stir-fry for us with the extra broccoli, snow peas, and French beans. After we had eaten our fill for lunch, she packed up the rest (perhaps ten pounds worth) and insisted that we take it with us. At first we refused — it seemed untoward that we take such a large quantity of food from a family of such humble means — but they insisted. It was not just that they were trying to be generous but that, as they told us, the vegetables would just rot since they cannot bring themselves to eat broccoli or snow peas. Food tastes — not just how we view food but also how things taste, what we like, what we put together on the plate, what we want deep down in our guts — are deeply ingrained, socially produced desires that are hard to shake.

Maya export farmers often speak of the contradictions of producing a product that is more-or-less useless in their local world. It is not so much that exchange-value is elevated over use-value as that it is nothing more than an expedient means to higher profits. Rather, the imperative to move the product before it rots often means that profits are elusive. In this context, not being wasteful, even if it means taking a financial loss, can be an important source of moral and cultural capital for farmers.

To ensure cosmetic quality requires farmers to apply large quantities of fertilizers and pesticides to broccoli, resulting in the crops being much more labor intensive than subsistence agriculture (see Watts 1992; von Braun, Hotchkiss, and Immink 1989). Farmers are often unfamiliar with the recommended application regimes and safety procedures of the products they apply. Many are illiterate, and often the labels are only in English. They need to adopt forms of knowledge and discipline that were not necessary just years ago. They need to be aware of the dangers associated with chemical use, proper usage ratios, storage requirements, and possible outcomes — agronomic or human biological — associated with chemical usage. Although few studies have been conducted, farmers themselves believe a number of health problems can be traced to the chemical fertilizers and pesticides they apply. Farmers report that chemical fertilizer "burns" the soils, slowly depleting them of their nutrients and thus requiring ever-larger doses. David Carey (n.d.) reports that Kaqchikel farmers simultaneously value chemical fertilizers for the increase in productivity they provide and lament the long-term costs they are taking on their lands and their vulnerability to price increases. He notes that an increasing number of farmers in the area are returning to organic fertilizers.

Changing forms of agricultural production in the Guatemala Highlands reflect general trends in global food systems. Smallholder farming still predominates in this area, but contracting production is the new model. Food-processing corporations transcend the fray of risk and uncertainty by contracting supply along a transnational chain of intermediaries. This leads to a paradoxical convergence of intensive production techniques and reduced prices — a detrimental trend for small growers on the margins of the global economy that highlights the human, environmental, and economic costs of food and farm labor (Thompson and Wiggins 2002; see also Hughes and Reimer 2004). Global food systems are often justified through recourse to an uncomplicated conception of desire: consumers want good-looking food year-round at low prices. But desire is not neutral. Desires arise at the interface of cultural representations, social experience, and large-scale systems of production and distribution — processes that combine, at the supermarket, for example, to determine for shoppers what is — and what appears to be — available, desirable, and affordable.

The Grocery Store

The fruits of alterity have acquired an immediate value even where the company of the people who harvested them is not itself desired.

— PAUL GILROY, *Against Race*

Supermarkets are important cultural spaces in the United States where consumptive desires meet the offerings of industrial alimentary capitalism and the two are reconciled through practice.[8] Supermarket shopping is one of the most widely shared quotidian experiences of adults in the United States, part of the daily rhythms of urban and small-town life for all but a very elite social stratum; the average American visits a supermarket about twice a week and spends half of his or her food budget there (Food Marketing Institute 2003).

Over several months in late 2002 and early 2003, we conducted surveys of 106 shoppers in a Nashville, Tennessee, Kroger supermarket to document their buying habits in general and their selection of produce in particular.[9] We followed up these surveys with ethnographic observation, interviews, and informal conversations with shoppers as they shopped for fruits and vegetables, as well as with conversations with produce manager and workers about marketing strategies and presentation.

While several national supermarket chains operate in Nashville, including

Harris Teeter and Albertson's, Kroger fills the local default category of "grocery store," blanketing the metropolitan area with its twenty-three stores. We focused on a Kroger in a busy commercial district of the Green Hills section of Nashville. For our purposes, though, we might as well have been in Cincinnati or Oklahoma City, since Kroger works hard to ensure standardization across its 2,300 stores nationwide. It is often precisely such mass production and uniformity that ironically produce feelings of familiarity among shoppers.

On average, U.S. produce purchased in the middle of the country has traveled over 1,500 miles to reach the shelves of the grocery store (see Pirog et al. 2001 on calculations of "food miles"). While the logistics are remarkable, our concern is with the social web that overlays this lengthy commodity chain: the hundreds or thousands of lives a given product has touched — the hopes, fears, and desires of men and women whose interconnectedness generally remains opaque.

The grocery store is a site of consumption and production. It does not simply respond to consumer demand but controls and produces demands that inform the broader agricultural market. Shoppers become certain kinds of consumer-subjects through specific consumptive acts, as even a single purchase plays a functional and productive role in broader discursive and economic formations. Here it is helpful to call on Crang's (1996, 63) view that "we consumers make all sorts of 'inhabitations' of commodity systems; and these ways of inhabiting result not in a simple alienation, a losing of our real selves under the pressures of various corporate and other institutional strategies and technologies . . . , but rather in a series of 'entanglements' of consumers and consumer systems, both being opened up to the other."

Shoppers enter Kroger with at least some vague expectation of what one can find there and of what one likes, expectations mediated by popular discourses on what is healthy, clean, a bargain, or good at this time of year, as well as by personal preference and the practical limitations of "making ends meet" (Lunt and Livingstone 1992, 89). In our surveys of Kroger shoppers, less than a third arrived with specific written itemizations. The rest brought only a mental or written tally of generalized "needs" (vegetables, meats, breads) that would be narrowed down to specific products in the course of shopping. While particular consumptive acts have the appearance of being spontaneous and willful, they are also conditioned by preexisting economic and political structures. Consumers enact a certain "vote," reiterating or performing the various cultural meanings that congeal around objects of desire (Miller 1997). A discourse of "options" and "choices" underwrites this sense of "freedom" — *at least* there is a choice — thereby making the grocery store seem optimal relative to less "democratic" or "free market" situations. In this sense, hegemonic power is exercised through the very existence and proliferation of choices, which act as limit points.

Although the act of consumer choice is not the altogether subversive moment anthropologists often romanticize, it does provide at least a modicum of cultural agency and material realization of desires. After all, the supermarket is a space in which consumer interests are ostensibly met, albeit through an apologetic "at least" stance toward the activity. This is seen in strategic trade-offs. One shopper showed us her cart, with a few gourmet-style frozen dinners, explaining that she dislikes buying such processed foods but is too busy to cook, and *at least* she buys healthy food, like her chicken and broccoli dinner.

In the produce section, shoppers are required to select fruits and vegetables directly from display bins. The determination of "quality" generally depends upon appearance, focusing on freshness, ripeness, color, texture, and consistency. Broccoli must be dark green as well as seductive in its size and buoyancy, buds flowering out and around the stalk like a mushroom cloud. Tungsten lights enhance the aesthetics, making the produce section an enticing palate of colors, with vivid orange carrots lying alongside deep green broccoli and exotic mushrooms and lettuces (cf. Freidberg 2004 on vegetable aesthetics in England and France). Kroger uses misters to sprinkle cool water drops on the fresh produce, a strategy that aims not only to increase shelf life but to forge a symbolic linkage between customers and the farms from which the vegetables come.[10] Cook and Crang (1996) point to the "double commodity fetish" of foodstuffs: an ignorance of the origin and conditions of production of the desired items combined with geographical and commodity "lore" about these origins (see also Cook 1994, Guthman 2003). Such lore, evident in shopping and over dinner-table conversations, operates by channeling consumer desires, not through overt coercion but by inspiring the consumer's imagination to want a certain product or self-image.

U.S. consumers happily, if also hesitantly, participate in global processes from the safety of their favorite supermarkets. And yet they often also lament or want to remedy the very site of the exploitative labor that makes that safety and that consumption possible (cf. Crang 1996, Moberg 2005).

Cultural studies of foodstuffs in the United States and Europe reveal how consumption plays into the commodification of identity and a fascination with exotic and foreign elements (Bell and Valentine 1997; Cook 1994; Watts and Goodman 1997; Kalcik 1984; Delamont 1995). Kroger strives to offer a year-round supply of produce, which generally increases and sustains demand as consumers become habituated. As we have seen, Guatemala, along with Mexico and several other Latin American countries, plays a central role in supplying produce in the "off season." Yet these connections most often remain opaque to both the producer and the final consumer (cf. Hendrickson 1996 on Guatemalan handicraft marketing). When we told shoppers in Nashville, Tennessee, that Maya farmers in Guatemala grew the broccoli they were buying, most expressed surprise. Their motivation to buy and eat broccoli came not from an imagined nostalgia of place but from popular contemporary discourses, or lore, concerning health, diet, and taste.

Broccoli holds contradictory images in the U.S. popular imagination: it is seen as a lackluster vegetable that is also an icon of health-conscious consumer culture. People for the Ethical Treatment of Animals (PETA) sponsors a dance troupe called the "Broccoli Boys," who, along with the "Lettuce Ladies," promote vegetarianism across the country. PETA's website features descriptions of each dancer, the ads taking the form of romantic "personals."[11] Here, broccoli consumption is linked to the production of lifestyles and identities that are removed from production and labor. And this is often done within an idiom of political activism, since broccoli, like other green vegetables, can be subtly associated with the ecological consciousness of "green living," even if the exact political dimensions of such a project remain undefined. One of the Broccoli Boys, Bruce, from Norman, Oklahoma, likes reading Chomsky but dislikes people who would eat meat or dairy in front of him without being willing to hear his counterarguments. This political idiom — using the symbol of green as a marketing tool and lifestyle marker — can play into the aims of agribusiness and global food chains, where the other sort of green is not evenly distributed. Dole Food Company's Barney Broccoli targets a younger audience ("I'm one SUPER VEGETABLE! Eat some crunchy, green broccoli today!"). His catchy funk-rock theme song goes in part, "Broccoli's the veggie that looks like little trees/Your family's favorite veggie/And you can eat it several times a week."[12]

In many ways, broccoli is an easy sell. Low in calories, virtually fat-free,

Lbs per capita

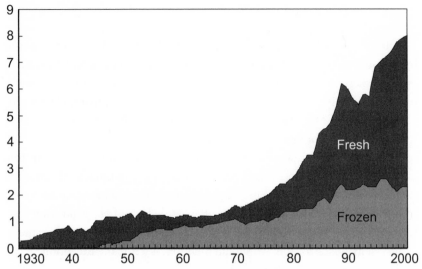

U.S. broccoli consumption since 1930. Courtesy of the Economic Research Unit of the U.S. Department of Agriculture.

and rich in vitamin content and antioxidant properties, broccoli has become a staple of mainstream, health-conscious cuisine in the United States over the last twenty years. An average-sized stalk of broccoli provides over 200 percent of the recommended daily allowance of Vitamin C, 15 percent of Vitamin A, 15 percent of potassium, and is a significant source of calcium and fiber. Studies have found that the phytochemical sulforaphane (found in broccoli) is an effective antibacterial against *Helicobacter pylori*, which is linked to stomach ulcers and cancer. Another phytochemical, indole carbinol, also found in broccoli, is associated with a reduced risk of breast tumors. Broccoli has similarly been claimed to help prevent or treat hypertension, osteoporosis, obesity, diabetes, even cataracts and strokes.[13] U.S. households consumed well over two billion pounds of broccoli in 2000, or about eight pounds per capita, putting it in the same category of produce sales as green peas, cucumbers, and celery. This is an increase of over 300 percent since 1980, part of a larger trend in Western countries of consuming more fresh vegetables (Friedland 1994). Such proliferation is due in part to the way broccoli is associated with public discourses about health and diet, and exotic and ethnic foods (perhaps best captured by cookbooks such as Mollie Katzen's 1982 *The Enchanted Broccoli Forest*).

"Health foods," a very loosely defined marketing category, are increasingly sought after by consumers (see Giard 1998; Watts and Goodman 1997). Supermarkets are keen to fulfill consumers' desires for healthy, gourmet, and specialty cuisines, all of which offer higher profit margins than regular products. A "low-fat" or Healthy Choice™ decal signifies much more than a description of ingredients. The upshot of this tendency is to limit critical inquiry into the possible health dangers associated with increasingly mechanized food chains, impossible-to-match body images, and obsessive exercise routines (see Guthman 2003). Health discourses, for example, ignore the fact that store-bought produce is often loaded with the residue of chemicals applied by far-off farmers struggling to address consumers' aesthetic quality demands. Broccoli, we should mention, is a notable exception.[14]

That broccoli has become a staple of many diets in the United States speaks to the ethically driven production of certain lifestyles and body types, the bourgeoisie cultural value of good eating and good living. Given this ethical pursuit, it is ironic that consumers have difficulty in making the ethical connection between their acts of consumption and the challenges faced by marginalized producers. For affluent Northern consumers, ethics becomes a project of self-fashioning and lifestyle embodiment far removed from a critique of global inequalities.

For John Ruskin, the ethical value of production derives directly from the moral utility of consumption. He writes that it is "the manner and issue of consumption which are the real tests of production. Production does not consist in things laboriously made, but in things serviceably consumable. . . . For as consumption is the end and aim of production, so life is the end and aim of consumption" (Ruskin 1862b, 47). The Tecpaneco position mirrors Ruskin's views of wealth. In Ruskin's view, for riches to be considered wealth they must be put toward virtuous ends that benefit the society and not just the individual; the fruit of selfish accumulation he termed "illth."

Our view is that the production of broccoli as desire is a social process that makes use of manifold webs of cultural meaning. This process is not confined to the supermarket, though shelf space determines the practical and conceptual limits on how broccoli is to be grown, seen, eaten, and experienced. Supermarkets draw on and in turn reinforce the cultural representation of food products, such that this space serves as a relay in the social production of desire across and beyond the material scope of the commodity chain itself. Desires are channeled in the supermarket in certain directions designed to extract maximal profit by leveraging both cultural and material resources. The upshot of this for U.S. consumers is that product shelf-lives are indeed enhanced and seasonal products are available year-round and at lower prices. Yet the very desire for these products and the high quality standards that most of us bring to the table must be approached with suspicion. Supermarket shoppers we interviewed expressed surprise and frustration when certain fruits and vegetables were not available, even if they were out of season. These shoppers expect shelves to always be fully stocked, a cognitive image supermarkets strive to reinforce. The social conditions that produce such expectations are neither natural nor necessarily optimal, but rather indicate a horizon where desires are transformed into commonsensical and even ethical approaches to eating. It is at such limit points that the social relations that make up global food chains become hegemonic, giving the impression that they are clearly victorious rather than contingent. Issues of power become increasingly important in this regard, particularly as we turn our attention from the abstracted commodity chain toward the small-holding farmers who perform the backbreaking labor of broccoli production.

The Moral and the Desirable

Ethnographers have long pointed out the special place maize holds in Maya material and symbolic culture. Maize is the staple of virtually all meals, from the humblest plate of tortillas and salt to the grand festive spreads of tamales. It is said that one cannot truly be satisfied at the table without consuming maize in some form, either by eating or drinking. The refined Tecpaneco palate, picking up on subtle differences of flavor that are elusive to the gringo palate, can identify the region of the country a particular batch of maize came from. Indeed, many claim that they can tell if a tortilla was made with maize from their own plots or not. Most Maya families in Tecpán plant plots of maize and beans, known as *milpa*, that will supply at least part of their families' subsistence needs.

Along with its central place in the local diet and economy, maize embodies key moral values for many Tecpanecos. Kanek López, an *'ajqi'j* ("day-keeper," or traditional religious specialist) and milpa farmer, explains that "maize has been a way to conserve our cosmovision, our cultural values, our relationship to the land." He goes on to outline a distinctly Maya view of agriculture and economics akin to Physiocratic notions (cf. Gudeman and Rivera 1990): "All humans live from the land. Even the petroleum that fuels machines comes from the earth. Even the elements that they use to make computers come from the land. When we die, we are going to decompose, but the land will always be there. Our corpses will fertilize the land. And another plant will be born. Maize, in its perseverance, is a symbol of the social and spiritual values of our culture."

Maize remains the material and symbolic staple of the Tecpán diet, simultaneously good to think and good to eat, but since the 1990s milpa has been increasingly supplanted on the prime lands around town by broccoli and other export produce. Maya farmers in the area have long grown cash crops such as tomatoes and wheat for urban markets, and they have been quick to adopt the new nontraditional crops. Surveys in 2000 of three rural hamlets in Tecpán found that 98 percent of households maintained subsistence milpa plots, but that 56 percent also devoted at least some land to nontraditional crops.[15] Of the nontraditional producers, 79 percent grew broccoli, followed by snow peas (57 percent), French beans (39 percent), mini-zucchini (18 percent), and blackberries (11 percent). Significantly, 78 percent of the farmers supplied all of their family's maize and beans subsistence needs for the year with their milpa land, using the earnings from nontraditional crops for cash expenditures and capital investments. As a result, the average size of the landholdings of nontraditional producers (20 cuerdas, or 2.3 hectares) was almost double that of the exclusively milpa producers.[16] In addition, the number of medium-size farms in the area has increased significantly, at the expense of very large and very small farms. Many of the large farms in the area used to grow wheat for the local mills. However, to bring itself into compliance with World Trade Organization (WTO) mandates, in 1997 Guatemala lowered the tariffs on wheat and wheat flour entering the country, as well as dropping government price supports for basic grains. As a result, private-sector wheat imports have almost doubled between 1997 and 2000 and the market for local wheat has collapsed, leading many of the large-scale ladino (non-Indian) farmers to sell their land to the mostly Maya nontraditional producers.

A central reason the broccoli trade has become compelling for farmers is that it provides a way to earn some extra cash while retaining control over

TABLE 1 *Farm Sizes in Tecpán*

	% OF FARMS		% OF LAND	
FARM SIZE	1979	2000	1979	2000
<1 cuerda	7.70%	2.80%	<0.04%	<0.20%
1–<7 cuerdas	27.10	16.70	2.60	5.00
7–<13 cuerdas	25.90	33.30	6.10	17.70
13–<30 cuerdas	23.50	33.30	12.30	39.80
>30 cuerdas	15.90	13.90	78.90	37.50

SOURCES: 1979 figures are from the 1979 Censo Nacional Agropecuario for the *municipio* of Tecpán; 2000 figures are from the surveys cited in the text.

NOTE: Cuerdas are a regionally variable unit of measure used by Maya farmers. In Tecpán, there are 8.6 cuerdas in a hectare.

their means of production, which is highly valued for both cultural and economic reasons. In particular, land holds powerful affective meanings for most Tecpaneco farmers, as a link to their ancestors, as a source of spiritual and material sustenance, and as a means for self-determination (see E. Fischer 2001, 229). "We want to take advantage of this area, its capacity for growing these kinds of crops," said Manuel Guarón, a middle-aged farmer from Tecpán. And for many, the shift to nontraditional crops has been an economic boon, allowing them to expand their landholdings at the expense of large ladino plantations. At the same time, nontraditional production raises a variety of new dilemmas. The qualifier "some," commonly used among farmers when discussing increased earnings, reflects this ambivalence. Nontraditional production becomes seductive because it is *at least* somewhat beneficial. Despite recognizing the considerable market, health, and social risks, most Maya farmers see nontraditional agriculture as a positive alternative strategy for holding on to their farms and, in the process, making some extra money. In random surveys conducted in Tecpán and neighboring communities in 1998 and 2000 (see Hamilton and Fischer 2003), 57.3 percent of sampled farmers saw their economic condition as becoming "better" or "much better" after the introduction of nontraditional crops (n = 211). An additional 36.5 percent of respondents said that there had been no change in their economic circumstances, with many reporting that they nonetheless saw the introduction of new crops as a positive development in that it provides an additional market outlet. Only 6.2 percent of the farmers surveyed reported their condition to be "worse" or "much worse" following the introduction of nontraditional crops (see Hamilton and Fischer 2003).

The simple answers required in surveys mask the complicated feelings Maya farmers have toward nontraditional production. They lament its demanding labor requirements, they express frustration with the involved quality control procedures, they worry about the heightened risks of crop failure. Yet, at the same time, they find value in it beyond the lure of material gain, such that it remains compelling despite the letdowns and short-changes farmers routinely experience. This is to say that there are complicated social and moral processes at work here that are not captured in narrow cost-benefit analyses. For example, a number of farmers report that their transition to export production has reinforced traditional family values. As one Tecpaneco stated, "These new crops involve the whole family, just like the milpa. It's not just the man that works in the field; the wife works, the kids work, everybody pitches in, which is to say it's communal labor. This is the way we [Maya] work, by doing things together. It provides unity. Let's take the case of broccoli. When it's harvest time, the parents, the kids, the aunts and uncles, the cousins and nephews — everybody — turns out to help harvest. This is the most important thing."

Thus, broccoli production becomes compelling for Maya farmers because of the way it fits into "traditional" forms of life. Nontraditional exporting is seen in certain respects as convergent with moral models involving family relationships, economic autonomy, and ownership, but is at the same time seen as an oppositional practice in relation to regional histories of labor migration. Many farmers with whom we spoke see the risks and added expenses of export production as worth it when compared to maquiladora and plantation labor, which is generally seen in Maya communities as the most odious sort of wage labor, an avenue of last resort. Many of the growers around Tecpán had been recruited for decades to labor on coastal cotton and sugarcane plantations and at Highland coffee plantations during harvest season. The working and living conditions at such places are notorious: workers sleep in overcrowded, makeshift dormitories, are exposed to malaria and other tropical diseases, and are paid below subsistence wages. It is not surprising, then, that working on local nontraditional farms is preferred. In the hamlet of Paquip, just outside Tecpán, almost all the able-bodied men migrated to coastal plantations until about a decade ago. Now no one does. They sell their labor, even at "exploitative" (below market) rates, to neighbors and kinfolk involved in exotic produce export production because it is better (less alienating) than the alternative.

Yet the literature speaks persuasively of the other side of the deal, the risks involved as compared with traditional milpa production. The tenor of much research on global food systems portrays top-heavy commodity chains and corporate operations built on the impoverished conditions of poor workers in the South. Yet, we find that small farmers in the Guatemalan Highlands enter into the global food system, with its risks and uneven benefits, as a way of resisting, or at least avoiding, other alternatives. The risks entailed in independent contracting — job insecurity, crop failure, price fluctuations — are more than offset, most Maya farmers report, by the independence and flexibility such production allows. To work for someone else, more than one farmer told us, is a form of slavery. Retaining control of their means of production is an important gain. Still, the emergence of agriculture exports in the Highlands does not only reflect a simple peasant desire to hold on to the land rather than migrate; the shift is compelling for other reasons, local and global, which means that this production is principally about earning "something more" and not just about doing "something else."

Farmers and the Future

Luis Tecum, a Kaqchikel Maya farmer in his late fifties living in a hamlet outside of Tecpán, works land that has been in his family for generations. He speaks nostalgically of the long days of hard labor he and his father put in when he was young, and of his regret at having to quit school when he was fourteen to work full time in the fields. Tecum is fortunate to have inherited nearly two hectares of land, more than enough to support his family of five with maize and beans. In fact, Tecum plants about half of his land with broccoli, snow peas, and French beans. He sells these nontraditional export crops through a regional cooperative, and has earned enough to buy a pickup truck and expand his house. At times, Tecum speaks enthusiastically about the potential for farmers to break into the export market, proclaiming it "the wave of the future" for smallholders who are willing to "work hard and take advantage of the opportunity." He says the export trade has provided a means of making some extra cash and that, compared to just a few years ago, "things are better now." At other times, in other moods, Tecum is less ebullient, saying the new crops are just "okay" and that the additional economic risks brought about by the export trade outweigh the benefits.

There are contradictory truths in Tecum's characterizations. The export business has left him and other farmers shortchanged. They work very hard for the *algo más* that never seems to arrive or, at least, always comes up short, providing only a little extra money and little chance for substantive economic change. Despite the 2001–2002 growing season when world prices plummeted, many farmers only became more hopeful and invested in the export trade. Whatever the vagaries of the market, Maya farmers' sense of locality is increasingly seen within expansive flows of goods and desire, such as the alluring "elsewhere" of global imagining.[17]

Within this changing world, where economic autonomy meets a felt lack of control, some farmers have done better than others because they have better access to markets and are more attuned to new technologies. The non-traditional markets around Tecpán are "like the Wall Street of vegetables," one observer noted, "because there they determine the prices. These are 'virtual markets' because you don't see it in any one place. It's not in the Plaza. It's in houses, it's in the street with cell phones; they're looking for prices, they're setting prices." When we spoke with him in 2002, Jesús Batz, a Maya farmer from the remote village of Paquip, just north of Tecpán, had just returned from Yonkers, New York, where he had gone to meet with a produce importer. Batz does pretty well by local standards, growing broccoli and other export crops, and with the earnings he has been able to buy a cell phone — a car phone hooked up to a battery and occupying the centerpiece of his modest dining table — that he uses to check prices in various markets and make contact with new distributors. Farmers like Batz, who are able to compare market prices and get the best price available for their product, have a distinct advantage.[18] Access to such information allows markets to work more efficiently and provides the possibility for producers to bypass chains of intermediaries and establish links directly with importers and distributors in the United States and other importing markets.

Probably owing to his class position as one of an emerging class of Highlands entrepreneurs who are better equipped to tap into the global food system than their neighbors, Batz has an idealized vision of the United States as a land of spectacular abundance where only the best is consumed. Growers and exporters frequently talk about the U.S. market as a good opportunity, referring not simply to its size or to the money that can be made there, but

also to the idea that Guatemala is competing with California and other foreign producers, which is a source of pride for them. Batz says that if consumers in the best and biggest market are consuming his products, then his
products must be the best.

The packing plant Batz sells to uses terms like "Exotic" and "Producto de
Guatemala" on its packaging. This is a direct way for them to reach consumers since, even if these signs go unnoticed at the market, the comfort of
knowing where one's food comes from — as we learned from shoppers in
Nashville — can provide a feeling of security for consumers, a way of supporting the Third World, or even a way to remember trips to faraway places.
For the Nashville shoppers we interviewed, the specific origin of a product
(such as broccoli from Guatemala) does not have as much resonance as the
simple fact that it is from elsewhere, a vague notion that nonetheless grounds
production in a personally meaningful cognitive geography. On the other
hand, for producers the image of the marketplace as spectacularly abundant
brings insecurities and anxieties since it means that they must meet aesthetic
standards because only the best will be purchased at packing plants.

Export agriculture is also compelling in reference to the emerging sense
of modernity in Guatemala that entails greater political participation and
cosmopolitan connections for a burgeoning class of educated and upwardly
mobile Maya. Such new identities are reinforced by economic structures that
bypass national markets from which the Maya have historically been excluded. In this context, the more-or-less direct link to international markets
found in export agriculture buttresses feelings of local or regional pride and
development. Among some farmers, particularly those like Batz who have
years of experience in exporting produce and are more able to use the market to their advantage, there is the hope that revenues from nontraditional
production will be used to enhance the local educational and community
infrastructure and in political organizing at the regional and national levels.
Batz reports:

> Some producers have begun to fund the Maya ethnic revitalization move-
> ment, bilingual education, and political activities. The Maya movement has
> never really linked up economics with politics, never had a self-sufficient
> source of money, but here in Tecpán because of the agriculture, and also
> the sweater trade, we do. Lots of producers are still interested in their
> culture. So it is an opportunity to raise consciousness. But we need to

stay focused on the *pueblo* and the *aldeas*, because this is where the education and participation must begin to be most effective. This is a chance to link economics with politics for the benefit of the movement, but a local movement with local interests and activities.

In this local setting, a vernacular cultural modernity must be distinguished from, even if it is also linked to, the process of social or economic modernization (see Knauft 2002; Appadurai 1996; Briggs 2001; Ferguson 1999). This is not to justify or celebrate one and not the other. The Maya Highlands remain poor. The broccoli trade has brought some added cash, but only for some of the farmers. There are the crucial issues of how this trade is creating new class-based tensions in the Highlands and contributing to a technological divide, if only at the level of cell phones and truck farming; and, thus, for many, survival remains a pressing concern. But if we distinguish between different registers of what it means to be modern, then in the Tecpán context, being poor intersects with the imagination and expectations of modernity that make the global promise of "something better" only more nefarious, since it is embedded in collective desires (affective and corporeal) and not just enacted as a predetermined routine or adopted as a simple consensus.

Batz's operation is a good example of how compelling the trade can be, even during tough times, and of how economic inequalities on a global scale can dig deeply into a local world, not simply through crude forms of extraction and force but through subtle channels of desiring. Having committed himself to nontraditional agricultural production for about a decade now, Batz has been forced to accept and endure the risks involved. Prices began dropping in the summer of 2001: "There was more competition," he told us. "Then, after September 11, we could not sell because the market was saturated and we lost our connections with New York City because of problems at the airport and customs. The demand in the United States dropped. If there were risks with these products a year ago, now there are too many risks." Despite this downward turn, Batz insists that he will continue to grow export crops. If anything, the price drop paradoxically intensified his desires to export. He told us, in a tone both optimistic and sarcastic, that the market can go nowhere but up. With farmers in Mexico, Argentina, Ecuador, and elsewhere increasingly vying for a portion of the U.S. produce market, it is more likely that risks will intensify. While the price crisis pushed many out of the business, Batz is now working harder than ever to strengthen cooperative associations with other farmers, to protect against another crisis, and to take advantage of the additional knowledge they all now have. In his case, the future is being organized around desires that are maintained even where expectations come up short.

It is not enough to simply point out that great risk accompanies the potential benefits of nontraditional agriculture; farmers themselves recognize this fact. One farmer admitted: "We have done just alright, making a little extra money, but not a lot. We know this is the danger, and maybe we will make more later, but for now we are making a little." Farmers are cognizant of the risks involved, almost too cognizant, for this recognition brings to bear on their small operations the anxiety and the pressure to perform that the global marketplace is all about. They realize the almost unattainable aesthetic regime, the increased labor and financial burdens, and the threat of crop failure. This is a dilemma not so much of knowledge but of control, at least from the standpoint of farmers. Knowing the risks but having little control is at once compelling and debilitating, since aesthetic and quality standards for broccoli are dictated from a distance, influenced by the desires of grocery-store consumers and channeled through regulations and restrictions. This is one of the great dangers of broccoli production in the Guatemalan Highlands.

Knowing the risks becomes a way for farmers to justify taking them. They "know the risks" involved, even though they have only an inexact understanding of the various dimensions of the global broccoli trade, including the decisions of competitors, desires of consumers, or changing regulations and restrictions owing to concerns about food safety. Nor can they control the desires of consumers. Packaging and branding have become strategies among growers and exporters, but these play into the consumer's scheme of desire rather than bringing it into question. The fact that the label on a package of broccoli says that it is from Guatemala may be a source of pride for growers. But it also confirms for the consumer that his or her broccoli has come from a place that is exotic enough to be appealing, enticing enough to buy, and understated enough to avoid asking how producers live and why they do what they do.

Luchando por la vida. Fighting to survive. This is a common response among the farmers to our break-the-ice inquiry of "How is it going?" Indeed, Maya farmers are struggling to survive. The shift to export agriculture is accompanied by a shift in the social and moral experience of farmers. Collective forms of labor and cooperation — not to be romanticized but still acknowledged as less alienated — have given way to a system in which the pressures of putting food on the table weigh heavily on the shoulders of smallholders. If world events have always had a great impact in the Highlands, the feeling that local outcomes are shaped by global events is ever more acute as farmers need to observe world market prices and be cognizant of regulations and opportunities. If anything, a keen consciousness of the various dimensions of the political and economic situation in which they work is being produced alongside pervasive forms of exploitation and short-changes of the global promise of something more or better. Again, the danger is how a global expansion of desire and expectation plays into local worlds that have historically been economically and politically marginalized and, in this case, brutalized across decades of war and social suffering. On the one hand, to say that farmers have no other choice, that they are acting out of desperation, is — as we have cautioned against — making need and desire into mutually exclusive spaces. On the other hand, to say that farmers are doing what they desire, pursuing their self-interests — simple as that, no questions need to be asked — is to ignore how desires take shape across geographies of class and capital, and are thus irreducible to the isolated interest of an individual or group. There again, desire and need would be held apart. What makes broccoli so compelling for growers has to do precisely with the ways that the desire for something more emerges out of and folds into an everyday fight to survive.

Luchando por la vida. This phrase combines the sense that life is dangerous, desperate, and precarious with the sense that life is also a fight or a struggle to be engaged. Broccoli has become compelling not because these poor people have no other choice, nor because growing broccoli is simply what they want to do, what is in their best self-interest. Broccoli farming is not a way to survive or a way to make a living. It is, itself, a living, a struggle or fight to survive, embedded at the level of need and desire, where desperation and expectation are inseparable. This fight is not figured and enacted between the weight of the past and the exigencies of the present, between how things have been for decades and how things ought to be today. Broccoli production is figured in terms of an emerging sense of modernity in which the future becomes compelling although deferred, seductive although short-changing.[19] This is an intermediate future (Bhabha 1994) in which desiring remains tied to basic needs, affirmed in the present, and connected to the past. This future, this form of desiring, is a practical and pragmatic one. It is open toward some *algo más* that remains an elusive goal. Farmers explain that they are in the broccoli trade because they seek to maintain their land, strengthen family values, acquire something more, or engage in community organizing. But each of these particular goals, if achieved, would not diminish the felt sense that — like ordinary people everywhere — they remain wanting and needing in other ways. *Algo más* remains compelling and close, even if never actualized, because of the ways it is embedded in social experience. But this also makes the idea of *algo más* dangerous — sticky, compelling, directive, and seductive, despite the risks involved, the fall in prices, and the broad view of inequality across the global broccoli trade.

The global broccoli trade reinforces certain structural inequalities and political economic structures, but not through simple coercion or deterministic consensus. The broccoli trade can extend relations of power across geographies of class and capital because it runs parallel with the expansion of expectation into local worlds. Power relations are extended, in this way, as the global broccoli trade plays into a sense of the future as open and ambivalent, capable of being practically engaged and realized. Our findings do not support the argument that power operates on an ideological or epistemological level only, such that for Highland farmers the promise of "something more" would function simply to conceal more basic realities of economic inequality and heightened risk. We are pushed toward a more concrete explanation of how control is extended and negotiated through socially produced desires.

Farmers are aware of the economic inequalities that make their life chances quantitatively and qualitatively different from those of the broccoli consumer. Yet we find them nonetheless compelled by an idea of something more that includes but is irreducible to basic needs or monetary gains. They seek a more expansive and inclusive sort of global marketplace, not a romanticized subsistence enclave. For most farmers, their savings are tied up in crops — the dried corn in the crib, the wheat or broccoli in the fields — and crop failure can easily bankrupt a household. Devoting all of one's land to nontraditional crops might actually provide more effective opportunities for getting ahead. Yet the key cited by most farmers is to balance nontraditional with subsistence production, simultaneously engaging the world market and maintaining the family's land. When asked about their vision of the future, many farmers insist that their children will maintain the land and will themselves be farmers. But most also speak of sending their children to school, having them get an education so that they may do "more in life," such as becoming a schoolteacher or opening a store. The decision to enter nontraditional production reflects and reinforces these desires for "something better" and an emergent sense of modernity related to transnational connections.

In thinking about the problems associated with export agriculture, as with other global food systems, it is important not to subsume an ethnographic examination of a local setting to distant deliberations about how things ought to be. This is not to justify current circumstances as natural or inevitable, but to point to quotidian structures and pragmatic desires upon which viable alternatives are built. Assumptions about what "something better" means often gloss complicated and ambiguous interfaces between globally expansive desires and local commitments and concerns. Our ethnographic examination of the export trade reveals neither a top-down imposition nor local "resistance" to market "hegemony." In coming to know Maya farmers and what matters to them, we have attempted to provide "a subtle reframing of experience . . . on behalf of different issues at stake in their lives and local contexts" (Kleinman 1995, 150). The sense of "something better" that farmers put forward to justify their engagement in the global broccoli trade reveals not a banal idea of the future opposed to the present but a vision of the future as an ongoing struggle between the past and the present. Here the future is always deferred, even as it enlivens risky practices. Global economic linkages, even where they have not brought the expected or most desirable material changes, are making possible transformations in the cultural and political imagination in the Maya Highlands, changes that are themselves complicated by local politics.

Something Better

Growing and exporting broccoli has become a lived *lucha* for the farmers we know. It is a life project that will not be easily forsaken, even when prices fall or risks rise. This is a real danger. There are practical benefits for farmers, and our research shows that farmers themselves emphasize the benefits over the risks and shortchanges. But their optimistic tone and commitment to stick with export agriculture may reveal that their desires are clinging around power, that they actually have little control. Affluent consumers enjoy a host of benefits, often at the expense of these producers. An expansive geography of economic and political difference becomes durable as the promise of *algo más* becomes embedded in life projects and everyday desires. As wanting and needing combine in the Highlands, growers become enmeshed in global flows that provide some opportunities, limit chances, and leave risk and responsibility on their shoulders, reproducing a great divide of capital and class between producers and consumers.

What is dangerous about global food systems like the broccoli trade is that they become livable for both consumers and producers. On both sides, the system is naturalized. Consumers enjoy year-round broccoli and may even feel comfortable with their purchases, from a moral perspective, despite the inequalities involved. Purchasing broccoli does not presuppose knowledge of its chain of production — although, such knowledge, insofar as it may appear somewhat ugly, may prompt in the consumer certain political sensibilities vis-à-vis the distanced laborer. In describing her purchases, one shopper noted that they are healthy foods, and she notes, "At least I'm not eating at McDonalds." "At least" — with this hedge she explicitly invokes a limit point of desire, revealing it for what it is. *At least* she is not eating unhealthy food — she will go home to eat at her own hearth and prepare her food with her own hands, unsullied by the rocks and accusations that José Bové and his compatriots hurl at the golden arches. "*At least* we are better off than they are." "*At least* we are not hungry." "*At least* I'm not eating at McDonalds." There is always something worse, and so one's activities are defined comparatively as morally superior.

The same holds true for producers like Xul. Recall his desire for *algo más*, a "something more" temptingly offered by the market. Some would be inclined to analyze this practice in terms of what James Scott terms "weapons of the weak" (1985).[20] This framing sees the global marketplace and the local world as opposed in an embattled relationship of hegemonic imposition and grassroots resistance. For Scott, weapons of the weak include those tactics that do not change large-scale structures but do provide at least some purchase and a chance to attain "something better," a phrase that ends his book (1985, 350). For example, growers like Xul would be seen as engaging the market, using the limited opportunities they find there to their own ends even as large-scale inequalities remain. In this framing, what counts as resistance is determined by the conditions in which an action takes place. Peasant actions, because they are levied from a situation of poverty, struggle, and need, are forms of resistance, regardless of whether the actor sees it that way or not. At the same time, Scott insists that one must know at least something of the intentions or the context to call an action resistance: if a peasant soldier deserts his post he is implicitly enacting resistance because he is a peasant, whereas resistance might not be the most appropriate term for a soldier of a different class position (1985, 301). Scott thus locates the analysis of resistance on the plane of class interests. He writes: "When such acts are rare and isolated, they are of little interest; but when they become a consistent pattern (even though uncoordinated, let alone organized) we are dealing with resistance" (1985, 296). Resistance is identifiable where a practice is coordinated as a pattern across a dominated class (cf. Scott 1990).

In this view, desires and agency are thought of as existing in opposition to power. But the global broccoli trade reveals something else — desires that are shaped in relation to fields of power, structures of inequality, senses of modernity, and limited life chances. In striving for a better life on the market's terms, what of the paths not taken by Xul and other growers? To give energy, resources, and time to one moral project is to sacrifice, silently or explicitly, other potential ways of engaging and envisioning the future. Something better comes to mean one thing and not another. Weapons of the weak and hidden transcripts are what make the existing order livable, enjoyable, acceptable, solidifying particular limits around a comparative or relative sense of something better, and thus these minor practices are part and parcel of the fields of power they seek to oppose (cf. Knauft's 2002a discussion of recessive agency). The crucial difference between our approach and Scott's has to do with the key phrase "something better." Scott *ends* with "something better." That is where we begin. These final two words in *Weapons of the Weak* seem to redouble on the book's primary thesis — that weapons of the weak, even where they offer no challenge at the structural level of domination, ought nonetheless to be recognized, at the ethnographic level, as valuable and significant. "Something better" is defined in terms of the past rather than in terms of future-oriented desires and projects. Consider the section titled "The Remembered Village" in Scott's book (1985, 178–83). Here history is the touchstone for thinking about the present and the future. There is a struggle, Scott tells us, between what has happened and who is to blame, over how the present situation is to be defined and interpreted. Having lived through this history, every villager is entitled, indeed required, to become something of a historian — a historian with an axe to grind . . . to justify or condemn the existing state of affairs. . . . The ideological struggle to define the present is a struggle to define the past as well. . . . They have collectively created a *remembered village* and a *remembered economy* that serve as an effective ideological backdrop against which to deplore the present. (1985, 178, emphasis in the original)

We push toward a richer examination of what "something better" might mean in particular local worlds. The aim of a specific weapon of the weak may not always be directed at structures of domination (see Gutmann 2002). The relation of power and resistance is usually less straightforward than this model implies: an ambivalent and multisided struggle over moral values and cultural meanings. Collective desires take shape amid such struggles (and are thus never on the side of either power or resistance only). What "something better" means is not just figured with an eye toward the past, a remembered economy, but also in terms of how the future is framed. Hegemony is an ongoing process of framing this horizon, involving consensus and the confluence of desires, which is not the same thing as dominance (Greenhouse 2005). And desires are deeply conditioned by social, political, and cultural interests, not just class ones. Weapons of the weak may just as readily be deployed in a Nashville supermarket as in a Guatemalan broccoli field; their effects may solidify or erode the relationship that subordinates the Maya farmer to the U.S. shopper. "Something better" becomes ambivalent and variable as it is taken up in different social fields along the broccoli trail. We see this in the variable discourses of progress used within agricultural cooperatives, government agencies, and exporting firms, which we examine in the following chapter.

Discourses of Development

Maquilas, Cooperatives, Government Directives

Life in Guatemala takes shape amid social, political, and economic conditions in which feelings of danger, uncertainty, and avarice have become pervasive and routine. The figures speak for themselves: Guatemala's relatively
low per capita GDP (US$1,512 in 2001 dollars) is exacerbated by highly
unequal land holdings and income distribution, resulting in one of the highest poverty rates in the hemisphere (between 44 percent and 80 percent,
depending on the methodologies and political sympathies of the authors of
the particular studies cited). By virtually any indicator (income, land holdings, life expectancy, access to potable water, literacy rates), Maya peoples
make up the overwhelming majority of the Guatemalan poor. While there
are many poor ladinos, it is also true that the country's political and economic elite are overwhelmingly ladino.

In the postwar period, these conditions have given rise to a new kind of
wishful thinking. Catch-phrases such as development, progress, and economic growth are bandied about as the means and the ends of the country's
problems. Yet, a palpable feeling of uncertainty persists, as desperation and

despondence exist alongside expectations of progress and modernity and the demands of development.[1]

In the decades following World War II, government officials promoted economic development with import-substitution industrialization policies. In the 1980s, burdened with a growing debt that had been eagerly supplied by the World Bank and private lenders, the Guatemalan state shifted course and began implementing neoliberal export-led development policies.[2] Neoliberalism has provided economic elites and technocrats with a compelling channel through which "desiring" can be translated into the concrete desire for "something better," while also limiting the range of expression to the selective idioms of development, progress, and reform.[3] Guatemala's entrepreneurial nouveau riche laud neoliberal reform as the heir to a venerable tradition of anti-monarchical liberalism (which also conveniently converges with their own economic self-interests). In this fashion, elite desires have been channeled and dialectically redefined in a complex calculus involving economic interests and social affinities. In cocktail party conversation and on the editorial pages of the respectable press this position is expressed in the discourses of multiculturalism, empowerment, and decentralization that mask residual paternalistic attitudes toward the masses (the Maya masses in particular). Such views are held not just in the upper echelons of government and finance but trickle down in the language of naturalness (e.g., "free" versus "distorted" markets), subtly conditioning the general space of public debate.

By 2000, the most dynamic sector of the economy was "nontraditional exports," led by apparel from maquiladoras — sweatshop-style factories where brand-name clothing is assembled for export to the United States. Close behind was production of broccoli, snow peas, and other nontraditional agricultural exports. These two modes of production affect local realities in ways that are at once convergent and divergent. It would be a mistake to simply collapse nontraditional agriculture with nontraditional manufacturing; yet it would also be a mistake to isolate the new forms of agricultural production from the larger context of Guatemala's position in the global political economy.

This chapter compares Tecpaneco perceptions of maquiladoras and of nontraditional agriculture. We examine how these formations are theorized, interpreted, and negotiated locally through the lenses of social experience, politics, and morality. The key difference between these two kinds of work has to do with autonomy and alienation. Labor in the maquiladoras is highly

alienated, whereas nontraditional agriculture is simultaneously entrepreneurial and embedded in social networks and cultural tradition. The great
risks and insecurities that broccoli farmers contend with, for example, do not
detract from the feeling among farmers that they are more autonomous than
their counterparts who work in factories. We then turn to the discourse of
development as employed by farmers, cooperative leaders, and government
officials. Development becomes a point of contention among those actors
who are not satisfied with the particular shape of local realities in the face of
global potentials. Development is a discourse, practice, and field of power/
knowledge through which problems are addressed, responses negotiated,
resistances met, and empowerment variously realized and impeded. We find
different, although overlapping and interrelated, economic and political
agendas at work in the private sector, cooperatives, and state agencies. In
each of these arenas, the vocabulary of a globalized world dominates: free
trade is either good or just a given, but it is widely considered the principal
means of shaping the future. Each cohort deploys discourses on "progress"
in particular ways that foreground certain truths and foreclose others. In this
way, widely accepted, indeed, hegemonic, discourses about development and
progress that are codified in state apparatuses emerge and reside in ideologies and practices at the local level.

Labor and Alienation

Emblematic of the dangers of global capitalism and neoliberalism are the
maquiladoras, offshore assembly plants that have sprung up along the Pan-
American Highway in the Highlands. Mostly owned and managed by South
Koreans, and assembling clothes for export to the United States, the Guatemalan maquiladoras have a reputation for recruiting vulnerable young
women, placing them in harsh working conditions that approach forced
labor, enforcing these conditions with plenty of heavy-handed guards, and
exercising biopower through pregnancy tests, limited access to toilets, and an
often overtly sexualized hierarchy.[4] Some maquiladoras are better than others (and such news travels widely in the towns from which workers are
recruited), but overall the conditions are deplorable.

While recognizing these problems, we must also be cautious in applying our moral valences to distant practices. The harsh conditions of maquiladora production that seem so clear-cut from afar are more complicated when viewed from a local perspective in which labor, class, and social experience intersect to make this kind of work simultaneously compelling, dangerous, and conflicted.[5] Christopher Jones (personal communication) points out that some young women working in maquiladoras see them as a liberating way out of the traditional obligations of early marriage and household chores — a lesser-of-evils choice, to be sure, but nonetheless revealing of their desires and tactics of resistance. These women have complex reasons for taking up maquiladora employment, and these reasons change over time. Green (2003, 53) emphasizes that "poverty not liberation is what has obliged many women to seek employment outside the household." Yet we must keep in mind that what appears hegemonic from one angle (the exploitation of maquiladora labor, say) may also comprise resistance from another perspective (such as young women chafing at parental control). When set within the frame of localized and domestic resistance, this production becomes especially compelling, for it is not simply about the desperation of poverty, although that is a key factor, but also about a social world that involves others types of suffering, limited life chances, and changing structures of opportunity.

Alberto Simón, who works out of his house in Tecpán making sweaters, sees the maquiladoras as both beneficial and exploitative. His concern is not with maquiladoras in general, but with the specific form that this labor has taken in his local world, especially regarding gender relations, education, democratic politics, and family life. Thus, he is careful to distinguish between the general form of globalized production and the particular hold that such a mode of production has upon everyday life in a given place and time. He makes clear that global processes are nothing apart from the way they take hold in the lives of women and men. During a conversation in 2002, he described his vision for an alternate model of outsourcing:

> [In the maquiladoras] there is low pay and sexual harassment; they don't permit pregnant or fat women, or married women either, and if they miss a day of work for whatever reason they have to pay. The workers are the ones that have to pay for every day no matter what the reason. There are clearly more negatives than positives, but what is important is that *at least it is a source of work for Tecpán and other towns.* The workers get an opportunity to learn the trade, and they might be able to use that to work for

themselves or their families in the future. That is how the sweater businesses got started, a few families had the knowledge and were able to train others. This is especially effective since most of the women workers don't have education and can't afford it, so they get training in another way. Also, I say that it's better to have that sort of job than to get involved in gangs or prostitution, for example. Look what happened: during the recent protests [on June 10, 2001; discussed in Chapter 4] we had gang members who wanted something free, they looted and stole what wasn't theirs, and that's dishonorable. I'd say better to have a job than to get involved in that.

What would be really great for the people would be a Kaqchikel-run maquila with Kaqchikel owners and workers. The working conditions and wages would be different, and with the money earned we could also support the people and the schools in different ways, or by funding the cultural movement, contributing to schools and the economy. And it would be a thing of pride because it would be with our people and our language. We already have the knowledge and the connections with the sweater trade. Tecpán already has that, and we are known for our sweaters. When I go to the capital city they know us because we are from Tecpán, they know and respect the sweaters that come from Tecpán, we already have a reputation, and this is in the indigenous community.

What we need to work on is raising consciousness, but most especially in the rural areas where political participation is weak and unorganized, and where the education system is not functioning properly, where the kids don't go to school or stop going — to build a force for political participation so the people will be just as interested in politics — and they will better understand who they are voting for, what they need to do to participate in the process, they will recognize their efforts as democratic and will be able to aid our process. This will improve democracy here in Tecpán, if people begin to get educated and interested in the process.

Maquiladoras often serve as poster children for all that is wrong with globalization and free trade: the loss of jobs in the United States, exploitative working conditions abroad, the creation of a race for the bottom in terms of wages among developing countries. Maquiladoras have not created the smoothly symbiotic web of relations that the exporter Tom Heffron (see Chapter 1) attributes to free-trade policies. Simón expresses a point of view not uncommon in Tecpán and elsewhere in the Maya Highlands. Tecpanecos are by no means anti-capitalist or even anti-free trade, but most do feel exploited by enduring inequalities in the system. This is to say, Tecpanecos we have talked with do not lay blame on the structure of capitalism for the circumstances in which they find themselves, but do place blame with the way the system is manipulated for gain by particular individuals, with apparent disregard for the moral dimensions of life. In some ways, this perspective seems inconsistent. Capitalism is about pursuing self-interest (the invisible hand and so forth), so how can Tecpanecos condemn the success of the player without condemning the game itself? But, of course, capitalism is not monolithic. There is no natural or inevitable reason why capitalism has to adhere to free-market fundamentalism. And here, Simón proposes a clever use of tactics of resistance: co-opting the terms of exploitation — the ideas of neoliberal economics, of outsourcing, of maquiladoras — toward the fulfillment of a vernacular modernity suited to located circumstances and conditions. Simón's is an inspiring vision of participatory democracy — that is, that a fully informed and engaged electorate makes its voice heard at the ballot box to affect change — and of a local prescription for stakeholding capitalism — that is, that a local enterprise can benefit from free trade and outsourcing.

Such tactics constitute a limit point, a regional horizon that becomes the target of localized criticism and a cipher of social energies, thought, and practices. In this way, limit points inhibit broader considerations and possibilities, not by repressing them but by disclosing a world of other problems. Such a horizon of disclosure and possibility puts the expansive interconnectedness and interdependence of things in a spatial and temporal context. We see how the very terms of empowerment and practice that Simón deploys limit the consideration of other possible orientations. Note his invocation of "at least" statements. Such hedges index a limit point in his discourse: "It is better than . . . ," Simón says, and here we could fill in any number of disparaging alternatives for Simón's specter of gang violence. Such statements define a pragmatic morality by implicitly investing some practice with the quality of being right and good while negating other comparisons ("It is still not as good as . . . ," e.g.). In this way, the promises of progress, development, and modernity are built around the generation and reproduction of individual and collective desires in the service of certain political-economic ends (see also J. Collier 1997; Ferguson 1999).

The rise of maquiladoras along the Pan-American Highway cannot be understood as simply an economic trend. Various kinds of globalization interact and compete in the postwar Highlands, each related to competing models of progress, development, and moral propriety. The paradox of Maya individuals recognizing that this kind of globalization is economic exploitation while justifying it via comparison to the past pushes us to understand attitudes about maquiladoras and other forms of nontraditional export production in relation to local moral models and cultural desires. This is not to justify this mode of production because "they want it" or "they are not opposed to it," but to complicate the polarized terms of acceptance versus opposition (Errington and Gewertz 2004, 21–24). The value of maquiladoras in Tecpán is figured in relation to the emerging threat and nebulous reality of gang violence, ideologies of democratic reform, and expectations about what a growing or prosperous community should look like. Part of this involves employment, no matter what kinds of violence are encountered at the workplace. Simón invokes a cynical "any job is a good job" attitude, which is not simply a personal preference but reflects a cultural trend that runs together with and reinforces the sometimes uncomfortable economic changes taking place. "It is much better to have a job than to get involved in crime or gangs or drugs," he reiterated. Seen as a limit point, Simón's statement highlights a particular moral orientation while ignoring other critical stances. His commentary speaks to conflicted moral experiences and reveals an acceptance of a world in which life chances are limited and locally emergent desires cling to the immediacy of pragmatic alternatives.

In an attempt to get away from the notion that global processes emerge primarily in a handful of especially cosmopolitan, or "global," cities, Alphonso Lingis (1998), in his essay on "Anger," proposes a model of a technocratic-commercial "archipelago" of urban and suburban areas ("the inner zone") where dynamism is not a product of industrial production or the possession of raw materials but is rooted in the organization of information and the manipulation of technologies. This inner zone is set apart from an "outer zone," the six-sevenths of humanity who live in out-of-the-way places like Tecpán, where the stuff that is consumed in the archipelago is extracted, manufactured, packaged, and exported. The archipelago is dependent, desperately so, on the outer zone, even as it seeks to cut itself off by portraying a world of discrete "players" and rational actors (cf. Cardoso and Faletto 1967; Frank 1967; Wallerstein 1974). Semi-urban places like Tecpán in the Maya Highlands are "global" places, although still peripheral in many ways to the mainstream of economic prosperity, healthcare delivery and services, and cultural capital (Lingis 1998).

Likewise, Simón notes that divisions within the globalized world system are cultural and moral as well as geographical. In suggesting that there should be a "Kaqchikel-run maquila with Kaqchikel owners and workers," Simón envisions a local world that is *within* the archipelago, as opposed to its current role as a producer of raw materials for international businesses. We noticed similar desires among nontraditional agricultural exporters, for whom retaining the means of production and exporting directly to overseas markets constituted a form of cultural empowerment even if the economic returns were disappointing. When Simón clarifies that "the working conditions and wages would be different," we see that becoming a part of the modern archipelago, in this view, is not simply about economic returns but involves the cultural and moral production of a place. He talks about the pride that this ownership would mean for the community. In envisioning this moral transformation, realities of the local situation, such as gang violence and crime, are seen to be out of place. They do not really belong in the community, even as they happen. The construction of the local world as progressing and modern depends upon the construction of specific aspects of that same world as retrograde, dangerous, threatening, and immoral. Here it is impossible to untangle economic trends from cultural and moral determinations, since even the most brutally exploitative relationship is now coded as job creation and supported by governmental initiatives that are part of larger peace and security processes.

Indeed, despite the recognition of oppressive labor conditions, maquiladoras still find support in the local world of Tecpán. Many, like Simón, see them as not as bad as the alternative, namely gang violence, unemployment, and petty crime. To understand how this specific form of violence — the violence of the workplace — gets overlooked, and even accepted, one must understand the force of affective desires that compel persons toward visions of something better, no matter what the costs. If desires sometimes point beyond the dominant state of affairs, they more often than not get routed along lines of what is practical or possible. Simón does not talk about collective resistance against the factories but about an incorporation of the factory model into local hands, a process that, although pitched as collective and communal, would likely benefit established or emergent interests and be no more "democratic," to use his words, than the extant factories.

Risk Management

Agricultural understandings and practices are composed of disjunctive and
incommensurably hybrid discourses. . . . Discourses of agriculture are not a
closed field of meaning and action but are profoundly shaped by the politics
of caste, class, and gender differentiation.

— AKHIL GUPTA, *Postcolonial Developments*

Contracting export vegetable production in Guatemala differs significantly
from maquiladora labor relations. It brings new possibilities, predicaments,
and more wishful thinking than do the factories. But, as we shall see, discussions of vegetable exporting still reflect the dichotomy of good-versus-bad
globalization. They are then used to theorize local–global connections and
make practical claims about progress, development, and the future.

Labor and ecological constraints favor smaller producers in the exotic-
produce market, and this allows smallholding farmers to retain access to
their primary means of production, land.[6] Maya peoples have strong affective
ties to their land,[7] and here the currents of globalization have reinforced
rather than eroded control over the material bases of culture. In particular,
agricultural exporting does not reconfigure the sense of place in rural areas
as do other varieties of industrial export production (see Green 2003).

In many ways, nontraditional production complements subsistence farming and builds on economic models that are familiar, comfortable, and culturally valued by most Kaqchikel Tecpanecos. Nontraditional crops are
more labor intensive than milpa, but the work regimes are similar and allow
for a highly valued degree of flexibility in work schedules. As one farmer
explained, "No one tells me when to go to work, when I can take a break, or
when I should go home." In fact, this man, like most nontraditional farmers,
generally leaves for his fields before 5:00 in the morning and often gets home
ten or twelve hours later, but he takes great comfort in his independence and
freedom to take off a day if he likes. Nontraditional crops require a lot of
care, and the high labor input results in an inverse relationship between plot
size and productivity that favors smallholders. Smallholding farmers are able
to subsidize labor inputs with parallel subsistence production and keep costs
down by exploiting unpaid household labor. On the one hand, this results in
the disruption of certain social patterns; women, in particular, are required

to work more in the fields and thus spend less time in the home and engaged in social networks. On the other hand, nontraditional production allows households to leverage the marginal value of their labor, increase economic efficiencies, and potentially to realize greater returns. Most importantly, nontraditional production allows at least a certain class of Maya farmers to pursue a new and profitable economic strategy while retaining control over their means of production.

Control over one's means of production is highly valued by the Kaqchikel farmers we have interviewed. In surveys conducted in 2000, 77.1 percent of respondents said that is it better to work as a farmer than in a factory. Their reasons all revolved around a common theme of controlling one's own means of production and destiny: "One is a slave working as an employee," "One wants his own land," "It is better to produce one's own necessities," "[In agriculture] one can decide when and how to work," and the most common response, simply, that in farming, "It is one's own" (*es propio*). Thus, while the contract model of agro-export production first arose in the Highlands in response to macroeconomic conditions, it has succeeded because of its convergence with local cultural logics, offering farmers a potentially lucrative means to get ahead while maintaining their own land.

Yet, critics argue that rural farmers growing broccoli and other nontraditional crops do not understand the risks of new global markets, so that when prices fall they are the ones left most vulnerable. Such assessments run the risk of ignoring the complex and contradictory motivations that propel farmers. To be sure, profits unevenly flow northward and there are greater risks involved in this sector. But those involved — farmers, packers, and exporters, each with different moral stakes and economic aims — readily acknowledge these risks, noting that they are precisely what justify the higher potential rates of return as compared to subsistence production. The problem, as they see it, is one of control. Maya farmers and packers have highly imperfect access to market information, belying any certain calculation of risk or return, though this is rapidly changing with cell phones and Internet access.

The complexities of technology use and access to information, risk management, and agricultural cooperation undermine views that, if well intentioned, victimize and often patronize Maya farmers, devaluing their capacity to strategize, exercise power, and organize futures. Maya farmers are not merely enacting the mandates of international capital but are, even as they recognize the asymmetries involved, rechanneling capital flows in the service of their own self-conceived futures. And, crucially, these futures are not defined simply in terms of economic returns, for the frames of "something better" among farmers encompass affective desires and social sensibilities.

One of the most effective strategies for smallholding farmers has been to join a cooperative organization, which allows collective bargaining and provides greater access to market information. About 20 percent of nontraditional producers belong to a cooperative. One of the most successful has been Aj Ticonel, funded in part by non-governmental aid organizations such as Oxfam and the Soros Foundation. Aj Ticonel exports fresh squash, French beans, broccoli, and other produce to the United States, and works with forty-seven different organizations throughout Guatemala's Western Highlands, including widows' associations and less formal farmer groups. Most of their associates are small-scale producers with less than one acre of land. The organization provides technical assistance, production credit, and access to a stable market for their products. It works hard to develop *confianza* (trust) among members, non-contractual trust relations that ensure steady supply, risk distribution, and voluntary labor in times of need. *Confianza* helps negotiate producer needs and consumer demands, maintain a balance between the two, and construct a non-alienating labor environment in which farmers feel more invested in the system.

One July day in 2001, we met with Aj Ticonel's operation managers, Alberto Monterrosa and Armando Maldonado. They showed us to a small office, reached by a set of industrial metal stairs rising above the packing plant floor, with walls of unfinished plywood, a small air conditioner running loudly in the corner, and a poster that read "El Equipo de Fútbol del EZLN" (The Zapatista Soccer Team), which implied something about their political sensibilities.

Monterrosa and Maldonado, both university educated ladinos, are dedicated to rural development and work closely with the local Maya population — their desires manifesting a complex blend of altruism and market savvy, multiculturalism and sub rosa paternalism. We sat around an old conference table, and after offering us drinks (rum, whisky, or bottled water), Monterrosa began:

> Our goal is that campesinos maintain their milpa, but just as a cultural force. They should leave the milpa only on their most fragmented lands. The best lands, the ones with irrigation, should be dedicated to the most

profitable crops. Garden horticulture, such as mini-vegetables, is highly profitable but requires a lot of manual labor. And this is to the benefit of the small campesino.

Aj Ticonel's managers seek to "train" the campesinos they work with — discipline them in the fickle ways of international markets. While explicitly seeking to change local cultural norms, they hope to do so in a sensitive way, introducing neoliberal market reforms but always with the goal of alleviating poverty.

Like many others we met along the broccoli trail, Monterrosa and Maldonado hold conflicting perceptions of the Guatemalan economy. On the one hand, they advocate neoliberal reforms as a moral project to make the world a better place. On the other hand, they see themselves as activists and advocates for rural Maya farmers in a struggle for economic equality. For them, the notion of "something better" becomes a dominant image of the future filled with a peculiar blend of left- and right-leaning sensibilities.

Incongruously, Monterrosa and Maldonado employ a language of class (e.g., they almost invariably refer to the Maya farmers with whom they work as "campesinos," or peasants, emphasizing class over ethnic inflections) and promote the benefits of cooperative association while also embracing a capitalist ethic of individual responsibility and the reigning paradigm of neoliberal reform. Monterrosa explains: "We privilege individual effort. Socialist countries and all the other collective systems have failed because they did not privilege individual effort. And so we say, if you work more you earn more." At one level, Monterrosa strategically situates himself and his group within the still salient paradigms of Cold War politics. It was not long ago in Guatemala that involvement in an agricultural cooperative was a dangerous proposition, placing one within the sights of army and paramilitary surveillance anxious to stamp out any inkling of communism. At another level, Monterrosa expresses a view of compassionate neoliberalism, a sort of Third Way to economic development that would be familiar to Tony Blair and Britain's "New Labour" movement.[8]

Long celebrated as sites of resistance, co-ops are also disciplinary operations, imposing strictly defined schedules, procedures, and codes that regulate supply structures, farmer training, and crop packing. Such discipline is not unlike that required by the factory or the plantation — the difference, of course, being that in co-ops farmers voluntarily submit to the disciplinary regime. As it conforms to broader trends of biopower (i.e., the organization and control of productive populations), Aj Ticonel's system is often beneficial for farmers, especially when it involves the devolution of power mechanisms at the local level. Thus, the larger global systems in which Maya farmers find themselves operating need not be oppressive, even if they are in some ways "hegemonic" and productive of politically inflected desires via new forms of training.

Juridical changes over the past few years have exacerbated the risks and challenges for smallholding farmers and yet at the same time strengthened the importance of and security provided by cooperative arrangements. U.S. customs crackdowns on residual pesticide contaminants, new rules governing what can be called "organic produce," and post–September 11 security measures have forced Aj Ticonel and other producers to implement costly reforms. They are working through David Food Technologies, a multinational firm that has the authority to inspect and certify farming conditions for the United States Department of Agriculture.

"The United States, President Clinton, said that bad, rotten products were coming into that country," Maldonado explains, "that Guatemalan products were making U.S. residents sick and contaminating the supply of food. The campesinos know what they have to do to stay in the market and to compete now." Aj Ticonel has begun a series of reforms (known as *buenas prácticas*) to enhance the marketability of their products and achieve certification standards. As an outcome of cultural representations, an anxious age, aesthetic standards, and geopolitics (Friedberg 2004), *buenas prácticas* and other sanitary standards intertwine the moral, political, and economic. In February 2002, Aj Ticonel replaced the plant's cement floor with a tile one to avoid dust contamination. Sanitation is stressed for the mostly female assembly-line workers, who now must use rubber boots, coveralls, gloves, and face masks. "The bathrooms are nicer than hotels," Maldonado explains.

> We know that all those handling the vegetables are clean. We agree with the U.S. law, you need to receive the best product possible, but that means we have to work hard to better our system, from field to plant to market. The campesinos are pissed off, but little by little they are coming to agree. They know what they have to do. But there are some things they actually appreciate, the better bathrooms, for example. It is not just for the products, these *buenas prácticas*, but also for the health of the workers. But sometimes it is difficult because there is only one bathroom on a farm and you may have

to walk a distance to use it. This always annoys the workers. They tell us: "Why can't I just go here behind the tree or in the field." We didn't make these regulations, but we agree with them, and that is what the farmers must do also if they want to sell. There is no choice in the matter. They must protect the crops, and we feel that it is also a way to protect themselves. In our fields, to have certification and health safety, you just can't go to the bathroom wherever you want.

This is not a clear-cut case of either opportunism or exploitation, knowing the risks on one side or being duped on the other. Maya farmers are trying to take advantage of new market opportunities and routes to economic power, and yet such maneuvering necessarily flows through channels not entirely of their own making. Even as they are critically reshaping the edges of capitalist expansion, they are also, through that very gesture of subaltern resistance, shoring up its course.

There are desires of consumers to be contended with — North Americans with expectations of hygiene and sanitation that are obsessively different from those of Maya farmers — and these get encoded in federal regulations and the unwritten market text. Maya farmers must conform to these discursive formations without really having chosen to become involved in them and without any ability to participate in their ongoing organization, a distant mode of discipline in which how to grow and harvest broccoli is determined by a removed collective consumerist regime of eating healthily. Many of the dangers involved in export agriculture have to do with the fact that farmers in the Highlands have little experience with these codes and the technology needed to comply is expensive. Farmers run the risk of producing a worthless crop that would be rejected in the United States because it does not meet these standards. In this case, the hegemonic character of global trade — the promise of extra cash running alongside the realities of risk and uneven returns — is sustained, in part, through subtle discursive and disciplinary procedures ostensibly aimed at regulating the enterprise and making it equitable.

Maldonado and Monterrosa tell us that they see themselves as the "voice of the campesinos" and they marshal a repertoire of success stories: one farmer who started out with less than a quarter acre of land earned enough money in just a couple years to buy two additional acres; another family with a modest-sized farm is said to have earned Q5,000 (about $640) in one four-month period. In our conversations with farmers bringing their produce to be weighed, washed, and packed at Aj Ticonel, we heard somewhat less rosy stories, too. "These products have done just average because we have to invest a lot of money in them," said one farmer. "When prices are good, we make a little money, but not a lot." He also contrasted his cooperative association with Aj Ticonel to the less-than-ideal situation of selling to coyotes.

As Maldonado sees it, the problem is not the coyotes per se but access to information. If farmers had reliable access to information about price variations between markets and to world-market prices, they would be better able to demand fair prices for their product. In this case, it would not just be a matter of "knowing the risks," but of understanding more fully the various ways that global markets and forces operate at an intimate level. New technology affords nontraditional crop producers access to these foreign markets and information systems. Greater access to media means that homes and communities are "potentially, much better informed," allowing the viewer to "situate oneself at a distance from the (national, local) viewpoint" and gain a more cosmopolitan perspective which might subvert local and global controlling processes (Tomlinson 1999, 115–16).

There is a problem though, as Maldonado points out, because "at the same time as prices are dropping in the market in the U.S., the costs are rising because of these new rules and requirements. But we hope that little by little, with better products, if the organizations and cooperative can comply perfectly with these rules, they will have better products and be able to beat the competition. This is the strategy, to work hard now preparing, but through the low market, and then to put out a product that can earn more." If such arrangements uncannily intimate a patron/client relationship, they carry with them the comfort and security as well as the dehumanizing victimization of such dependency.

To further illustrate the ways ideas of progress and development condition desire we turn to the case of the Proyecto de Desarrollo Integral de Comunidades Rurales (Integrated Development of Rural Communities Project, or DICOR), an executive-branch organization charged with rural, mostly agricultural, development efforts.

Desiring Development

With a US$15 million budget, DICOR works in seventy-seven municipalities in the poorest areas of Guatemala. Its purpose is to operationalize a particular model of development, supported by the state and international consensus, that seeks to leverage private investment in bureaucratically identified sectors of the economy and geographic regions. This logic emphasizes the use of private capital for common social welfare and utilizes the form of conventional top-down development schemes in which the state targets "populations" for development. DICOR's projects include construction of connector roads, potable-water systems, and other small-scale infrastructural projects — making marginalized areas more attractive to private capital investment. At the same time, they have a number of agricultural, fishing, forestry, tourism, and micro-enterprise development projects — providing technical assistance and credit access to producers too small and risky to be attractive to private investors. This model reflects a shift from a state-controlled political economy to one governed by private enterprise. The global division of labor — in agriculture as well as manufacturing — increasingly depends on cheap, docile, and flexible workers (Hardt and Negri 2000; Ong 1999). DICOR adopts the neoliberal emphasis on free markets and flexible accumulation, although we also find a potent desire for industrial development and a romantic, post–World War II plan for import-substitution industrialization programs.

Danis Romero and Milhelm Orozco, earnest state employees, were pleased to share their vision of the country's future. We met with them in DICOR's conference room in an old industrial complex on the edge of the capital city. In many ways, they represent bureaucratic hegemony in action, agents of the government seeking to discipline categorical populations according to prescribed models of "progress." It is tempting and relatively easy, at least in the Guatemalan context, to demonize and criticize such actors, even if Romero and Orozco come across as sincerely well intentioned. Yet, recognizing that power and knowledge are formative and productive, we can both understand their desires as genuinely heartfelt and discriminate the ways that power and domination are working through their preoccupations. Romero and Orozco are men with projects and plans, with a vision for the future, a with a sense of good work and public service. But they are also the product of certain forms of discipline and training. Instrumentally and sincerely, they have come to adopt the broadly neoliberal philosophical principles and discourses of multiculturalism promoted by recent government administrations. They turn these broad ideal-types to their own ends, and the presumed neutrality of scientific development is compromised by their earnest feeling that certain stances and cultural attitudes hold Guatemala back from the progress that should be its birthright. They present a neoliberal, Washington-consensus model with a tinge of Guatemalan nationalism and the patina of lingering paternalism. They sometimes seem uncomfortable with the mantle of neoliberal multiculturalism and fall back on an idiom that portrays the country's rural population as helpless and backward.

Romero and Orozco sat across from us at a long mahogany table, seeming to compete for our attention, aggressive in their turn-taking tactics. They may work together and share broadly similar goals, but there is a noticeable tension. A stocky man, Romero is drinking coffee and the caffeine seems to be getting the best of him as his speech becomes more and more energetic and his gesticulations more and more emphatic. A slight man in comparison to Romero, Orozco is more subdued, waiting for an opportunity to intercede rather than forcefully plying his views. At one point, Romero draws an elaborate diagram of an idealized family farm on a whiteboard. With duck coops built above a small pond, the droppings fertilize aquatic plants and algae that the fish will eat; in turn, the ducks eat fish meal. The farm includes a sty with pigs that will eat the household refuse, and an elaborate system of crop rotation for the fields that surround the homestead. Romero argues that subsistence farmers must be encouraged to pursue such self-sustaining agricultural techniques, using simple technologies they already command. Orozco responds: "The model my friend just drew is great . . . if everybody had land, if they all had water, if they were all knowledgeable; if they had gone to school they could understand this system. Since they don't, it is going to take a while to realize." Not to mention that duck, like broccoli, is hardly a staple of the Maya diet. Orozco goes on to advocate a "basic necessities" paradigm of direct aid and infrastructural improvements, which resembles Aj Ticonel's *buenas prácticas* program, to educate and disseminate knowledge into marginal locations.

Orozco and Romero both view the alignment of cultural attitudes and modes of production as crucial, but just how such an alignment will take place remains up in the air. Orozco realizes the shortcomings of his colleague's idealized model; for his part, Romero seems to realize that what appears to be a grassroots approach is actually a form of control and governance. Both models hinge on remaking local worlds and the people who inhabit them, and both run into trouble where the abstract ideals of neoliberalism do not map onto the gritty reality of Highland Guatemala.

Despite their debate over the means of development, Romero and Orozco do share a view of a future industrialized Guatemala. They present a compelling argument for the need for neoliberal reforms in Guatemala's economy, harnessing private capital to do the work of socioeconomic development. Yet this is no undigested regurgitation of formulaic models. In fact, we find an approach that seeks to marry capitalist profit-seeking with social conscience, DICOR acting as a facilitator, encouraging corporations and venture capitalists to invest and become invested in certain prescribed sectors of the economy. Romero and Orozco do not see this as simple privatization, but as creating new governmental alliances, which, in their opinion, will benefit society as a whole and for the long term, and help realize their personal desires to contribute to a social and moral cause in which they strongly believe.

There are contradictory images of the intended beneficiaries of DICOR's efforts. On the one hand, there is talk of empowerment, simply providing the opportunity for "peasants" to progress into capitalists and proletarians. At the same time, there is a clearly modernist vision that many Maya farmers would find disturbing. Orozco notes that "What interests us is agricultural industrialization," and Romero adds: "What we need to do is modernize our agriculture in order to focus on industrialization, which is what we need to get out of our situation of underdevelopment. No other way is economically viable. Nor will it be technically efficient if we don't take into account agricultural modernization so that we can move to industrialization."

Implicit in this desire is the notion that Maya small farmers stand in the way of development (see Nelson 1999; E. Fischer 2001). They stand in the way not only of national progress but also of the development of these two men as professionals. This is not the Maya's fault, the officials emphasize. (Like many ladino civil servants in Guatemala, they find recourse in multicultural discourse as a means of suturing the impossible yet necessary categorical role that Maya campesinos secure in their own modernization plans.) To our ears, however, their words, if sometimes compelling and optimistic, are also edgy and biting. Orozco says, "We have to take advantage of the resources that already exist. The majority of the population are campesinos. They are knowledgeable about agriculture, and so this is where we have to start. We cannot industrialize them because they are not educated in a general sense. They are not prepared for that." At best, the campesinos are seen as misguided, lacking fundamental capacities to manipulate their own lives and in need of patronistic direction. Romero continues: "We hope to help the campesinos identify their problems because they do not know what they are. But when they can identify their problems they will be able to solve them. They are going to learn to make their own decisions. And we as the state are just facilitators — they are the ones who are going to do it all. This is sustainable development." Indeed it is: punishment may be a deterrent and economic reward an incentive, but internalized discipline and fomented desires are the surest routes to realizing visions of transformation and models of development (see Oglesby's 2004 analysis of these processes at work in the Guatemalan sugar industry).

Romero and Orozco reiterate what the farmers had earlier told us — that there is indeed some extra cash to be made in exotic-produce exporting — as evidence of the kind of economic "progress" they advocate. But one must remain suspicious, for the other attitudes expressed by farmers are not part of the picture presented by such advocates. The nontraditional export trade opens up a gap of dissatisfaction for both farmers and development workers, delivering only some extra cash, and this is exactly what sustains it, like so many other global industries, as an ambivalent coincidence of exploitation and "fair trade." Though it is important to emphasize the increased dynamism of transnational subjectivities and new modalities of local consumption or production opened up within this milieu, we must also bear in mind that precisely because aspiring political and economic hegemonies are looser, potentially less efficacious in a global setting, operating at distances and indirectly, they are often more subtle and exploitative (see Nash and Fernandez Kelly 1983; Salzinger 2000).[9] "Exploitation is not simply opposed to justice," Žižek reminds us. "*A worker is exploited even when he is 'fully paid'*. . . . There is one commodity (the workforce) which is exploited precisely when it is 'paid its full value'" (1999, 180). This rings true in the case of the broccoli farmer, as exploitation moves beyond the economic to encompass new forms of governance and compliance.

The workers do all the work, Romero and Orozco readily admit, and the distant work of governance remains understated. DICOR, as with other state agencies, denies playing any effective role in organizing and mediating local articulations with the global marketplace. Neutral "facilitators," like an open door neither inhibiting nor screening the global commodity flows, DICOR appears democratic, not class compromised, and so is able to rhetorically "give" all the risk and responsibility over to the worker-citizen, even as the "rewards" of nontraditional production may not be as fairly dealt (see Offe 1984, 119–29). Participation in this industry itself is portrayed as a free gift, a space of opportunity for farmers cleared by the state, and so when the chips inevitably come up short it is indeed convenient that the farmers all along "knew the risks" and "made their own decisions." The idea that exploitation may be taken up as a moral project among those being shortchanged is troubling.[10] Yet it is exactly what makes the broccoli trade so compellingly dangerous. This creates a theoretical dilemma for those who view the penetration of transnational markets into marginal communities as unilateral, either cultural imperialism or local subversion (see Eagleton 1991; Žižek 2000).[11] From a more modest perspective, with a slight swivel of kaleidoscope eyes these binary oppositions fold into complex, variously dimensioned, often paradoxical interactions in which multiple forms of governance and corporate hegemonies overlap, sometimes at odds and sometimes in mutual support and determination. A critical and engaged ethnographic inquiry must address the multivalent nature of these interfaces, the many ways that selves and others are defined and divided through their efforts to make the world a better place.

THREE

Ultimatums, Moral Models, and the Limit Points of Hegemony

We have to push the notion of hegemony into the lived space of realities in social relationships, in the give and take of social life, as in the sweaty, warm space between the arse of him who rides and the back of him who carries.

— MICHAEL TAUSSIG, *Shamanism, Colonialism, and the Wild Man*

Guillermo Rodríguez, a Kaqchikel Maya man in his mid-fifties, grew up helping his father in the fields and attending school only irregularly. Largely self-educated, he is now a well-respected social scientist working at the national university. One evening in the summer of 2001, sitting around his family's kitchen table in Tecpán, a cooking fire filling the room with equal amounts of warmth and smoke, Rodríguez responded to our question about the many economic changes faced by Maya farmers. He is energetic and wants us to know that he has thought through the issue. We take heed of what he has to say — an organic intellectual, a spokesperson for the Maya community, an advocate with an agricultural background, someone who speaks our academic language. But we are also wary. He is no longer a farmer, and his middle-class lifestyle means that he does not face the risks and uncertainties about which he so energetically speaks. "It is not true that they don't understand the risks. They do understand what the risks are. If you analyze the costs of production of beans, of corn, these really aren't profitable either. They never have been. But these new crops provide some benefit to families. They know the risks."

Rodríguez points to a certain freedom that local producers enjoy in "knowing the risks" and not simply being broadsided by capitalist expansion, and this knowledge presumably enables potentially profitable economic relations for local producers. At the same time, Rodríguez stops short of critiquing the unequal distribution of information and capital that conditions risk in the first place. The idea of risk functions prominently in this discourse to justify things as they are.[1] Because farmers "know the risks" they are able to derive some profit, and yet this very knowledge constrains possibilities for farmers to complain about, and resist, the practical dilemmas they face. Their awareness of the risks means, effectively, that the responsibility is theirs — the perilousness and the rewards.

The theoretical and political positioning found in studies of nontraditional agriculture tends to either critique the economic exploitation and increased risk of global capitalism or celebrate local resistance to the world market (AVANCSO 1994; Goldin 1996; Goldin and Sáez 1993; Hamilton and Fischer 2003; Thurpp, Bergeron, and Waters 1995; cf. von Braun, Hotchkiss, and Immink 1989; Immink and Alarcon 1993; Carletto, de Janvry, and Sadoulet 1999; Klak 1999). In this chapter, we interrogate theories about hegemony, global processes, resistance, and social action. We contend that a critical ethnographic examination of moral orientations and desire can move us beyond the dichotomy of hegemony and resistance. We argue that the turn to export agriculture in Highland Guatemala is neither simply empowering nor totally debilitating for Maya farmers. Rather, it is an ambivalent cultural practice in which multiple struggles are at play and in which there are various tendencies that converge with and diverge from dominant forms of social organization. Shared aspirations for "something better" (along with a shared moral orientation about what is fair and just) constitute a real sense of transformation and progress given the daily struggle of *luchando por la vida* and yet, at the same time, limit possibilities for social change. This framing is in no way to "denigrate the importance of the human justice issues" (Massumi 2002, 132). It is to be pragmatic. It is to acknowledge that the global broccoli trade is a fact, a material reality that embodies hope and a contradictory relationship between American consumers and Maya farmers.

Grounding cultural analysis, ethical questions, and political strategies in how things are rather than in how they ideally ought to be, far from justifying the status quo, can allow the global connection to be "re-posed and operated upon in an entirely new problematic, one that may even now be waiting for us around the next node" (Massumi 2002, 132). We consider the cultural meanings and moral valences to be as consequential as the economic facts. When we talk to a Maya farmer who continues to grow broccoli in the face of the new risks involved — despite having lost money last season, despite the fact that switching back to milpa would (from our perspective) make more sense — for us to adopt a posture of condescension or pity would mean sacrificing a unique opportunity. This would be simply equating the "interpretation of some person's or some group's suffering as the reproduction of oppressive relationships of production" (Kleinman and Kleinman 1991, 276). Using our approach, however, we can create bridges across patterns of desire that push against the tendency — noticeable in both neoliberal and anti-global commitments — to keep desire in its place, individuated and localized.

The projects through which futures are envisioned and the world made can be said to be "moral projects," in the sense that they matter deeply and are defined with reference to what matters (see Kleinman 1999a). Because projects connote the act of taking up stakes in a world of desires and values, there is at least some collective dimension to their formation and actualization. Moral projects enact the shared or contested investments of locally figured worlds.[2] They are also embedded in large-scale political and economic processes, which in turn impact local worlds. This is what gives hegemonies and worldviews their durability and capacity to dwell deeply in the desires and aspirations of people. Hegemonies take root in social experience. Worldviews get rooted — often dangerously so — in life worlds. Localized, even idiosyncratic or personal moral projects, articulate with expansive ideologies, shared practices, collective moral commitments and beliefs, and socially produced desires.

One advantage of ethnography as a research method is that it pushes us to take seriously people's motives for becoming involved in activities that, from another — perhaps our own — perspective, seem to involve certain forms of danger and inequality. This involves stopping short of universal ethical claims that impute our desires onto others, but it need not imply a relativistic disavowal of moral responsibility. It is useful to maintain both a critical account of political and economic relations and a humbler appreciation of our informants' and our own desires.[3] Such methodological patience demands an analytic shift from an overarching theory of power as a totalizing, top-down force to an analytic of the multiple, often contradictory ways that desire, power, and cultural meanings intersect in specific situations. Rodríguez, critically optimistic, points us in this direction: "Neoliberalism is an economic current. The fact is: it's a worldwide economic current. Nobody can halt or stop this flood. It's like the Rio Grande, you can't stop it. But, where is this river coming from? What purpose does it serve? When we understand the source and causes of this river, we can use it [e.g., a global flow] to our own advantage."

Equality, Morality, and Exploitation

Let us begin by recounting how local moral models of fairness and equality can trump, or at least temper, hegemonic market impositions that are often assumed to promote competition at the expense of local solidarity. In Tecpán, a number of cultural traditions reinforce moral values of reciprocity and cooperation: communal harvesting, ritual exchanges of sweet-rolls on Maundy Thursday, collective obligations for the town fiesta, and so on (see Fischer 2001; Fischer and Hendrickson 2002). This is not to be romanticized as a subaltern anti-capitalist stance — as we have seen, most Tecpanecos value just rewards for hard work and want to better their own material circumstances. At the same time, the Tecpaneco vernacular of capitalist meritocracy (valuing hard work and the fruits of affluence that are honestly come by) is tempered by deep suspicion of those who get too rich too quick and who are stingy with their resources. Morality tales are told of greedy individuals' Faustian pacts with the devil, hidden chests of gold, and connections to the drug trade (see Chapter 1). Most of the Maya farmers with whom we have worked express a strong preference for cooperative behavior while also recognizing the realities of market competition.

Further proof of such a moral orientation comes from economic experiments, particularly the Ultimatum Game, conducted in Tecpán in 2003.[4] The Ultimatum Game offers a robust experimental method for documenting the limits of self-interest and rationality in actual behavior and the competing pulls of competition and cooperation in the context of anonymous game-play. Such experiments, predicated on unpredictability and open-ended interactions, allow us to get at future-orientations and how outcomes are projected on the basis of durable moral models, practical concerns, and social values. In the Ultimatum Game, two players are anonymously paired with one another and a sum of money (*x*) is given in cash to Player A. Player A's sole move is to offer Player B a portion (*y*) of the total *x*. Knowing the amount (*x*) that Player A has received, Player B's one move is then to either accept or reject the offer. If B accepts, she keeps the money offered (*y*) and Player A keeps the rest (*x–y*). If B rejects the offer, the money is returned to the main pot and neither player receives anything. Thus the game consists entirely of Player A making an offer and Player B either accepting or rejecting that offer.

In terms of maximizing one's material utility, the most rational move for Player A is to offer the smallest unit of account (10 percent if playing with ten bills) and for Player B to accept the offer (since any amount will have more utility than zero, which is the alternative). In fact, in several rounds of the Ultimatum Game played in Tecpán (n = 72), we found unusually high offers, suggestive of a high degree of cooperation. The average offer in Tecpán was 51 percent of the total, among the highest recorded anywhere in the world (see Henrich et al. 2004). The modal offer was 50 percent, while fully 76 percent of players offered half the pot; hyper-fair offers (those of more than 50 percent of *x*) made up 16 percent of offers in Tecpán.

Our results are consistent with the hypothesis advanced by Henrich et al. (2004), Ensminger (2004), and others that market integration results in more cooperative game playing: Tecpán is a booming market town tightly linked to the national economy through the broccoli trade and other venues. Although market integration shows a strong correlation with cooperative game behavior, equally important for understanding Ultimatum Game results from Tecpán are vernacular rationalities built upon moral conceptions of equality and fairness, socioeconomic differences between individuals and communities, and the local history of violence and activism. When questioned after the game about why they offered what they did, players who offered 50 percent or more of the total told us that they imagined their partner needing the money as much or more than they did, and in this light they did not feel right taking more than half. Most players who offered less that 50 percent similarly reported that they felt that they probably needed the money more than their partner and thus felt morally justified in making a lower offer (and a few invoked a clear income-maximizing rationality to justify low offers).

While the broccoli trade has become a compelling way for some Tecpaneco farmers to earn some extra cash and to achieve *algo más*, the very act of getting ahead financially is fraught with moral dangers inasmuch as it contests norms of equality. To elide such dangers and the fate of social ostracism, farmers are expected to reinvest profits in the local community by supporting local causes and community events, as well as through funding the business ventures of their extended families. Critics point out that this can create patronage networks that reproduce exploitative relationships, bringing global dependency down to the local level.

One key contradiction between producers and consumers in the broccoli trade involves how people feel responsible for their involvement in the trade and the ways they benefit or lose out. Moral models in the Highlands emphasize cooperation and interpersonal connections in ways that most consumers do not recognize. This allows Northern consumers to benefit from Maya norms in a sort of moral arbitrage. Farmers in the Highlands realize that export agriculture disproportionately benefits consumers, whereas consumers are often cynical, even escapist, about their involvement in the economic inequalities of the global marketplace. Some purposefully purchase Guatemalan produce to allay these political-economic anxieties by "supporting" growers in a part of the world they only know through tourism and cultural simulations. This is a cynical kind of owning up, delivering personal relief over collective responsibility.

Hegemony and Desire

Some critics of nontraditional export agriculture in Guatemala fear that it is simply a new form of economic colonization: foreign concerns entice and coerce poor Maya peasants to produce luxury goods and commodities for more affluent markets, profits are asymmetrically distributed, and farmers bear the brunt of market fluctuations and failures. One might call this process hegemony. It is part of the overall domination of "the West," or "Empire," or "McDonald's," that is thought to characterize globalization. Neoliberal regimes and world markets are strengthened as ideologies of "something better"—of progress and of the future—drive the desires of producers and consumers in the Global South to engage in practices that are, from a political-economic perspective, exploitative. The domination of capitalist food production is linked to ideologies of progress that are used to justify (through images of something better) differential geographies of class, access to opportunities, and exposure to risks. Among farmers and exporters in the Guatemalan Highlands, the global broccoli trade does not involve absolute acceptance, clear consensus, or practices of resignation. It also involves skepticism, cynicism, disbelief, and even resistance.

Farmers see broccoli production as a way to co-opt global flows toward local and personal ends, to hitch personal and collective futures to new economic opportunities. Along the broccoli trail, we find individual and collective actions that are neither merely reactive — neither opposing or adopting hegemonic impositions — nor freely proactive, but worked out through practice and within fields of desire. Taking seriously Maya farmers' desires to achieve *algo más* — not reducing universal aspirations such as "something better" or "progress" to Western impositions — also means that we must rethink what is conventionally understood as hegemony and global processes.

Following Gramsci (1971) and Comaroff and Comaroff (1991), hegemony may be understood to be manufactured consent, where a particular political ideology becomes embedded in a cultural model so as to seem natural, acceptable, desirable.[5] Hegemony refers to the way that common-sense thinking benefits a ruling class, ensuring that things are the way they are supposed to be and thus limiting critical inquiry into those conditions. Hegemonic processes condense historical blocs of political force and economic clout, supplanting the need to use brute force to maintain a social order (although, as Barry Lyons [2005] argues, hegemony is not inconsistent with physical and martial coercion, and in practice, coercion, persuasion, and consent are often hard to distinguish). Hegemony is basically a struggle to define the "universal," to elevate contingent, local sets of ideas to the status of normal, true, and good such that they seem commonsensical (see Butler, Laclau, and Žižek 2000).

Hegemony does not merely react to or repress desire post facto; it "constrain[s] in advance the kinds of objects that can and do appear within the horizon of desire" (Butler 2000, 149). All cultural production is in some sense hegemonic — or is part of this social process of hegemony — in the sense that forms of knowledge, expression, and discourse frame thoughts and desires, induce people to think and act in certain ways, determine what can be said or heard. But to meaningfully distinguish hegemony from that other problematic term, culture, it must point to at least some form of economic exploitation, such as a class structure. The flow and stitching together of desires in the social world often reveals a patterning that plays to the political and economic advantage of some groups ("classes") more than others (Deleuze and Guattari 1983; Massumi 2002).[6] Yet, one limitation of such a view is that it tempts us to view hegemony as a "thing," owned by someone or some group and unilaterally imposed on the masses. Power is thus seen as a possession, not as a flow or force. Hegemony is an incessant, ultimately open-ended process involving competing discourses, contentious practices, and the ongoing production of desires. Ambivalence is at the heart of hegemonic processes precisely because such processes always produce collective desires that are divergent and resistant, no matter how tightly consolidated a hegemony may seem. Hegemony is not the imposition of a group in opposition to the resistance of those being dominated. It is a social process that occurs *between* people, such that collectives do not cause or control but are themselves an outcome of this struggle to transform, strengthen, or reverse relations between people (Buchanan 2000, 30).

As a social process, hegemony stops being something that is "bad" — to be analyzed and opposed from the outside — and becomes a necessary aspect of the social world, a process to be studied, engaged, and inhabited from within. To account for the ways that power shapes how people want, how desires are channeled and constrained socially, is not to justify those relations, but to put the analysis of power on pragmatic footing. For example, to claim that some Maya farmers desire deeply to engage in nontraditional agricultural production is not to overlook the economic inequities structuring the commodity chain as a whole, or to justify those inequities because, as is often said, "People want it." Rather, by taking into account how people want and how desires enliven sometimes risky or impractical practices we achieve at least two pragmatic effects. We get a more concrete sense of the existential depth of hegemonic and controlling processes, which makes such processes only more available for critique. And we also get a sense of the many levels at which power operates across global processes, and of the multiple, often contradictory effects of hegemonic processes as they are embedded, challenged, and transformed in practice (see Greenhouse 2005). Thus, this conception still points us in the direction of economic exploitation and political control. But here the production and accumulation of surplus value is not reducible to the hidden or explicit agenda of a class that utilizes the forms of public culture to produce false consciousness. As Weber showed, the accumulation of wealth is not a natural desire but is itself an historical and cultural outcome linked to moral orientations, values, and the pursuit of status. Added to that, surplus accumulation strengthens forms of political domination and social organization, such as colonialism, nationalism, and empire. But economic exploitation runs together with multiple, competing discourses about what is good and bad, right and wrong, fair and just, framing desires for those left out of the mainstream of economic prosperity as much as those benefiting from it.

Hegemony, it turns out, is not fundamentally about cultural domination; it is about moral orientation, the pursuit of happiness and well-being, desires and aspirations, and conceptions of normalcy and the good life. Hegemony succeeds when what people are concerned about is brought into line with the pursuits of making money and the benefits realized by a slice of the stream of humanity. It is in the lived process of desiring that hegemonies take hold, producing certain kinds of producers, consumers, and subjects. Individuals and groups become firmly attached to the social formations from which their potent sense of identity, security, or power derive. Hegemony as a social process actualizes a double bind in the context of everyday life, where people are shortchanged, both empowered and constrained, in struggles to define how the world ought to be.

Hegemonies do appease subjects, providing at least a modicum of agency, a vote, a chance to respond or disagree, a venue, or, in the case of export agriculture, a chance to maintain the means of production and to earn some extra cash. Often, so-called "weapons of the weak" and "hidden transcripts" actually play into hegemonies — are the real basis upon which they are sustained — because they serve as limit points, points of appeasement where there is at least some sense of freedom, some critical purchase, such that the overall formation becomes desirable and satisfactory. Think about the fact that nontraditional agriculture does provide "at least" some extra cash, and farmers feel some degree of comfort and security in "at least" knowing the risks. Such affirmations are key to the ways that this mode of production and the promise of extra cash have become embedded in the Guatemalan Highlands and, in fact, are integral to neoliberal justification of that system.

Limit Points

It is around limit points that hegemonic processes achieve stability and yet also become ambivalent. Limit points emerge within discourses as collective desires condense around particular objects, as in the narrowing of aspirations among Maya farmers onto "something more." These desires get condensed around this image because export agriculture has, in the experiences of most farmers, provided a little extra cash, even though the desire for *algo más* is never fully satiated. This limit point — accruing in the local discourse about what "better" means — limits the possibilities for changing the organization of broccoli production because collective energies are routed toward what is practical, obtainable, and realistic (i.e., a little extra cash). Thus, we did not find the sort of collective resistance among farmers that we initially expected, but rather a convergence on key limitations, pragmatic footholds in a pre-carious world.

Limits points are also evident on the consumer side of the food chain. For example, think about how well-intentioned consumers buy fair-trade coffee as a way of casting an economic vote for labor justice and ecological conscientiousness. Fair-trade coffee acts as an objective, coalescing the desire to "do something," to be good global citizens, perhaps even to change things. And yet it also stabilizes the food chain in ways convergent with neoliberal interests and, indeed, the maintenance of asymmetrical geographies of class and capital. It reinforces preconceptions about agency and power, with the Northern consumer deciding what is fair and equitable in the lives of others. The political sensibilities expressed through the purchase of fair-trade products and organic foods become commodified in a way that privileges the sign over the signified. Julia Guthman (2003, 54), in her insightful study of "yuppie chow," observes that for affluent and progressive California consumers of the 1980s, "eating organic salad mix connoted a political action in its own right, legitimizing a practice that few could afford," while the "subtle conflation of aesthetic reflexivity (that of the gastronome) with political reflexivity added an extra ingredient of desire." In a similar vein, Mark Moberg (2005) shows how the well-intentioned politics of fair-trade banana consumption in Britain brings benefits to only a small group of Saint Lucia growers and poses a new set of risks associated with the certification process. He concludes that, "among consumers in the developed North who believe that their purchases will fundamentally reform the global commodity system in which Fair Trade farmers participate, such hopes may prove as elusive as the condition of postmodernity itself" (2005, 13).

Limit points divert attention away from contradictions, problems, and inconsistencies in how social life is explained.[7] But they are different than so-called "structures of the mind," because in reconciling certain contradictions they also reveal others. In addressing, even allaying practical dilemmas, limit points do not purge social experiences of ambivalence and uncertainty. Fair-trade purchases, for example, bring consumers into new kinds of relationships with producers that agitate ethical questions and keep the anxieties of the consumer in play. Limit points must be understood as relational, not operating in a vacuum. In coalescing desires around particular objectives, they also disclose alternative models, competing ways of seeing things, looks beyond and around what is taken for granted. Limit points only work because they are ambivalent, because assumptions about how the world works always takes shape in relation to other possibilities, thus leaving the struggle to define common sense open. Common sense demands some "common" that is never fully made clear, not least in its moral orientation. So limit points are not limits in the sense of being final, as in a border without a beyond, as "structures" are usually conceived. Limit points are best thought of as constituting a horizon — this horizon being "hegemony," a horizon of intelligible thought, limiting in advance what can be seen or heard, what is desirable, what counts as true. This is not unlike contingent points of equilibrium in a simple supply-and-demand curve, except that the complexity of desires and the inevitability of danger lend a certain depth and instability to axiomatic values.

This conception of hegemony — as the struggle over and about limit points — shifts the work of power from the epistemological level to an existential, moral, and social level. Limit points are not simply a matter of cognition or discourse. Limit points operate at the level of social experience, at the basic level of desiring. At this level, limit points are pragmatic handles in everyday life. They can assure people that they are doing a good job, doing the best they can, living up to their abilities or according to cherished principles, that they have a handle on things and that things should not be different. Limit points are thus crucial to processes of subject formation, relay points between desire and power, where individuals and collectives come to desire *in certain ways only*. The Maya broccoli farmer does not expect more than the little extra cash he earns, is not compelled to demand more from the system, because value is added *at another place*. Ideas about propriety, individuated responsibilities and rewards, and distinct spheres of action punctuate the reality of interconnectedness that exists along the broccoli trail. These attitudes and beliefs are limit points, framing the way the broccoli trail is seen by producers and consumers. Most consumers feel no stake in the futures of broccoli growers for basically the same reasons — these are different activities, different worlds, distinct forms of desiring and living. The consumer is not compelled to partake in the struggle to improve the living conditions of those who grow his or her vegetables because, it is assumed, *that is just how they live there.* It would be a mistake to see these attitudes and ethical orientations as "repressed." They must be understood as having been produced, affirmed, incited at limit points. Global food chains sustain dominance and their current organization — in which consumers benefit much more than producers — not because people do not know any better but because this mode of production is linked to cultural forms, hegemonies, that massively produce collective desires. The desires that are effected include, paradoxically, desires to actively avoid change, desires to affirm the way things work today.

Notice, however, that in the specific situation of broccoli farming, there is not just one single hegemonic process at work. Local versions of what progress means are both conditioned by and different from the models that circulate globally. "Empire," the current phase of global political-economic organization, "pretends to be master of the . . . world because it can destroy it," Hardt and Negri write. "What a horrible illusion! In reality we are masters of the world because our desire and labor regenerate it continuously" (2000, 368). Hegemonic struggles depend on people becoming stakeholders in collective processes, believing deeply, sometimes dangerously so, in certain models about how the world works. Hegemonic struggles do not proceed by way of rational calculations or abstract ethical deliberations but through the ongoing process of regenerating the world.[8]

The upshot of this is that hegemonic struggles are necessarily fractured, ambivalent, because no single framing of common sense maps directly onto how things actually are. People have multiple commitments and concerns. In the context of everyday life, multiple hegemonic struggles run together, strengthen, transform, or reverse each other. In the global broccoli trade, for example, there is the global expansion of desires and expectations regarding "something more," and then there are more regional or local struggles within which globally circulating ideas get embroiled. These limit points — what counts as "better" or as "progress" for Maya farmers, exporters, and community leaders — are defined not as such but *in relation to* other values and alternative models. In this way, as hegemonic struggles come to define individual and collective desires, they are also productive of divergent practices.

Resistance, Desire, and Global Connections

Hegemonic struggles are inherently ambivalent — never fully achieved and yet a necessary component of social experience. We must be careful, then, not to portray those practices that diverge from hegemonic tendencies simply as resistance, since such divergences take shape in relation to power. What "something better" means for Maya farmers diverges from the assumptions of both neoliberal and anti-global advocates, and yet we have also shown how their participation in the global marketplace, coupled with their belief in progress, involves the reality of economic exploitation and various forms of subjective training. This participation thus plays into the desires of consumers and, therefore, one could argue, absolutely sustains the hegemonic form of global food production in particular and global capitalism in general. Yet such a view neglects how this participation rubs up against regional histories of wage and migrant labor, is experienced as sustaining local cultural traditions, and can be linked to political organizing on community and national levels. We would be hard pressed to quantify the importance of the global versus the local in this instance. Neither global images of progress nor local appropriations, neither the appeal of making some extra cash and retaining the means of production nor the local aversion to migrant labor, by themselves make export agriculture compelling for farmers. It is a combination of all of these factors. Various localized effects diverge from the overall effect of exploitation and domination noticeable on a global level. They certainly do not constitute a form of "resistance," and yet they also persist as ambivalent outcomes within the broader "hegemonic" organization of this global connection. The sort of localized cultural adaptations that Bruce Knauft (2002b) terms "vernacular modernities" often resist the particulars of the outside imposition of "progress" while embracing and fortifying the abstraction of material progress (and the real-world inequalities that it entails).[9] It is useful to focus ethnographically on the workings of global flows themselves and not simply on "the power of local culture over global forces of apparent homogenization" (Marcus 1998, 34–35).

What is resistance and what is hegemony is often a matter of perspective. A middle-aged Kaqchikel Maya man we know in Tecpán critiques capitalist expansion by lamenting the penetration of Pokémon into the local cultural world — his children watch the cartoon videos and eagerly collect the toys that accompany bags of corn chips — and yet such resistance also underwrites gerontocratic authority. Export agriculture recalls an egalitarian ideal of communal family labor and thus seems to be a resistance to the cultural homogenization often said to characterize globalization. But it also reifies neotraditional gender relations through the division of labor on farms and at packing plants. It is often remarked that women are better suited for harvesting delicate export crops because their more nimble hands are less likely to bruise the produce. In this way, "Mayan women are seen to be doing what comes naturally in the home . . . while simultaneously participating in modern production methods and the participation of modern selves" (Nelson 1999, 360; see also Green 2003). And yet the participation of Maya women in export agriculture must not be understood, despite this strict division and its associated gender stereotypes, as a continuation of "traditional" cultural hegemonies. "Mayan women's decisions to participate in these activities are complex," Nelson writes, "responding to economic and familial pressures as well as hopes and dreams of their own, which often include both pride in their Mayan identity and the desire to be modern" (1999, 361).

While theoretical understandings of persons as the dupes of hegemonies and cultural traditions must yield to humbler considerations of what matters to people, it is also critical that we not romanticize resistance or agency (Abu-Lughod 1990). What is articulated and felt as resistance can play into that which it seems to oppose, a limit point at which satisfaction and gratification are guaranteed, but never absolutely and never with any real consequences (see Willis 1977; Gutmann 2002; Knauft 2002a; cf. Scott 1985, 1990; Pile and Keith 1997). Seed stealing, for example, the classic "weapon of the weak," is both a mode of power for poor people and a way that force relations are sustained because this specific practice becomes an object of desire itself, a release and source of satisfaction. The overall organization of force relations (i.e., power) is not brought into question because hegemonic convergence is actualized not through force but rather through appeasement.

This process of appeasement is apparent for both producers and consumers along the broccoli trail. How things are in each specific setting — in the cool Highland fields and in air-conditioned supermarkets — is basically justified because it is desirable compared to something else. For example, although broccoli farming is not the greatest, it is seen as better than the migrant labor to which farmers have become accustomed. For consumers, things in the United States are not perfect, but at least there is a year-round supply of broccoli, choices at the grocery store, and good food at a cheap price. These experiences become limit points that, because they are real, because they do indeed provide some sense of satisfaction around which desires coalesce, turn attention away from other possible ways of organizing life.

Global processes bring different individuals and groups into distant relations, such that power becomes diffuse and variable (even as it can also seem direct and divisive [Lingis 1997]). Here we have identified how a particular kind of organization — global food production — is linked to ideologies of progress. This, we contend, can be considered a hegemonic process, a global hegemony, although such a label demands a thorough reworking of the concept in light of everyday desires, the moral life of producers and consumers, and the practical limits that make life livable.

Simplistic models of hegemony and resistance have little purchase in the context of global connections, where the effects of power are multiple and depend on how the analysis is framed. Terms such as "compliance" and "resistance" often obfuscate this complexity (Abu-Lughod 1990; Lyons 2005; Ortner 1995). Our reframing of hegemonic processes focuses on how desire is conditioned in everyday life, amidst collective processes and changes, and in historical time. The advantage is to move us away from the temptation to see globalization as either "all good" or "all bad," the engagement of the local with the global as sly resistance or cultural imperialism (see Joseph 2002; Marcus 1998; Miller 1995; Tsing 2000a). In the case at hand, Maya broccoli growers are either needing to survive in structural conditions that ensure overwhelming poverty or they are actively pursuing the "something better" that veils their best interests. It is either needs or interests. Somehow the social world of desire is left out, the world of experience where what they do matters in pragmatic and abstract ways. The ethnographic imperative to understand where others are coming from is lost as practices are transformed into determinations of large-scale processes. It is in desiring, really caring about how things turn out, that people act in the world. This is the case for poor broccoli farmers as much as for affluent consumers. Our findings challenge the ways in which scholarship on food assumes that poor producers act according to structural determinations whereas wealthy consumers act according to their own agency and preferences.

Ethnographers are well positioned to investigate how life projects are shaped and influenced by broader political, economic, and historical processes. We take this to be a crucial element of studies of global processes. To bring desire into the study of hegemonic processes means examining how moral projects are actualized amid both the "accretion of historical experience"[10] and aims for the future. It is crucial to examine how large-scale processes come to shape what matters to people and their life chances, while also relating how the locally emergent projects and forms of desiring complicate global theories about domination, progress, and change.

The mayor's house in Tecpán, burned during the June 10, 2002, protest. Note the advertisement for Olympia beds ("To rest and sleep well") and, on the far left, the three-finger symbol of Rios Montt's FRG party (whose slogan is "Justice, Well-Being, Security"). Photograph by Carol Hendrickson.

PART TWO

Violence, Victimization, and Resistance

FOUR

Social Suffering in the Postwar Era

"Things are better now," it is said by many, "not like before" — a "before" understood to be *la situación, la violencia*, the war of the 1980s, the genocidal baseline for measuring "normalcy." In 1996 wide-ranging Peace Accords were signed between the Guatemalan government and an umbrella organization of rebel forces, formally ending the country's long-standing armed conflict. Looking at newspaper photos of the negotiations and signing ceremony, one is hard-pressed to tell the revolutionaries from the functionaries — an almost undistinguishable group of middle-aged men, their well-fed frames filling up slightly tight suits, all looking as if they could be on the society pages as well as under the headline. These men hailed the Peace Accords with grand speeches filled with grand promises, but living the peace has proven to be elusive.

It is true that in "postwar" Guatemala the number of deaths has decreased, the massacres and wholesale destruction of villages have died down. It is also true that the average Maya income has risen steadily since the late 1980s and that Ministry of Education efforts have increased education levels. Yet Guatemala is still a country wracked by violence, gruesome acts carried out with such frequency that they have become commonplace — mundane if not banal. Images of bullet-ridden cars and bloody corpses fill the front pages of the tabloid press — even as (with the novelty wearing off) such stories have migrated deep inside the more respectable dailies. Judges and lawyers working on human rights or drug trafficking cases have to fear for their lives. Kidnapping for profit is rampant. Gang violence is up not only in the capital but also in cities and towns throughout the country. The wounds of *la violencia* have morphed into ever more virulent and elusive forms as the so-called peace sets in. The rough and careless suture of the Peace Accords treated the symptoms and not the underlying causes of the violence, allowing it to spread like an infection, unseen at first yet all the more pervasive and deadly.

Emergent forms of life in Guatemala involve violence and social suffering, but because this is not "war" there is the impression that the postwar phase has delivered the "something better" promised for so long. This is an outsider's perspective but one actively shared by politicians and leaders within the country — those with a stake in restoring a more positive and tranquil public image. That folks across the Highlands still say they are aspiring to "something better" — whether by working in nontraditional agricultural production, as we saw in the previous chapters, or by becoming politically and culturally active, the subject we examine here — should give pause to any argument that "something better" has finally arrived. Indeed, the projects of export farmers and cultural activists should give pause even to those who say that the postwar present is "at least" somewhat better than the past even if social suffering is still massive.

In this second section of the book we look at social suffering as it plays into the changing stream of social and moral experience in postwar Guatemala. We follow Arthur Kleinman, Veena Das, and others in our conception of suffering as social, embedded in certain experiences, and tied to moral stakes (see Kleinman, Das, and Lock 1997). Suffering can be said to be social in the sense that the origins and outcomes of suffering are collectively dispersed and often structurally legitimated. Infectious disease, mental illness, substance abuse, and other local health problems are irreducible to biology; they also feed on political, economic, and social processes. This orientation tilts against the common tendency to regard suffering as a private matter and to explain it in terms of local causes and effects only. Suffering happens in the real time of quotidian experience — it is affected by and in turn shapes changing social practices, norms, and routines. Suffering is embedded in moral experience, depending on cultural valuations of right and wrong and producing effects that threaten what is most meaningful and valuable for people, be they victims, observers, or caregivers (Kleinman, Das, and Lock 1997; Das et al. 2000; Kleinman 1999). In the following chapters, we examine the emergent kinds of social suffering and collective violence evident in Guatemala's postwar era. We focus attention on everyday forms of speech, memories of violence, narratives of global and local events, and ongoing forms of cultural activism to show how the Maya actively engage the dangers of social suffering.

We begin, in the present chapter, by examining postwar forms of violence in Tecpán. We consider the political appeal of a former dictator, describe the rise of gang violence, and analyze a violent protest that occurred on June 10, 2002. We argue that today, as compared to the early 1980s, the violence in Guatemala is more fluid, and as a result more difficult to represent in scholarship and to engage politically. In addition, it is more difficult to bring this violence to the light of "capital-J" Justice, which is different, we conclude, from the procedural kind of justice that has been sought and achieved or denied between Maya communities, the Guatemalan state, and foreign actors and agencies in the postwar period.

Today, clandestine terror squads attack individuals in ways meant to look like common crime. The papers are full of accounts of horrific drive-by shootings, kidnappings, and home invasions, a number of which just happen to target human rights workers, judges and lawyers, union organizers, and so on. The current state of affairs may be understood as the neoliberalization of violence — an outsourcing of what the state once took to be its exclusive function, that is, the exercise of coercive force. There are covert organizations and informal groups that now carry out functions of power traditionally thought to be the exclusive right of the state government, although in such a way that their pursuits do not threaten but attenuate state control. We see this even in the assistance provided for victims, as well as in the marketing of images of suffering and violence. Here, an ethical imperative to respond is subsumed to mediated forms of interaction that are themselves linked to systems of profit, governance, and even violence. Today, more than ever, image control is a central function of violence. But whereas before the effort was focused on secrecy, now it is just as often focused on public relations, media spin, and exposure. Just as democracy and free-market capitalism are said to operate hand in hand, so too — in a sad ode to Marx — does the culture of violence in

Guatemala evolve and advance with late capitalism. But the Maya in places like Tecpán are not incognizant of these emerging forms of violent life and are not passive in the face of these experiential changes.

El General Returns

General Efraín Ríos Montt talks to God. To hear him tell it, they are good buddies — two old, privileged white guys sharing their disgust at the state of affairs in the world today, from the rise in crime and corruption to the decline in family and faith. Ríos Montt's God speaks in Old Testament tones and calls for vengeance rather than forgiveness, the need for discipline more than compassion. And it was this God who told the former military dictator, head of Congress, and born-again evangelical Christian to run for president in Guatemala's 2003 elections.

Through the summer of 2003, the legality of Ríos Montt's candidacy was in doubt. A quaint section tucked away in Article 186 of the Guatemalan Constitution bars those who have participated in coups from being president, and it was a military junta that first brought Ríos Montt to power in 1982. On this basis, the Supreme Electoral Tribunal ruled in June 2003 that he was ineligible to run for president, a decision at first upheld by Guatemala's Constitutional Court. Ríos Montt, however, continued to campaign, confident that he would prevail. On July 24, "Black Thursday" as it came to be known, the Ríos Montt campaign organized demonstrations that shut down Guatemala City and cost millions in property damage. Thousands of rural supporters were bused into the capital city and armed by campaign workers with machetes, sticks, tires, and gasoline; organizers, cell phones held up to their black ski masks, then directed the protestors toward targeted courthouses, government buildings, and private businesses, a number of which were looted while police looked on, unwilling to intervene. As the smoke from burning cars and buildings filled the Guatemala City skyline, Ríos Montt announced to the press that he would not be able to control his supporters, that the people must be heard and their will heeded. Following this none-too-subtle flexing of muscle, the Constitutional Court overruled itself and, citing international accords, voted 4 to 3 that to retroactively apply the 1985 Constitution to Ríos Montt's 1982 actions would violate his human rights.

One might have hoped that donning the mantle of a human rights victim would be uncomfortable for El General (as he likes to be called). Various human rights monitors, from Amnesty International to the U.S. State Department, hold him largely responsible for the displacement, torture, and death of tens of thousands of noncombatants during his 1982–83 reign, at the height of Guatemala's long civil war. Overwhelmingly, the victims of that war were rural Maya, leading a U.N. Truth Commission to declare the violence a case of genocide. But politics can make for strange bedfellows, and in 2003 it was the poor, rural, Maya peasants — the very targets of Ríos Montt's scorched-earth campaign two decades earlier — who now formed the base of El General's popular support. As the former majority leader of Congress, Ríos Montt cultivated this allegiance by pushing through huge subsidies for fertilizer and increases in the minimum wage, and by making large payments to those who had served in the country's notorious 'civil patrols' of the early 1980s.

Ríos Montt spoke one Saturday afternoon in June 2003 in Xenimajuyu, a small hamlet on the outskirts of Tecpán. In Kaqchikel, Xenimajuyu means "at the foot of the mountain," and true to its name, a dramatic peak rises over the village, overshadowing the distant volcanoes. Before the arrival of the Spaniards in 1524, the mountain had served as an outpost of Iximche', the nearby capital of the Kaqchikel Maya empire. Climbing its preposterously steep slopes, one can see why — the mountaintop offers a strategically unencumbered view for dozens of miles around. Today, the ground is littered with potsherds and broken obsidian blades churned up by subsistence farmers who have been pushed off more accommodating lands by the expansion of nontraditional agriculture. In contrast to its environs, Xenimajuyu appears somewhat drab: a few cinder-block buildings (the school, the health center, a few small churches) compete with the wood-plank and adobe houses than front one of the village's two dirt roads, kids play in the street, women dressed in vivid, handwoven blouses go about their daily chores, and men can be seen walking to and from their fields.

On the day of the rally, more than a thousand people gathered in a large field on the edge of the village. This turnout was surprising — both because of Ríos Montt's reputation as an iron-fisted dictator and because the sole publicity for the event consisted of a few members of Ríos Montt's advance team going around that same morning recruiting supporters. Several people came to the rally because they were promised information about the next installment of payments the government was promising to the men (or their widows) who had served in the army-led Civil Auto-Defense Patrols (PACs) during the early 1980s.

The PACs had been a bad idea to start with: villagers charged with protecting their towns from "subversives" had been forced into paramilitary service and often given quotas of the number of suspects they needed to hand over to the local military garrison for "questioning" (see Carmack 1988; Montejo 1992). Many of these "suspects" never returned from these interrogations, their bodies showing up days or weeks later by the side of the road, perhaps missing a hand or covered with cigarette burns. During the civil war, the PACs were responsible for thousands of extrajudicial killings (as the Guatemalan legal code delicately phrases it), working with the army to instill a quotidian terror in Guatemalans that we can scarcely imagine even in this age of terrorist threats. Yet the civil patrollers were also victims. Coerced to do the army's bidding under the threat of persecution and death, these poor Maya farmers had been forced to turn in their neighbors and friends, also poor Maya farmers, in this hot spot of the Cold War. It is for this suffering that the Guatemalan Congress, led by Ríos Montt (who, twenty years earlier, had overseen the expansion of PACs and sanctioned their atrocities), now authorized cash compensation for the former civil patrollers. The payments were to be disbursed in three parts. The first payout of 5,000 quetzales (about $640, a year's income for a poor farmer) per claimant was made in April 2003. Although 600,000 applications were filed, only 250,000 claims were paid, to those whose names appeared in the official, if incomplete, government registry of eligible patrollers. Still, the payout represented a half-billion dollar expense that Guatemala could ill afford, and so the program was frozen in 2004.

The 2003 campaign was Ríos Montt's fourth attempt at the presidency. In 1974, he lost an election under suspicious circumstances. While early reports in that election gave him a decisive lead, television and radio broadcasts of the results mysteriously ceased on the night of the vote count. The next morning, when broadcasting resumed, it was reported that Ríos Montt's rival, General Kjell Laugerud, had apparently pulled ahead in a decisive lead to win the presidency. Fearing for his life, Ríos Montt fled to California, where he made contact with Pat Robertson's Church of the Word. Born again as an evangelical Protestant, Ríos Montt came to believe that it was God's will that he lead Guatemala in the battle against communism that threatened his land. Toward this end, he returned to Guatemala to head a 1982 coup that overthrew another military dictator, General Romeo Lucas García. Ríos Montt's reign as head of state lasted only eighteen months, but it was the bloodiest year and a half in the country's ongoing civil war. Tens of thousands of civilians were killed, often in horrific ways: pregnant women were eviscerated, children were swung by the legs to shatter their skulls against walls, men were castrated and decapitated. In scenes reminiscent of the Holocaust, victims frequently had to dig their own mass graves before being executed. Whole villages were bombed and fields burned to the ground, forcing hundreds of thousands to flee into the jungle or to the anonymity of Guatemala City's slums. By 1983, Ríos Montt's megalomaniacal excesses became too much for even the hardened army brass, and he was overthrown and replaced by a reformist general who oversaw a transition to democracy, at least nominal, in 1986.

In 1989, Ríos Montt mounted another campaign for president, but his candidacy was blocked by the electoral tribunal and the Constitutional Court. He went on to found a new political party, the Guatemalan Republican Front (FRG). Courts again barred Ríos Montt from the 1994 FRG presidential ticket, but he was elected to Congress, where he served as majority leader. In 1998, the FRG ran Alfonso Portillo as a stand-in for Ríos Montt in the presidential elections. Portillo, who as a young leftist living in exile in Mexico had killed two men in a 1982 political dispute, was able to spin scandals about his past in his favor ("A man who can defend himself to defend our country") to win the five-year term that ended in January 2004.

In 2003, the FRG government (which held the presidency, a majority in Congress, and great sway over the judiciary) was troubled by corruption scandals involving shockingly large amounts of money (hundreds of millions of dollars), even for a system long accustomed to high levels of graft. After leaving office in 2004, former President Portillo fled the country (and is believed to be living in Mexico), and his vice president was arrested on corruption charges. Ríos Montt, who was campaigning on a platform of greater security (to combat the wave of crime that had swept in the country in the years following "demilitarization") and an end to corruption, found himself in the position of having to distance himself from Portillo and other officials of his own party. Arguably the most powerful man in the country, El General ran as an underdog who promised to fight corruption and the entrenched oligarchy.

In 2003, Ríos Montt arrived in Xenimajuyu in a red helicopter, accompanied by a fanfare of firecrackers and campaign songs ("My mommy votes for Ríos Montt, my daddy votes for Ríos Montt . . ."). Like private jets in the United States, helicopters are de rigueur for serious Guatemalan presidential aspirants, allowing them to navigate the campaign trail above rather than on the country's poor roads. (Just outside of Xenimajuyu, the Pan American Highway — the country's primary transportation artery — is a poorly paved, two-lane road that looks like a county highway in rural Alabama.)

A sprightly seventy-seven, El General roused crowds with the fervor of an evangelical pastor. He railed against corruption: "I am not a rich man. I started out with three little quetzales [about $3 at the time], and I am where I am today because of my hard work. But I am not rich." He inveighed against political patronage: "Who does your mayor work for? Who does your congressman work for? Who does the President of the Republic work for? You, that's right. And so why should you have to enter their offices with your head bowed and hat in hand to beg for a little favor? This is wrong. You are their boss." And he preached against infidelity and loose morals: "I have been married to the same woman for almost fifty years. A man should have just one wife, just one woman. If any candidate — even the FRG candidate for mayor of your town — cheats on his wife, I urge you not to vote for them." After this last remark, the mayoral candidate, who was on the dais, looked sheepish, and a wave of muted giggles passed through the crowd.

El General took no note, moving on to embrace Pedro Palma, a former guerilla leader, holding his hand tight while declaring that "the past is behind us and we must leave it there. We must move forward. Together." The contrasting appearance of the two men was striking: Ríos Montt wore a cheap, slightly ill-fitting gray suit and looked like a humble man who had dressed up for a special occasion; Palma, in contrast, sported black designer jeans and a stiffly pressed guayabera shirt and looked like a dandy who had dressed down for a trip to the countryside. Palma, who had lived for years in the jungle fighting the Guatemalan army, appeared unbothered by the irony of running for Congress on the ticket of his former mortal enemy.

Pointing to one side of the stage, Ríos Montt stated, "There is the plantation of yesteryear," and pointing to the other side, "There is the nation of tomorrow." He then said that Guatemala was walking the treacherous path from plantation to nation while dark forces were trying to pull the country away from the straight and narrow path. Yet Guatemala should fear no evil — El General had his eye out for evil, and like the national patriarch he seeks to be ("I am Guatemala," he is fond of saying), he would guide his Guatemalan family to safety. This would not be easy, Ríos Montt admitted, but he claimed to have the moral fortitude and the *mano dura* (hard hand) to see it through. Like the protagonist of Miguel Angel Asturias's novel *El Señor Presidente*, Ríos Montt is a man fighting demons of surrealistic proportions, but his demons are of a particular fundamentalist variety.

The day after his visit to Xenimajuyu, Ríos Montt made an ill-timed campaign stop in Rabinal, an Achi' Maya town that had been hit hard during the civil war. Forensic anthropologists have been working for some time in Rabinal, excavating clandestine graves and identifying victims' bodies in order to document what happened there during the violence and bring some sense of closure to still-grieving families who never knew for sure the fate of their "disappeared" loved ones. On the day Ríos Montt arrived in Rabinal, several bodies were being reburied in marked graves. The presence of the man many hold responsible for these deaths was too much for some townspeople, and they arrived at the rally with a coffin that had been painted black and began to jeer Ríos Montt. Not heeding the advice of his security team, Ríos Montt took the stage to try to calm the crowd, but he was met with a barrage of bottles, sticks, and rocks. After being hit on the head with a stone, Ríos Montt retreated to his helicopter holding a handkerchief to his bleeding forehead. The balanced editorials of the national press that followed pointed out that it had been foolish for Ríos Montt to go to Rabinal on that day, but they also condemned the protestors for using tactics of intimidation in a free election. Still, the editorials asked, who can really blame them?

In the end, Ríos Montt's vows to use overwhelming force to end crime and corruption in Guatemala did not carry the day, and he finished the presidential race in third place. "I don't care what he says," declared one Maya at the Xenimajuyu rally, "we remember who he is and what he has done. We have suffered enough. I will never vote for him no matter how much money he promises."

June 10: Popular Protest and Residual Violence

No he said, tell them *no concessions.*

His voice above the fire as if there were no fire —

language floating everywhere above the sleeping bodies;

and crates of fruit donated in secret;

and torn sheets (for tear gas) tossed down from shuttered windows;

and bread; and blankets, stolen from the firehouse.

— JORIE GRAHAM, "THE HIDING PLACE"

The 1990s in Guatemala saw the historic signing of the Peace Accords, an aggressive program of privatization and liberal economic reform, a new attitude toward Maya peoples that sought to provide new opportunities for a historically excluded group, and a sharp decline in massacres and other large-scale military actions. Amidst these changes, there was also famine brought about by droughts and declining coffee prices, as well as a sharp increase in street crimes, gang violence, kidnappings, and robberies, along with a resurgence of right-wing political activity. These and other changes were more than just ominous rumblings or glitches in the democratic system — they were mutually entwined with the country's more progressive moments.[1] Considering the postwar peace process in terms of "successes" and "failures," therefore, becomes a dubious task, for it must proceed according to certain typologies and hierarchies of violence.[2] The waning of a certain type of violence might be considered a "success," even though new and subtler forms of economic and symbolic injustices may have emerged. Likewise, the strengthening of indigenous political rights might be seen as a "success," even though, at the same time, bureaucratic authority has been extended. It all depends on where one is standing.[3]

On the morning of June 10, 2002, thousands of farmers stood along the Pan American Highway just outside Tecpán, preparing to protest against a new tax-reform measure.[4] Estimates of the number of protestors range from 3,000 to 45,000, but whatever the number it was a remarkable show of public dissent, an act that would have been suicidal in the not-so-distant past. The leader of the demonstration was a Kaqchikel-speaking human rights worker who lived in the municipality. In late 2001, he had begun organizing opposition to the new property and estate tax measure called the Impuesto Unico Sobre Inmuebles (IUSI). As part of the implementation of the Peace Accords, the collection and administration of the IUSI was to be devolved from the Ministry of Finance to local municipal governments, a neoliberal approach designed to improve accountability and transparency while also empowering the local population. Despite the efforts of local officials to convince people that decentralization would be good for them, however, there remained great ambivalence and resistance, further evidence of the Peace Accords' lofty ideals breaking down in practice.

Many Tecpanecos will tell you that local government is no less corrupt than government at the national level — and that local corruption was all the more apparent, in the mayor's new house and his shiny red BMW. Said one community leader who observed the protests from atop a friend's house in town:

The mayor treated us poorly. We tried to discuss the tax with him. We told him it was impossible to afford, but he was rude and would not hear our demands. I don't discount that the mayor was robbing money from the *pueblo*, but all I know is what I have seen: he didn't have a car before he assumed office and just afterwards he has a new, nice car, one of the nicest in town.

At nine o'clock the protestors marched into town and quickly inhabited the central park in front of the municipal building. They carried signs and banners and documents demanding the resignation of Mayor Chepe Morales, a member of Rios Montt's FRG Party. In front of the mayor's office they were met by a phalanx of local police and were not allowed to get any closer than a stone's throw away. The crowd grew frustrated and anxious, but still no one anticipated the violence that was about to erupt. A youth, said by all to be a gang member, suddenly hurled a rock through one of the town hall's windows. Other protestors immediately followed suit. "The only thing certain was that nothing was certain," said one, "and I heard the first window shatter, then others, and all of a sudden it was out of control. I mean, no one knew what was going on."

Many participants, abandoning their pacific intentions, proceeded to set fire to the municipal building, the police station, and the mayor's home. The mayor's car was flipped over and set ablaze in the street. As in New York on September 11, firefighters and police acted quickly. The *bomberos* were already there because the mayor had called them, and when the buildings began burning they dispatched their trucks to a neighborhood where there was a water storage tank. The police reacted to the protest by throwing tear-gas bombs into the crowd, and protestors recovered those bombs and returned them to their senders. One also saw "weapons of the weak" at work (Scott 1985). Protestors used their cell phones to provide family members at home with live reports of the action, or as walky-talkies to contact one another and organize movements on the spot. Rumor had it that protestors also used their phones to coordinate looting and to relay information about the location of the police, who eventually were stripped naked by the protestors, their firearms stolen, their bodies beaten and bloodied and dragged through the street. The mayor, flanked by his bodyguards, hurried to his getaway vehicle as rioters pegged him with stones — some trying their best to kill him. Morales was the first mayor in Tecpán's history with a bodyguard service. The guards carried pistols and dressed like the mayor himself, sporting polished boots, sombreros, crisp Hilfiger jeans, and denim or plaid shirts. One protestor joked: "He's the first with bodyguards and the first with a burned-out house."

Despite the creative techniques employed by the protestors to subvert police authority and establish, if only momentarily, control over the town center, it would be dangerous to read this event strictly as the celebration of agency too often implied by the weapons-of-the-weak analysis. No one wanted June 10 to turn violent, except perhaps those eager to steal televisions, computers, appliances, and food from houses around the park. But it is also clear that "gang members" were not the only ones looting and torching. One organizer related the following rumor:

> I only know this from a friend. I wasn't there to hear it directly. Many say that the mayor mistreated the protestors when they wanted to talk to him, that he was rude and would not hear their demands. That is why the people got angry. Many say that it was just the gangs that were acting violently during the protests. But if the mayor was treating the protesters badly when they went to see him, the pacific protestors and even the organizers, then they had their own reasons for becoming violent.

This informant skillfully distanced himself from any complicity, denying that he was even there (when, on another occasion, he and other observers admitted the opposite), and at the same time vindicating the sudden use of violence among the angered protestors. It is as if the rumor itself violently commanded this skeptic to insist that he saw and heard nothing in particular. This central trope of the protest experience — "nothing was certain" (not "not a thing" [*ninguna cosa*], but precisely the positive claim of "nothing" [*nada*]) — allows blame to be projected onto the impersonal "street gangs." Rumor dismantles relations of trust at times of communal riot and becomes productive of skepticism — an unwillingness to take notice or the feeling that our sensations are not real. In both rumor and skepticism the signature and context of action are removed, absent, often anonymous. The danger is that these modes, or moods, can enable the abdication of responsibility and partition social relations (Das 1998). It is likely that the nominal "gang member" category serves as a generalized and immediate container for popular feelings of complicity and resignation, a way for protestors to remain skeptical about, abdicate, and yet silently make sense of their own participation in the violence. Protestors lamented that the *Prensa Libre* (and the rest of the free press) later characterized their well-planned and well-intentioned protest as "chaotic," that they were portrayed in the popular media as incorrigible and undemocratic. Despondence festers in this space where what is seen does not jibe with what is said and heard — the genuine motives and peaceful intentions of protestors who are treated skeptically in subsequent media reports. Inversely, popular rumors distance what is said and heard from what is seen — rumors that gangs are solely to blame cover over the reality of popular participation in violence. In this context, such rumors become understandable, if also dangerous, given a desired, perhaps willed, disbelief regarding complicity — a convenient inversion that allegorizes the postwar process of political decentralization, where circumscribed communities are set apart, such that shared responsibilities are disavowed, skeptically, and blame is incited through rumor. "We were interested in resolving real political issues," said one participant, who became noticeably upset as he added, "The gangs are to blame, not the protestors. But everyone ended up losing. The worst is that only 1 percent of the participants were ladinos. It was Indian against Indian. We didn't start the violence in this town, the violence has been here, but we are blamed and we are the ones who suffer."

Gangs

"You should take your car." We were up late one night, sitting around the kitchen table talking with a friend in Tecpán and decided to run to the store to get a few *cervezas*. The corner *tienda* was closed, and the closest place with what passes for cold beer was off the central park, a leisurely five-minute walk away. We were heading out the door on foot when our host stopped us with his warning. At first we thought he was just making a comment on what gringo idiots we were for having a car and yet choosing to walk. But then he explained: "It's better not to walk around here after ten o'clock," he said. "The gangs [*maras*] come out then, hanging out on the corners looking for victims. They would spot you blondies [*canchitos*] a kilometer away. You should take the car." And so we did, doors locked, eyes peeled for shady characters in the shadows cast by the intermittent streetlamps and houselights. We saw a few groups of rough-looking teenagers standing around or walking down the street. They could be gang members, we thought, and we had seen the spray-paint tags popping up on walls around town.

If *maras* and youth culture are blamed for much of the everyday violence that has emerged in the postwar era, in Tecpán there is still not much of a public transcript regarding gangs — maybe there is fear, maybe epistemic murk, as gangs are discussed privately but always without skepticism. Locals seem to be certain of the gangs' activities. Some have an idea about who their members are; some have witnessed gang vandalism; all have seen the graffiti signatures (Diamantes, Salvatruchas, Calle 17, Batos Locos, Patojos Locos) that increasingly demarcate gang territory. There are wild rumors of gangs robbing shoppers and vendors. Stories of gang violence have become commonplace in Maya towns and villages throughout Guatemala's Western Highlands. On one Thursday, market day, about a week after the June 10 protests, we heard that the gangs were out preying upon shoppers for fruits and vegetables in the narrow passageway that runs alongside the church. One woman supposedly was robbed of 700 quetzales (about $90) and spent the afternoon sobbing on the church steps, attended to by relatives and friends. She hadn't seen or heard a thing coming, they said. And this was not really surprising, a veteran fruit vendor said, as there is just nothing to do in Tecpán. The paradox being: "It is just too quiet and peaceful all the time, so what else than to hang out in the streets or the stores and look for fun or violence, and while at it they can make money."

Ten years ago, domestic violence, municipal graft, and petty theft were Tecpán's most pressing crime problems. Today, the perception is clearly that Tecpán is a much more dangerous place — and gangs have become the synecdoche for discussing violence. As in El Salvador, Nicaragua, and other Latin American countries, gangs have become a serious crime issue in Guatemala. The National Police have established a special anti-gang unit to track outbreaks of gang crime in the capital. Special squads are then deployed in affected areas to pick up youths who sport gang tattoos and colors, with little regard for due process. While gangs have been around for decades, if not centuries, in Guatemala City their size, strength, and sophistication has increased dramatically since passage, by the U.S. Congress, of the 1996 Illegal Immigration Reform and Immigrant Responsibility Act. The Act drastically increased the deportation of illegal immigrants who are convicted of even minor offenses. Chicano and Latino gang members in Los Angeles (and elsewhere) have been targeted, and many of them have been deported back to their countries of origin, where they have organized gangs that maintain ties with their U.S. counterparts.[5]

In Tecpán, they say that the gang leaders are mostly local youths who went to live in the capital for a while — looking for more opportunity than this small town can offer, and finding community in the street gangs. There are also youths who have moved to the town and who live there with no visible means of support. It is said that one gang leader runs a brothel on the outskirts of the town. The local youths said to be members of the gangs are, of course, known. We did not interview any gang members (we were really more concerned with the perception of gang violence), but one young man who knows several gang members told us that some physically intimidate their parents, others have moved out of their homes, and in a few cases, parents are ignorant of their children's activities.

The gangs are very real — but in Tecpán they have become larger than life. They seem to have lost that grounding in reality, in fact, since at the level of conversation, public or private, gangs can only appear as something mysterious, inexplicable, and somewhat anonymous. It may be likely that the gangs are a terror more than a real threat. People say that groups of very rough looking young men hang out on dark street corners and look menacing. Are they thieves and rapists or are they posturing teenagers, a Guatemalan version of the wannabe gangsters who hang out at suburban U.S. malls? And to what extent would a real gang member be different than a wannabe, given that imitators must, indeed, imitate that which they believe or want to be a reality? In the United States, does not the very idea that suburbanites are just wannabe gang members justify — through a class- and race-based logic — a fundamental inability to understand, or even to try to understand, gang culture in urban areas? That is to say, the "reality" of gang violence in those areas is already known in advance as the real thing, indigenous to an area, localized and distanced, so that when it is imitated in other places or times it does not indict, ontologically — does not say anything about the essence of — the performers. It is symbolic, a "performance" rather than an identity.

As we saw in the June 10 protests, the category "gang member" can serve as a useful container for popular feelings of anxiety, stress, and despondency, especially when the whole *pueblo* is being labeled — as it was in the wake of one popular protest — as chaotic and violent. Often, social analysts argue that violence is useful given a certain situation, that the rationalization or explanation of violent processes makes sense within a given context. Here we want to suggest that it is first the construction of a context that then makes violence useful. The discourse of gang violence reflects a fundamental shift in how violence is imagined and talked about in the Highlands. Within a postwar phase, one task is to determine who was and is responsible for the violence of the past and to bring those people to justice. But one of the key existential features of *la violencia* was that it was never clear who was responsible. The reconciliation process has had an unintended consequence of transforming this existential, ethical lesson into one of accusation, blame, and indictment — not unlike the events of June 10, in which, as one Tecpaneco noted, the only thing that was clear was that nothing was clear. In doing so, such a process risks playing into a discourse in which the context of violence is constructed in order to facilitate legal and political procedures. It thus also risks enabling governmental control — marking the context and the population available for inspection. This can render violence local, indigenous to an area, allowing the state to transcend the fray — either by withdrawing its presence and its services from the "chaotic" or "dangerous" area, as Bourdieu et al. (1999) describe, or by intervening through the use of the police or the military to counter indeterminate phenomena like gang violence.

Most of the people we spoke to in Tecpán have this sense about gang violence, that it is a performance. No doubt real and with concrete effects, it nonetheless seems like something out of place, something that has taken hold but from the outside. It is not, people think, indigenous to the community. Some blame the globalization of Western movies and other forms of popular culture that bring images of gang violence and delinquency to the Highlands. Others blame a political economy of boredom, saying that there is really nothing to do in the town and so delinquency is understandable. Still others blame a breaking down of the moral structure, ranging from the erosion of families to a declining work ethic. Blame, it seems, has become an ironic partner of "reconciliation" in these postwar times. Nobody we met in the town had been robbed or assaulted by a gang, but everyone seemed to know someone, a more distant acquaintance, friends of friends, who had, and they all said the threat was real.

Blame and Symbolic Violence

Let us return to the June 10 protest and its aftermath, a process of reconciliation with the mayor that left many protestors feeling blindsided. We can regard the protest as pointing to a number of contradictory processes at work in the postwar era in places like Tecpán. There is, for example, an emerging democratic public sphere where being seen or heard can be politically empowering but also potentially dangerous. This public sphere is structured around forms of symbolic violence, insofar as some voices are valued more than others. But more than this, the use of discourses of empowerment, compromise, and political participation are, in practice, seen to be limiting, since it is often the case that the kinds of compromises and agreements that are reached — the ideological limit points that are desired and valued — favor established interests. We can think of this emerging world of democratic ideals, mandates, expectations, and desires in Guatemala as a "social imaginary," "an enabling but not fully explicable symbolic matrix within which a people imagine and act as world-making collective agents" (Gaonkar 2002, 1). The diverse work of certain publics, such as the pan-Maya activists, language advocates, human rights advocates, labor organizers, religious leaders, and development specialists, has converged in this social imaginary. In it, economic liberalization runs together with political decentralization.

During the protest, there were as many intentions as there were participants, or observers, even if the multitude was discursively reduced to the more manageable and blamable figure of "gang members." We have seen how gangs have become a container for more diffuse, less personal forms of violence and social suffering in the postwar era. Think of the gangs as a "limit point," as the concept was developed in the first section of this book. It is at this point that violence becomes livable, even as the stresses, uncertainties, and anxieties of living in a social world transitioning between an overtly violent past and a more insidiously or symbolically violent present persist. It is at this point that popular feelings of blame, resignation, and complicity can be disavowed, responsibility and violence attributed to a group whose members' identities are nebulous, often no more than graffiti on the walls. But within the multitude of protestors there were significant group divisions: campesinos, teachers, curious onlookers, aspirant politicians, restless gang members, and other youth. The protests do demonstrate the emergence of a new political space, a space that people haven't felt comfortable or been allowed in for nearly a generation. Many folks felt that the protest was a success, even if the tax structure has not changed, since it taught local politicians and other ladinos an important lesson. This success would seem to be unproblematic, as the lingering hard feelings of the protest did find reconciliation in a series of democratic town-hall meetings in Chimaltenango between the mayor, protest organizers, and the departmental governor. "We got what we wanted," said one of the protest organizers. "A chance at a meeting with the mayor, a chance to talk. At least we got that."

Many of the protestors use this same term, *por lo menos* (at least), in describing the meetings: "The protests didn't work out as planned, but at least we can sit down with the mayor." The opportunity for a meetings itself, regardless of the outcome of that meeting, becomes the object of desire. Returning again to our concept of limit points, we can see how political commentary stops at a certain "at least" point that demarcates the horizon at which desires seem satisfactory, or "at least" somewhat fulfilled. It is at this point, moreover, that things seem good and just, such that the limit point is associated with moral values such as compromise, open dialogue, reciprocity, and recognition, even apart from any real evidence that social structures are being changed. The dominant order becomes desirable insofar as it can appear to be an oppositional order. It does allow political subjects "at least" some sense of enfranchisement ("I'm proud to be an American," a popular country-music anthem proclaims, "where at least I know I'm free").[6] But it is often just such a democratic or neoliberal concession that paradoxically limits the very terms of freedom that it purports to enable. "The discourse that makes people believe," de Certeau writes, "is the one that takes away what it urges them to believe in, or never delivers what it promises. . . . I call such a discourse a 'local authority'" (1984, 105–6).

At the reconciliation meetings, the mayor, by acquiescing, was able to co-opt protestors' sentiments and largely define the idiom through which social experiences could emerge. "We are all completely in agreement," he said during one reconciliation meeting. "You have the right to protest. I helped write those laws, remember. But what about those honorable people screaming 'kill him . . . kill him'? I want to work with these honorable people, but I don't want to lose democracy." One protest organizer responded:

> We too want a dialogue, but with no direct accusations or blaming. Because when you look at the press, it says we have no law here, that there is chaos in Tecpán, and that we the organizers are to blame, that there is no difference between what we did and what the gangs did. The same problems we are discussing here right now, we already met with you about this . . .

Quickly, the mayor stands up and moves toward the center of the meeting hall. The documents brought to him on June 10, he claims, were not official and so he could not sign them. Not only that, he insists that there is nothing he could have done about the tax. It is his duty as mayor to carry out the task of decentralization, not to call it into question. The governor reinforces the mayor's position: "The law is the law and the tax is the tax," he says. "Look, the law is *bonito* because it provides the mechanisms for our dialogue and equal exchange." (Throughout the meeting the governor's efforts to communicate with his audience led him to speak slowly and in a register of Spanish replete with errors of grammar and agreement that many ladinos associate with "Indian Spanish.") Here, as always, local authorities in Tecpán must occupy a "tenuous position between constituent mandates and state authority" (E. Fischer 2001, 57). The mayor now says that it seems to him that the protestors are laying the blame on him. The organizer must respond again: "We are not here to accuse you. When we're talking here, we are on an even level, in dialogue, it is a democratic process." The protest organizers, themselves not wanting to be blamed by the mayor or the media for the violence, are forced through this kind of rhetorical toggling to limit their critique of the mayor so that they themselves do not appear to have a finger in the wound (see Nelson 1999).

The notion of democratic compromise grows seductive as a presumably flattened space of voice and vision, and yet can become disappointing in its own blindsided way. While the discourse of harmony and reconciliation is ordinarily perceived as being advantageous to the "little guy," providing at least a foot in the door, such gestures almost invariably favor established interests in a way that encourages active acceptance by the opposition (Nader 1997). The mayor's position becomes privileged through the democratic gesture itself, since the protestors, if they do not embrace his rhetoric, are seen as stubborn, unwilling to listen. This was their critique of the mayor all along! The same protestor who was so enthusiastic about the meeting opportunity beforehand admitted afterward: "I am disappointed. The mayor just kept talking about his bad character. Yeah, that's a problem. But we all know that. That's why we protested in the first place. What is he going to do about it? That's my question. Apologies are nice but so are results."

Neoliberal Violence

Since violence lives in the memories of those for whom it remains a lived history of the present, the violence in Guatemala has not ended, even though we now refer to a "postwar" phase of Guatemalan history. Indeed, the naming of this phase as separate from the genocide is part and parcel of an ideology of reconciliation that actually facilitates the extension of new clandestine forms of social suffering. While the army presumably hunts drug traffickers (although more often than not it seems to be in cahoots with them) and cracks down on heinous crimes, political violence continues apace. But the execution of this violence has been divided up. It is carried out not by the thinly veiled heavy hand of the military or secret police, but by what appear to be common criminals and gang members. One result is that the death and suffering get washed away in the larger flood of violence overwhelming the country. It is the best cover for political violence. If dozens of people are being gunned down in carjackings and robberies every week, how significant is it if one or two of them are human rights lawyers or judges or Maya leaders? The current spike of common violence serves the authoritarian proclivities of the powers that be, shielded as they are from the consequences of their decisions by bodyguards and high walls. As attention is diverted to the terrors of violent crime, those in power can loot the coffers and fill their Panamanian back accounts which ensure them a comfortable retirement in exile, away from the havoc they have sown.

This is not to divert blame from the state and its armed services. The military is widely and credibly believed to be tightly connected with the drug traffickers; in 1990 members of the notorious presidential guard killed the Guatemalan anthropologist Myrna Mack; and government forces have been involved in other acts of intimidation and coercion. Yet the majority of the politically motivated killings in recent years seem to have been carried out by private death squads. And the sustained wave of common crime is largely the work of freelance criminals, who work for profit rather than for politics (except when politics are profitable). The ethical imperative in writing about the postwar situation would be to implicate the state and other agencies — indeed to implicate everyone — as culpable and obligated, even if they have not chosen to become involved.

In the 1980s, in the terminal Cold War mood of that time, it was obvious who the bad guys were (the army, the government), which made their actions easier to oppose in representational form (if also with more deadly consequences). Perhaps it is just hindsight, but the stark binaries of the late–Cold War conflict in Guatemala, the Manichaean choices that had to be made, seem especially clear. The quest was to shed light on and turn the world's attention to the atrocities going on in Guatemala, the genocide of the Maya peoples. The goal was for representation to simply be. It was one of those instances in which anthropologists could employ their on-the-ground understanding to uncover and expose to the world the horrible genocidal violence that was going on in Guatemala. It represented the best sort of ethical anthropology, a clear-cut case of how to be in solidarity with the Maya. This was part of the Cold War zeitgeist, in journalism as much as in academia — taking off the blinders of society, bringing secrets to the public. Today, symbolic violence takes new, more insidious forms. Since the end of the war, there has been a dramatic increase in clandestine groups that carry out assassinations; the "perpetrator" is now represented as the more anonymous and diffuse specter of "crime." As befits these globalized times in which we live, there is no longer a clear bipolar divide; the enemy is now fragmented and ever morphing; and there has been a semi-privatization of coercive powers that were once claimed exclusively for the state.

One dilemma is that foreign observance and attention to the social situation in Guatemala is in decline because the kinds of social suffering that now emerge in the wake of genocide do not, perversely, carry the cultural capital or marketing potential of all-out war. In the 1990s, foreign military aid to Guatemala dropped precipitously. With the Berlin Wall demolished and the Soviet Union disintegrating, U.S. strategic interests shifted dramatically to Eastern Europe. Meanwhile, in Guatemala the revolutionaries and the government continued their low-intensity conflict, which dwindled down until the Peace Accords were signed in December 1996. After 1996, military aid dropped further and the Guatemalan government began a major reduction in the size of its armed forces. Between 1999 and 2005, the number of troops was reduced by half and several major bases (notorious sites of torture and killings during the violence) were closed. The Peace Accords mandate that the military focus exclusively on external threats (of which there are none, really; the one possible dispute results from Guatemala's aggressive stance concerning its claim to sovereignty over Belize). But recent presidents have invoked special powers to keep the army deployed to help fight the wave of violent crime that has swept the country in recent years. In 2005, the United States resumed direct military aid to Guatemala following a ten-year postwar hiatus, while drastically cutting development aid.

While it is still too early to write a full postmortem of *la violencia*, as ethnographers working in Guatemala it is our duty to pursue a sort of forensic social science. Our *compromiso* (commitment), as participants as well as observers, compels us to pore over the corpus delicti of political violence and the detritus of broken promises, recording what we see and hear so that the horrors will not be forgotten, so that past mistakes can be corrected, and so that reconciliation, if not justice, can be achieved. Ravaged and torn during the civil war of the 1980s and the accompanying state-sponsored terrorism, the body politic of Guatemala was left with gaping wounds, pointed fingers, and fingers in wounds. These wounds have been partially sutured through the peace process and through countless small acts of reconciliation. But too often the recovery has been governed by a view of short-term political expediency rather than long-term social health. Too often the practical impossibility of ever fully actualizing "capital-J" Justice is forgotten, and the human suffering of the past tragically gets utilized, appropriated as a means in the reconciliatory procedures of the present. "The more I am just," Levinas declares, "the more I am responsible. . . . It is the exigency of holiness. At no time can one say: I have done all my duty" (1985, 105). Small-case justice is necessary, but violence doubles when society forgets that "it is not as just as the kindness that instigates it is good." And when society forgets that maxim, it can dangerously close in on itself, finding identity and purpose not in its basic motivations but in its self-defined, self-evident, and self-righteous goodness that risks losing the gift of generating new forms of human coexistence (Levinas 1981, 230).

Blame, violence, and retribution are usually discussed in terms of individuals and particular groups. Politically engaged criticism often begins from the perspective that one already knows who is to blame, who the victims are, and, accordingly, what must be done to redress those wrongs. Starting in this way — thinking about the law in terms of individual rights and responsibilities — overlooks the infinite ways that we are already connected to others. In recognizing that the cheap clothes one wears are produced under oppressive circumstances in Guatemala one might only be pushed further to disavow such a reality. Disconnects are formed to morally protect psychically bothered and socially agitated individuals and groups from the pathologized spaces and forms of life, the crimes and unjust practices, on which their own survival depends. Gates can keep chaos out of communities, but one must avariciously read the papers to daily underwrite the logic of security as a practical imperative. Even if located and contained in out of the way places, stressful specters of risk, danger, and violence impinge on the most serene settings of everyday life, in the guarded and rosy zones of society, like the shadows of barbed wire and glass-sharded walls cast into a cordoned courtyard in Antigua, Guatemala. What is called "stress" in the United States and, increasingly, among the emerging middle classes and the elites in Latin America, is a complicated blend of anxiety, despair, and dismay regarding the relation between what is important and what is thought to bring loss and ruin. Stress embodies spatial relations of tension and anxiety, figured out of representations of self and Other. We imagine a world of Others that is threatening, impinging, corrupting, even as we rely on so many Others to provide our food, clothes, shelter, and transit. Stress also embodies a temporality, emergent as an unrealized and ambivalent time produced by the history that compels us and lends certain expectations to our projects in the present.[7]

One of the unpleasant ironies of our time is that as living conditions improve, so too are collective and individual desires motivated along vectors that perpetuate underlying structures of exploitation and deepen inequalities across social classes and social groups. Life comes to be seen as increasingly desperate, dangerous, and hostile, even during a time that is described as "postwar," peaceful, or resurgent. Life comes to be characterized by ubiquitous danger because social experience becomes morally conflicted as people must depend on others in whom they do not trust, and because threats once thought to be apparent and clear become indefinable (Kleinman 2006). In such a context, the attainment of political recognition can genuinely limit the empowerment that is said to be fomenting. The waning of one kind of violence can bring into relief the residue of ongoing brutalities and disparities, or, put another way, the peace process can usher in new and subtler kinds of violence. The boredom of ordinary existence fragments into multiple kinds of violence and upheaval. The so-called violence of everyday life becomes a composite of interacting modes of violence, anxiety, distress, and distraction. Crime, stress, physical brutality, substance abuse, the thrilling shortchanges of economic transformation, the disobedience and restlessness of local corruption, the alienation and anxieties of living within a bureaucracy that can see without being seen — ordinary life is overwhelmed by processes that contradict moral sensibilities and threaten our dearest projects.

An anthropological look at violence in Guatemala should point to the ways that the current postwar phase is characterized by heightened suffering and ongoing violence. But to emphasize this point singularly would risk seeking too great a return on that violence. It would risk using that violence to the ends of scholarship, transmuting what is experienced as reality among those dwelling in this milieu into a smugly comforting anthropological irony. Truth commissions are important but insufficient because they always leave open a space for skepticism or outright dismissal. One cannot use a re turn to the violence inflicted upon and by the Other as an occasion for potential material or symbolic returns. This is also the risk of scholarship that sees in export agriculture *only* economic exploitation and abstracts from the affective desires and hopes of those for whom that project is pressing and of immediate consequence. This privileges a form of solidarity defined in terms of the self over a form of affliction emergent out of an initial acknowledgment of what matters most for others, in their terms, even or especially where the situation is marked by violence or domination (Das 1998). An acknowledgment that violence endures as a lived history of the present in the Guatemalan Highlands involves not simply solidarity, therefore, since such a reciprocal relationship would risk *using* suffering, making it useful, if only as an occasion for anthropological engagement.

Such a strategy would also risk ignoring the depth of the violence it seeks to understand, since it would contain violence, reduce it to a group or a location, and overlook how violence brings multiple groups and social strata into dense, although distant relations of responsibility, dependency, desire, and antagonism. In postwar Guatemala, forms of suffering are thoroughly social, implicating numerous actors and agencies, deep underlying structures, and policies. Violence — like politics — is never just local (*pace* Tip O'Neill's famous axiom). To say that violence is local is to reduce it to a context that, no matter how meticulously detailed or theoretically framed, is nonetheless arbitrary. The context of violence puts things in perspective, and this involves erasing the lines of human relations that exceed contextual limits by crossing borders or enduring over time. These are the perpetual agitations, lingering in the minds of many in the Highlands, that will not put a stop to the rustling of violence in the postwar era. Violence and blame disavow the basic primacy of global interdependence. The swelling currents of postwar violence do not only burden and threaten the Maya, nor only the poor. It is not simply that the visibility of counterinsurgency warfare is giving way to more mundane and transient forms of violence *in the Highlands* — or in poor urban pockets ignored by the state, or among communities of migrant workers and refugees. New currents affect everyday life across economic

SOCIAL SUFFERING IN THE POSTWAR ERA **115**

strata, social sectors and networks, and ethnic groups. The elite sector, behind its gates, walls, and blinders, is never *beyond* existence; it is always entwined in concrete relations and moral experiences with those without. This message needs to start being articulated by anthropologists, whether they are "studying up" in Guatemala City or working among poor farmers in the Highlands.

FIVE

June 10, September 11, and the Moral Understanding of Violence

Aq'ab'al, a Maya *ajq'ij* ("day-keeper," or spiritual guide) in his late twenties, is part of a generation of ethnically conscious young Maya who have come to embrace traditionalist Maya religion.[1] Called to his destiny through a series of dreams, Aq'ab'al sought out an elder *ajq'ij* and served as his apprentice for several years. He now has a small clientele of his own who seek him out to diagnose spiritual illnesses and conduct rituals. In May 2002, Aq'ab'al foresaw the June 10 protests in a dream. Still unsure of his divinational gifts, however, he did not warn his friends, for fear that they would not believe him. But to tell them now that he saw the violence coming would be an insult, for they would ask "Why didn't you warn us?" In this chapter, we track the aporia between acknowledgment and avoidance, between giving warning and taking notice in the dream. Aq'ab'al's telling, we argue, does not "refer" to the protests but allegorizes the very act of reference, speaks to the difficulties of remembering violence while retaining the felt power of warning, danger, and complicity. "The dream has not yet left me," Aq'ab'al intones, "and I still feel guilty."

In this chapter, we look to the lingering panopticonic effects of *la violencia*, the intermingling of the narratives of September 11 and of June 10, and at the dream of a possible future. We focus on a moral understanding of the meanings and effects of violence, attitudes toward the past and the future, and the construction of blame. By highlighting the ambivalence involved in memory and narrative, we show how the truth about critical events and the ascertainment of responsibility and blame remains indeterminate.

In looking ethnographically at local perspectives on local and global forms of violence, in speaking about memories of violence in the postwar era, we are drawn close enough to the moral experience of sufferers and survivors that their stories come to enable a powerful medium of cultural critique. In seeing how folks in Tecpán remember and respond to the experience of violence, we are pushed to think critically about how violence is managed, consumed, and made meaningful in the dominant framing of the global media. In other words, these stories constitute an ethical plateau (M. Fischer 2003), an occasion to reflect critically on the moral uncertainties involved in the experience of violence and to challenge characterizations of the "postwar" era that would ignore both the emergence of new forms and the extension of old forms of social suffering in the Highlands. These stories, as a medium of cultural critique,[2] also challenge the idea that in a post-9/11 world "everything has changed," suggesting rather that things have not yet changed enough.

Trust, Surveillance, and Moral Understanding

Tecpán is popularly regarded in the tourist guidebooks as being simultaneously a "sleepy little community" and a "vibrant market town." Locals often say that "there is nothing to see here." As one middle-aged man observed, "Tecpán is a nice and peaceful place. There is nothing going on. The government likes it a lot — that's why they are so often here." Accounts of *la violencia* in the Maya Highlands echo this sense of a social life constituted around nothingness, of the fear and uncertainty that characterize everyday existence. There is always a dearth of information, a lack of trust, a loss of family or community, an inability to make meaning or to make sense, of never being sure who one's neighbors or family members supported.[3]

La violencia permeated everyday life in Tecpán, as it did throughout Guatemala; it became routinized and internalized, normalized in a macabre fashion. The effects of *la violencia* linger on. Similar to how the Holocaust defines present-day Germany, *la violencia* defines Guatemala today through a multitude of complex, contradictory, and fluid personal and collective memories:

memories of the killings (of pregnant women, defenseless children, and eld-erly males mercilessly murdered, often in gruesome ways); of the everyday terror of the counterinsurgency (not only the checkpoints and roadblocks but the neighborhood informants and strategic kidnappings); of an atmos-phere in which one never knew who to trust and thus never spoke freely (fos-tering even more suspicion and social isolation).

During the early 1980s, the military almost completely usurped the local authority in places like Tecpán. Surveillance practices, quarantine, censor-ship, and mandatory military enlistment increasingly characterized everyday life. More recently, like most other Highland Maya towns, Tecpán has be-come a target for heightened bureaucratic attention and neoliberal economic reforms, the contentious tax hikes discussed earlier being a prime example. This historical backdrop conditions the irony that the autonomy now demanded by community leaders depends upon a certain juridical recogni-tion by an increasingly nebulous and decentralized administrative Other. Tecpán must become an object of administrative gaze in order to emerge as a recognizable subject of enunciation. To be publicly recognized — to be seen or to be heard — is especially crucial for communities long plagued by clan-destine warfare. Silence or speechlessness is one effect of violence, but polit-ical and legal agencies demand "words (or other signs) so that justice may be done" (Daniel 1996, 121). The closer one looks into the space of everyday terror, the more one encounters "epistemic murk" (Taussig 1987).[4] As inspection intensifies, so does, paradoxically, the deferment or transposition of the so-called source of the problem — the dodgy thing, like a weapon of mass destruction, generating a cycle in which the governmental gaze chases an impossible object-cause of terror and, accordingly, produces a context in which anyone can be considered a potential threat.[5]

People are still reluctant to talk openly about the violence, and with good reason: death threats, kidnappings, and assassinations of human rights activists, clergy, and social scientists continue, though not at the horrendous rates of the early 1980s. The moral life of sufferers attests to the fact that suf-fering and violence do not "put things into perspective," but usually ruin the stability and coherence of perspectives and narratives. That which is most meaningful — family and friends, a community or home or job, life chances — becomes endangered and menaced, perhaps lost entirely (Kleinman and Benson 2004). In order to understand the meanings and effects of violence in the lives of sufferers, one must look at how violent processes influence the structuring of everyday moralities.

Moral models, as abstracted ideal types, are at once widely salient, idiosyncratically diverse, and never fully realized. While there is no singular Tecpán Maya morality, certain moral themes are widely woven into stories and life projects. Across local worlds referred to as "Maya communities," with their great diversity of experience, we find shared moral orientations and values. We do not mean to imply that there is a fixed code of right and wrong, but rather we refer to a layer of human experience in which common things matter in different places (Kleinman 1999a). Thus, we refer not to essences or identities but to situated moral orientations expressed in practices and projects.[6] We have noted that by and large Tecpanecos are not anti-capitalist; an autochthonous ethic that stresses self-reliance and rewards for hard work has converged with the capitalist mechanism of incentives. At the same time, Tecpaneco conceptions of the self tend to be much more inclusive than Utilitarian philosophers and micro-economists would allow, at times encompassing not only the individual and immediate family but also extended relations and the community as a whole. This more inclusive notion of the self (and thus self-interest) informs a wide range of moral narratives that emphasize the collectivity over the individual. For instance, wealth by itself is not generally viewed as evil or bad; but wealthy individuals who do not freely share their good fortune with their family and neighbors are subject to sanctions through social exclusion and stories of Faustain pacts with the devil.

Such communalistic moral orientations are expressed in and reinforced by reciprocity. This happens in ritualized contexts (e.g., the exchange of sweet breads on Maundy Thursday in Tecpán or the role of civil-religious cargo systems in many Maya communities), as well as in quotidian social intercourse. The surveillance culture of *la violencia*, however, largely broke down the trust upon which reciprocity relies (in that giving implies a trust that one will also receive), replacing it with a more narrowly defined self-interest. In this way, the violence was even more successful than intended in supplanting communal tendencies with (neo-) liberal capitalist relations. Fear is the enemy of trust, and the fear instilled by the violence is only slowly receding.

November 1999, Nashville, Tennessee. César is up visiting from Tecpán and we go out to the Pancake Pantry for breakfast. Sharp, funny, and intense, César is a charismatic speaker. Today, the conversation follows a familiar path: catching up on news of family and friends, discussing our work, and, as always, winding up with the latest critiques of Guatemalan politics and society. At one point, the talk turns to the lingering effects of the violence and to César's own experiences in the early

1980s. At this point — in what he later described as an unconscious, reflexive gesture — César lowers his voice and leans in close across the table, periodically glancing around to see who is seated nearby. He tells the story — one that he has told before, but that never loses its emotional impact — of friends and relatives being kidnapped, tortured, and killed, of death threats he received, and of his years of internal exile. In César's town the violence had largely died down compared to fifteen years ago. The Peace Accords ending the war were signed three years ago, and a United Nations commission is in the process of collecting and publishing firsthand accounts of the massacres. Yet so ingrained is his suspicion of speaking openly and freely, that César, not normally a man to mince words, instinctively resorts to a hushed conspiratorial tone. As the Germans discovered after 1989, a wall in the mind can be more insidious than an actual physical barrier.

Yet, conditions are changing. In the years since that conversation with César, Tecpanecos have had a dramatic shift in their attitudes toward discussing their experiences during the violence. Sitting around kitchen hearths, drinking sweet instant coffee, people we have known for years are for the first time telling us stories about the violence to which they had only alluded before. These same friends are also suddenly much more open about criticizing the government; they are working in local political campaigns; and they are even once again starting agricultural and artisanal cooperatives.

Nothing to See Here

In the night, where we are riven to it, we are not dealing with anything. But this nothing is not that of pure nothingness. There is no longer *this* or *that*; there is not "something." But this universal absence is in turn a presence, an absolutely unavoidable presence. . . . There is no discourse. Nothing responds to us, but this silence. . . . *There is*, in general, without it mattering what there is, without our being able to fix a substantive to this term.

— EMMANUEL LEVINAS,
"THERE IS: EXISTENCE WITHOUT EXISTENTS"

Against this cultural and moral backdrop, when people in Tecpán insist that "there is nothing to see here," more than describing their material reality they are drawing the contours of their postwar moral understanding. After all, it is not all boring in town; residents also point tourists to the nearby archaeological ruins as something to see, brag about the new Internet café and the luxury hotel, and take pride in the thriving local woven sweater and textile trades. Asking what the claim "means" locally is already forbidden, since it functions precisely as an epistemological border, marking cultural intimacy, the privileged and protected domain of local knowledge that only locals can access, in relation to curious tourists, ethnographers, bureaucrats, and other outsiders (Herzfeld 1997).

The phrase "nothing to see here" encodes a fear that within the current postwar context, were there actually something to see, it might bring stigma, blame, or an occasion for heightened surveillance and control. Immediately after June 10, the locals, although aware that the media had come to town because of the protests, continued to insist that reporters and photographers were wasting their time. "What do they want?" one older woman asked. "They should forget it. There is nothing to see here." "They will say that we, the town, are to blame for the violence," a man responded. "But they are making this up." This claim reiterates what will be the inevitable conclusion of the investigation: of course, there is always something going on, but no matter how hard you look or listen, you will never find the thing itself, so, really, there will have been nothing to see here. "Yes," the old woman spoke up again, "they already know what they want to say, 'The town is to blame,' so why do they need to come here and ask us what happened during the tragedy?"

This claim simultaneously conceals and draws attention to the reality of social suffering in the Highlands — a reality evidenced in poverty, illness, substance abuse, and the stories and specters of state violence. A silent preface is not heard in the claim: "*Excepting all that stuff,* there is nothing to see here." And if suffering and violence signal, in their overriding residual presence, the impossibility of nothingness (Levinas 1989b, 40), then the claim becomes arresting, at least to the ears of an ethnographer studying the experience of political violence in the Highlands. It produces a surreal effect, where images and captions relentlessly contradict each other. The local world is literally defined by nothing in particular, but also by the impossibility of nothingness, given the silent rustling of social suffering. So the claim does exactly what it says, referring not to the lack of some thing specifically, no thing, but rather performing or miming "nothing" as such, as a pervasive structure of feeling that defined *la violencia* and endures in the postwar period (see Ulmer 1983, 101; Derrida 1981, 206). The characterization of community, of what exists "here," remains infinitely open, like a blank line after "There is . . ." (Levinas 1989a). It points to the promise and persistence of existence, even when all else has been stripped away, disappeared, and made silent. Martial technologies of governmental surveillance that look for an object, a target and a container of blame combine with the media's ability to categorize the local context as lawless, to produce an elliptical "aesthetics of ethical existence," deferring or denying the presence of any specific "thing" and emphasizing, instead, what is patently seen and felt but not talked about (de Certeau 1986, 197). The protests only become reducible to the local context of parochial unrest described in national media coverage of 6/10 if the silent presence of violence that already and still brings the "local" out of context and into the history of relating is tragically forgotten.[7]

We are reading this mundane claim ("Nothing to see here") as a dialectical or montage image (Taussig 1987, 369) that suspends meaning between image and caption, here and there, presence and absence. In montage, two or more unlike figures are brought into a zone of proximity such that inconsistencies emerge from the invisibility and silence gleaned between the lines. This is different from collage, the "transfer of materials from one context to another," since it disseminates or remakes "these borrowings through the new setting." While there is nothing essentially subversive about montage (Ulmer 1983, 94–97), storytellers can use it to bring hegemonic formulations of meaning and reference into relief. This force lies in the unique capacity to produce change or variation in a whole, in the very form of the narrative itself. Montage can alter a frame of reference by disclosing or referring to the act of framing itself. Sign and meaning can come unstuck through the discordant proximity of unlike images. There emerges a sense of the relation defined by nothing in particular, since this relation comes between the two sides, subject and object, running "parallel without ever crossing the dialectic" (Daniel 1996, 208). The claim that "There is nothing to see here" is marked by the internal contradiction, the spectral presence of all that stuff, the silence that occurs but does not put a stop to the rustling.

We began reading the claim of "Nothing to see here" as dialectical, arresting, and contradictory because of its resonance with a postcard photo, titled "Wish You Were Here," that appeared on the cover of the *Village Voice* after September 11. The postcard presents, as an apparition, the twin towers of the World Trade Center, immediately recognizable. With the intrusion of the postcard frame inside the photo, the towers — in their earth-shattering absence, precisely because within this frame there is nothing to see — these lost giants simultaneously do (not) signify the great thereness of being. The image both says that there is nothing to see here and fills in "nothing" with a spectral referent. Like a phantom limb or an invisible hand (Nelson 2001), these incorporeal giants now literalize that virtual, decentralized agency for which they once stood. "Seeing Manhattan from the 110th floor of the World Trade Center," de Certeau observed, "the tallest letters in the world compose a gigantic rhetoric of excess" (1984, 91). They are now themselves commodities, surreal speculations, futures, dreamy souvenirs, wish-you-were-heres. Through destruction and loss the giants have accrued magnificent surplus value, not only because that empty space is now worth more than ever, but also in the desire to fill in the excessive political and economic absence indexed in the giants by extending an invisible hand — on the one hand, through global gestures of amity, assistance, decentralization, and thus, conveniently (on the other hand), severing the retaliatory sword from the amicable and innocent body politic wielding it.

Within U.S. discourse of "the war on terror" there are two predominant ways of seeing things. In both cases, "they" hate "our" way of life. Those on the right oppose "the terrorists," and, more generally, critics of U.S. policy, whom they see as standing in the way of universal good. Those on the left often sympathize with these critics and see them as standing in the way of the global flow of goods, that is, as valiant opponents of capitalism and empire. But what if anti-American sentiment expresses something different — a "wish you were here"? Perhaps it is not simply about hating the American way of life, but rather: we hate your way of life so much that we demand you share. Read thusly, the postcard is not stating that the twin towers were here yesterday and gone today. A wish, the image operates in the future anterior, coming between the past and the present. The ruined towers allegorize the wishful, virtual operations of global capitalism[8]: enigmatic, opaque, distancing, and deterritorializing, a process that had never been fully actualized and yet remains ongoing, a promise that for many around the world still retains meaning and force.

We sense this ambivalent timing in the Tecpanecos' claim that there is nothing to see there. The June 10 protests demonstrated the "complications involved" in being recognized. Political recognition does violence to ethics where it renders citizens impersonal and anonymous. It does violence to a face. We are reading the claim as a hailing, then — not political interpellation but an ethical call. In the classic formulation, the agent doing the hailing is the state, in the form of the police, development officials, the mayor, or other functionaries. "The government likes [Tecpán] a lot," the joke went, "that's why they are so often here." By negating this surveillance — "There is nothing to see here" — the claim gestures toward a form of recognition that is prior and more personal than political relations, a feeling of wanting-to-have-really-been acknowledged. The claim becomes an everyday rustling of this wish, the longing of a public marked by the overwhelming absence of those who disappeared during the violence, a public now regularly accused, when it protests, of stirring things up, keeping a "finger in the wound" (Nelson 1999). This demand cannot be made, is impossible, must remain a wish, else it risks being reduced to resentment or blame, which is exactly what occurred, as we demonstrate below, during the reconciliation meetings after the protests. The desire to give warning about "all that stuff" meets the impossibility of taking notice, demanding an acknowledgment without recompense, a recognition or responsibility justified by no prior commitment (Levinas 1981, 127), an impartial ethics of nothing in particular. But this demand must remain silent, rustling within the assertion that there is nothing to see here, no recognition necessary — why . . . would you take notice if there were?

9/11 and 6/10: Two Days in Tecpán

In June 2002, while in Tecpán, Guatemala, I went to visit Don Domingo, a local day-keeper, farmer, artist, and grassroots activist.[9] Don Domingo is simultaneously reserved and gregarious — cloaking personal opinions in irony, using non sequiturs to keep friends a bit off balance. On this occasion, his greeting parodied and reversed the equation of terrorism and Otherness. After opening the front gate, he asked me: "Do you have anthrax? I need to ask before you enter. I'm worried because all the *canchitos* ["little blondies," here a playfully derogatory reference to foreigners] are the ones with anthrax." He seemed satisfied when I assured him that the anthrax letters in the United States were a case of domestic terrorism. He showed me to a dim living room, candles burning, coffee already boiled down. We sat at a squat table on fine wooden chairs, carpentry being one of his many hobbies, and he talked about September 11:

We saw everything. No one could miss the news from the biggest country on the planet. I had the television on the whole day. At first I didn't realize the size of the towers, so it wasn't so incredible, except that two buildings had fallen. But then a neighbor told me of their size. The whole event became almost too terrible. I felt for the sufferers, but I also wondered why the hijackers did this. I realized that they had political concerns, very serious ones.

Tecpán, as we saw in the last chapter, would witness its own arresting moment just months after the 9/11 attacks, when the anti-tax protest of June 10 turned violent. In the days and weeks following June 10, these events dominated local conversation. There were the bits and pieces culled from immediate memory, the snapshots and recollections of those locals bursting through front doors that first week, a response to the whole series of "Did you hears?" and "Listens!" as families mingled around the hearth to learn what participants in the protest saw and heard. One night, a man wearing sunglasses — strange, as it was already quite dark — came to the home in which I was living. We were finishing dinner and discussing the protests. But Don José, the father of the house, quickly cautioned: "Stop talking about it. We can't say a word about what happened." The stranger was still occupied at the door by the family's more curious children. "He was there. He works for the mayor and he was hurt. How embarrassing is that, to have been there on the side of the mayor? That is why he is wearing sunglasses, to cover over his injuries so that no one can see that he was involved." That Don José, who did not witness the event, was nonetheless aware of the man's participation speaks to the decisive and dangerous role that rumor played in popular conceptions of the protest.

When compared to the implicit presence of memories of violence in everyday speech, some narratives of the June 10 protests explicitly provoked broader questions about cultural politics, transnational linkages, and the ongoing history of state violence. In the wake of the protests and in televised views of the September 11 events, various kinds of discourse interacted, circulated, and were used against one other. The experience of the protest was shaped by locally prevailing idioms that increasingly privilege democratic ideals. Officials were able to use rumor, under the banner of dialogue, to incite blame and limit popular criticism of corruption. In the previous chapter, we demonstrated how the very idea of democratic compromise became a powerful and acceptable limit point during reconciliation meetings, one through which protestors, and of course the mayor, who got away with his life, could feel as if something had been accomplished, even if, as some protestors noted, nothing had changed. It was difficult to get around this discourse in the specific setting of the reconciliation meetings, since to criticize democratic compromise would make one seem, well, undemocratic and stubborn, which was, ironically, what the protestors were criticizing the mayor for being all along. But other narratives of violence, told after the protest and in the safety of people's homes, like the thoughts of Don Domingo, cast the ideal of democratic compromise in the light of global events. In these discussions, people were able to get beyond the dominant framing and respond to the experience of the menacing new modes of social control and violence that have arisen in the postwar era.

Much of this ability has to do with the creative use of collage or montage. Don Domingo's narrative of 6/10 and 9/11 is a collage, with its juxtapositions, although it only approximates the form of montage, which more explicitly points to the narrative framing itself, not simply the various spliced contents. "June 10th was already waiting to happen," Don Domingo went on. "It was meant to be. You can't treat people the way we are treated in this town and expect everything to remain *tranquilo* forever. This is a quiet town, but the people have anger inside of them. This is why the protests became violent." Suddenly, he took a line of flight, a seeming non sequitur that effectively folded together global and local situations of violence, using the one to make sense of the uncanny appearance of the other:

> The hijackers were not terrorists. This is the problem here in Guatemala. They were guerillas, they were revolutionaries, but there developed a discourse of who is to blame and who are the victims. History talks about guerrillas terrorizing towns, killing women and children, but it never discusses the complications involved, the violence committed by the state, the difficult choices that people, my friends, needed to make, the fears people faced. Terrorist is a name, a way of disqualifying a critique, creating an enemy that poses some threat and is totally different. Their critique is never heard because it is based on violence.

In the weeks after June 10, many Tecpanecos would compare that event to the hijackings, mainly local activist types who, like Don Domingo, are proud of their cosmopolitan perspective and closely followed all the television news on September 11. Don Domingo watched the same broadcasts that the mainstream American viewer watched. He gets CNN, too. But his impressions are figured against a different moral background. He knows the ambiguities and dangers involved in facile notions of blame and unilateral restitution. The communalistic leitmotif of Tecpaneco moral models, along with a discursive penchant for strategic ambiguity, has been adopted into a subjectivity that is hesitant to lay blame. Don Domingo refuses to see June 10 or September 11 as parochial eruptions of madness dissociated from larger political and economic designs. "The people have been made angry since the 1970s," he said of the protests. "It was coming because of the poverty and crime, and then they ask for more taxes." Now he shifts again: "It is the same with September 11th. The hijackings were crazy, of course, but I was really not surprised. People have had different opinions about the United States for a long time. This is a lesson to be learned, if your country can learn anything, especially since animosity has made it impossible to communicate."

Don Domingo is skeptical of the conventional wisdom that images of violence will, eventually, lead to popular outrage and resistance. Don Domingo stresses that popular perceptions of violence all too often lead to habits of blaming the victim, and here he may be speaking from personal experiences, as his family was often endangered during *la violencia*, suspected of collaboration with guerillas and forced to hide for years in the countryside before being comfortable returning to Tecpán. On September 11, for example, viewers fixed to televisions across the country felt as though they themselves were being attacked, experiencing a visceral response that made it very difficult to substantively or critically discuss the event beyond sentimentality. And just as the problems represented in media images are distanced, so too can their solution be. This is best seen in the modern U.S. military preference for high altitude warfare, the discourse of which produces the impression for some soldiers that dropping bombs is like playing a video game and distracts media and audience attention from the harsh realities of warfare that is close, intimate, and face to face.

By comparison, Don Domingo identifies with the hijackers, not out of solidarity or because he supports their efforts, but because, as he stresses, there is value in understanding the Other apart from structures of blame and vengeance that — and he finds the same process at work in *la violencia* — turn the Other into an enemy. But this kind of understanding is not about democratic compromise or reciprocal dialogue, as was the ideal during the June 10 reconciliation meetings profiled in the last chapter. Here, a pedagogical imperative emerges precisely where there is nothing to see or hear, here at the limits of dialogue, at the extremities of power and the ends of compromise. Don Domingo is witness to two violent events, certainly, but he is also witness to the event of witnessing itself, to the imperative of acknowledging or taking notice of the "difficult choices" and "serious concerns" of others, even or, as he emphasizes, especially, where it is impossible to communicate. Even where literal Others — hijackers, for example — are on another plane altogether, Don Domingo, without ever having decided to be involved, becomes bound, in the televised face of others' suffering, to their motives.

We can understand Don Domingo's views in part through his personality, always curious and critical, looking beneath the surface of things, never one to be duped. But we can also understand his commentary within a larger moral and cultural universe in which blame is more deliberately approached and deployed. Testimonies of violence from Highland Guatemala have been a powerful witness to, and also a buffer against, recurring state-sponsored violence. But they have also created a meaningful and thoroughly practical moral discourse for thinking about violence in Guatemala. If it is clear who the victims and the perpetrators in this genre are, it is just as clear that complicity and blame are immensely diffuse and are only dangerously attributed to specific groups or individuals (see Menchú 1983; cf. Stoll 1999 and Arias 2001). Global human rights efforts have brought Guatemala into articulation with an international public of journalists, monitors, ethnographers, development specialists, and humanitarian workers whose project is tensely caught between a solidarity (grounded in the history of violence and discrimination) for a particular segment of the population, the Maya, and the premise of a nation-state that must partly dissolve racial and cultural differences, and in many ways neglect that past, in order to guarantee equal rights and protections.

If the postwar and post-September 11 framings find repose in familiar binaries like victim and perpetrator, then between these poles there is a space where observers and actors are related in feelings of complicity, and are pushed into new dimensions of understanding, especially where communication breaks down. The reflections of Don Domingo are located in this in-between space. Here, local and global forms of violence are seen as interactive and reflective. He sees counterinsurgency warfare as neither something altogether in the past nor something hermetically confined to "Guatemala." In Don Domingo's own words:

> Democracy is something politicians say to win affection but this is often a lie. Before June 10th, the mayor did not listen but talked a lot about democracy. He talks about it even more now, but how is this different? In the United States, there are problems — an elite class with money and power, and there is violence. September 11th occurred for a reason. The hijackers had a problem with the government, not really with the people, just as the problem during the protests was with the mayor. And who suffered there? The people suffered, the protesters, shop owners, the community. The protestors wanted to be heard but it doesn't matter because it was violent. The political concerns are not taken seriously. Even if the United States has its problems, the interests of the people are heard. So sometimes I wonder if it is better in the United States. There are social problems there, but *at least there is no war.* There is still a war here. Not a *war* war, but there is a war that has been with us for years.

A few Tecpanecos working in the New York City area at the time actually witnessed September 11 firsthand. Although in Guatemala the fear of being seen too clearly or heard too loudly — by the state, for example — limits what people are willing to say about violence (Warren 1998, 93), many locals wanted to discuss September 11. The creative appropriation of the discourse on terrorism here at the margins of an emergent West-versus-rest dichotomy is especially relevant to the context of what is being called "postwar" Guatemala. Marcel Xuya, a broccoli farmer from Tecpán, was in New York on a trip to establish contacts with importers on September 11, 2001. He was staying with relatives in Newark when the two planes hit the towers:

> When the first hit, we got a call telling us to get up to the roof. Just a few flights of stairs, looking across the river. Smoke rising. We assumed it was an accident. Then we saw another plane flying low to the ground, it passed the towers initially, then turned around, it came back straight into the second tower. Wow. Ok, that is no accident. A few days before I was down near the towers. We have some flower vendors down there. And a few days after I was in the subway with some friends. We were coming back from a meeting in Yonkers. The subway stopped, lights went out, couldn't see a thing. We thought it might have been another attack. We stayed in the

subway for an hour, waiting, not knowing what happened. We found out *that* was just an accident. There I was less than a year before, watching something that would appear again in my own community. They were different, but almost too familiar. On June 10th it seemed like I already knew what was going to happen. I was right there in the middle of what I saw from a distance. Now I felt what it was like around the towers.

Xuya relates a similar sense of resignation that occurred during the June 10 protest, which he watched from a neighbor's rooftop. He remembers: "I saw smoke bombs going back and forth in front of me. I knew right away that this was more than a problem of the mayor. It had become a problem for the whole *pueblo*. I thought, here I am again on a rooftop, with smoke rising up from the ground, and I cannot do anything but watch."

Shifting back and forth between the local and the global, the distant and the intimate, Xuya acquires a personal double vision, a strange and uncanny feeling all his own that, simultaneously, prompts an acknowledgment and sense of the suffering of others, such that experience becomes social, inter-personal, attached to transnational affective flows. For Xuya, perhaps more than the others, June 10 is directly related to September 11. Not only because he witnessed both events, but also because he attributes the eruption of violence in Tecpán to the local economic decline, one result of the hijack-ings in faraway New York.

> September 11th affected us a lot. We depend on the U.S. economy so much. When ports closed down after September, we had difficulty ex-porting produce. The problem was timing. I call it the "coincidence of June 10th" rather than the tragedy. Most of those protestors grow export crops, and so when the U.S. economy sunk there was nothing to do but take up against decentralization, the new tax. But how can we make political demands without funding?

Even while he condemns a unilateral fight against decentralization, Xuya suggests that an attack on the inequities of the global market — even if it takes the form of terrorism — is justifiable: "The hijackers had some reason and motive because of American business throughout the world. Look, there is a McDonald's in Antigua. More and more that town is becoming a little plot of the U.S. It was a good lesson for your country to have learned, if they have learned anything." It is interesting that Xuya, who might be situated in

Tecpán's middle to upper class, who has arguably benefited greatly from a liberalization of global trade, expresses latent sympathies with a broadly anti-globalist position. Such irony is highlighted by the words of other Tecpa-necos who take a very different view of September 11 and the global econ-omy. One local restaurant worker, Felipe Gómez, complained:

> I went to New York and saw the towers right in front of me. I worked there and was there on September 11th. Before that I worked for an Arab three years in Guatemala and he never paid me. Three years and [he] never had money for me. But *he* had the money. He kept it all. Arabs are crazy, fucked up. In New York it's like this: one hour worked, one hour paid. You get the money right away and do whatever you want. I am angry about what happened in New York. I worked five years there.

Gómez went on to relate a popular June 10 rumor that we had already heard on numerous occasions:

> One guy was captured by the police and put in jail that day. People said it was for looting during the protests, and he was indeed looting. That is certain. People said he deserved it, being put in jail, he got what was coming, not because he was looting but because he was the owner of a cantina on the central park known locally as a fence for prostitution and criminal activity.

Juxtaposing the two events in this pair of stories, Gómez elaborates a partic-ular moral perspective on labor and entitlement in Tecpán. Such moral cat-egories are also invoked, although differently, in Xuya's narratives. Both men admit dependence on the U.S. economy. But whereas Gómez uses this dependence as a means of critiquing local economic and moral conditions, Xuya argues that the U.S. got what was coming to it.

These two perspectives reflect prevalent tensions in emergent Tecpaneco moral models in an age of rapidly changing economic and political circum-stances. On the one hand, there is a realpolitik approach that views the tra-ditional Maya work ethic as convergent with the rewards structure of global capitalism. The political-economic hegemony of the United States may be viewed as positive or negative but, regardless, it is taken as a given that must be worked with. In this context, nontraditional agriculture and anti-tax demonstrations are seen as risky but ultimately rewarding endeavors. On the other hand, a more critical local model sees export agriculture and local protests as what we have termed limit points. From this perspective, more radical change is not only possible but necessary, a view that finds support in traditional notions of reciprocity and karma-like justice. We must be ever careful of romanticizing a presumptively more communitarian past as opposed to an alienated present, but when our Tecpaneco interlocutors put forth such comparisons their significance moves beyond the curiosities of native historiography to the construction of moral projections of the future.

A Good Night's Sleep

Modern demolition is truly wonderful. As a spectacle it is the opposite of a rocket launch. The twenty-storey block remains perfectly vertical as it slides towards the centre of the earth. It falls straight, with no loss of its upright bearing, like a tailor's dummy falling through a trap-door, and its own surface area absorbs the rubble. What a marvelous modern art form this is, a match for the firework displays of our childhood.

— JEAN BAUDRILLARD, *America*

Something comes along. Something else comes along. They collide and stick. They stay together, perhaps combine with something else again to form a larger combination. . . . Over time, under pressure, sediment folds and hardens into sedimentary rock. . . . The connective syntheses that made the muck and turned it to rock were passive. No concerted action by an isolable agent was involved. The disjunctive synthesis that made it a building was active. . . . It swoops down to capture connective syntheses, but also rises from them . . . block by block, a wall is built. . . . A courthouse is more than a building. It is also a conjuncture of judges, handcuffs, law books, and accused.

— BRIAN MASSUMI, *A User's Guide to Capitalism and Schizophrenia*

Deleuze observes that "it is between the visible and its conditions that statements glide, as with Magritte's two pipes. It is between the statement and its conditions that visibilities insinuate themselves" (1988, 66). Text and image, sign and referent, in contradiction, appear as two highly charged magnets constantly attracting and rifting off one another, never collapsing to produce "a pipe" or "nothing" as either truth or non-truth. The image of the mayor's burned house in Tecpán achieves the same effect. If critics of the mayor found the arson itself ironic and somewhat amusing, even more hilarious was the slogan inscribed across the outside wall: "Para Dormir y Descansar Bien" (For a good night's sleep). The text contradicts — is literally inscribed on — the detritus of burnt walls, broken windows, and hard feelings. Along with his wife and older children, the mayor ran a mattress and bedding business out of his home. Some locals saw it all along as a front for the political corruption and money laundering that they knew was going on and heard lots about but could never really see. Others saw it as a symbol of increasing class polarization in Tecpán, consumer goods becoming a preoccupation and luxury of urban elites like the mayor.

Class distinctions and corruption remain, many locals insist, despite the idiom of equality. "He keeps saying we are equal," one protestor commented on the mayor's behavior after a reconciliation meeting. "We are equal in some ways: we are flesh and blood, human beings. But we are not equal in many other ways." "Look at the mayor's house," said another protestor, chuckling. "He won't be sleeping so well anymore. We gave him something to think about, and whether he takes our demands seriously or not, he's at least got something to keep him awake at night." The constant disavowal of this nightmare, of inequalities and corruption, conditions the possibility for the postwar phase as a dream of a good night's sleep, a wish you were here, a wanting-to-have-really-been.

Aq'ab'al, a Maya spiritual guide and day-keeper from Tecpán, tells of the dream he had forty days prior to June 10. Aq'ab'al and I met for a few hours one evening in July 2002, sitting in his kitchen on upside-down plastic buckets that had been used just a few days before to store a potent homemade fruit concoction used in religious rituals. One wonders whether his premonition really occurred prior to the protest. Part of this ambivalence has to do with the intensely playful way about him. Like Don Domingo, Aq'ab'al regularly destabilizes conversations through humor or seemingly illogical injunctions, and he prefers the power of imagery to the verity of evidence. It may be just such an undecideable reading effect, characteristic of montage (Ulmer 1983, 99), which propels this uncertainty and which Aq'ab'al finds so relevant.

The protest [*manifestación*] already happened in the dream but it was there even before that.[10] The dream has not yet left me and I still feel guilty. There is a meeting with thousands of participants. Their faces, their identities are hidden. There are expensive trucks around the central park, weighted down in the rear with anxious passengers. They circle the park again and again, *mucha gente* with bats and guns. They want to assassinate President Alfonso Portillo because he can do or say anything. "Vámonos," say the people, "Vámonos." I am there among the crowd but I am not a part of it. I observe and listen but I feel ill prepared, not ready for what is going to happen because I know something is about to happen. I see the whole thing from the outside. I see it but am not participating. But the participants do not see what I see, the dangers and the people becoming angry. The mayor is not there. Instead, it is Portillo inside the municipal building. He is playing the role of mayor, but this is not the mayor.

Let us first note that the mayor and the president become fractal aspects of a decentralized government. The dream suggests that although decentralization may enable local political autonomy, the process has also provided more subtle paths for extending bureaucratic control. The notion of decentralization seems to gloss over this fact — that the president, whose authority often goes unseen and unheard, muffled in the exigencies of local politics, deflected around the corruption of local officials, is never not in a relation to the Highlands. The dream imagines power as a diffuse flow traversing and bringing into distanced articulation "apparatuses and institutions, without being exactly localized in them" (Foucault 1978, 96). The dream conjures the mayor and, as a caption, insists, "This is not the mayor" — creating a nightmarish gap between distraction and warning in which a "third phenomenon" emerges, beyond the "two elements [seeing and hearing]," that "unknown, unseen and unsaid" mode of control (Deleuze 1988, 81). The dream insists that, really, power in Guatemala is not decentralized enough. The local cannot be regarded as completely autonomous. The protests are irreducible to parochial unrest. The president remains accountable in this local world. To paraphrase Don Domingo, the local can become "a name, a title, a way of disqualifying a critique or creating an enemy," of reifying "who is to blame and who are the victims."

In his dreams, Aq'ab'al is (from) "there" (but who knows where?) and yet is "not a part of it." He observes from the "outside," as Marcel Xuya had done on the rooftops, as Don Domingo had done on his television, an outside that nonetheless grows close and murky, epistemically speaking. Aq'ab'al can see and hear things that the faceless and nameless participants cannot, and he is at pains to put a name or a face to this anonymity — impossible, for that would identify actors and perhaps impart or parcel blame. Already the dream echoes Levinas: "Violence can only aim at a face" (1969, 225). Violence betrays an interpersonal relation more ancient than the individuation of anonymous and autonomous subjects, and then violence redoubles as blame is allocated along those lines. In his dreams, all politics is not local but remains open to an outside. "I can see the participants meeting on the outskirts of town," he continues, "very far away, but who knows where?"

> I don't know who the leaders are, but they want to talk with Portillo, with the mayor. He cannot hear them because he is not there, because he is not the mayor. But then I see *mucha violencia*. No one dies. I know that no one will die. The violence occurs because of emotion. It was not thought out.

An unseen line emerges between "there" and "he is not there," between "the mayor" and "he is not the mayor," effectively miming the work of decentralization, seeing without being seen, and deferring the assignment of blame by resisting identification. Protestors blamed the mayor. He blamed them. They blamed the gangs. Yet the dream does not know who was in charge or where the violence originated: "I won't be able to name it, a seismic jolt that came from far away and that carried very far" (Derrida 1992, 348). Aq'ab'al goes on:

> The violence came from energies and emotions. It was coming already. I dreamed it and it was already occurring in the history. It came forty days before the protests but I sensed even earlier that people were becoming angry. The people came to talk at three or four in the morning because they work or have to travel and can't meet at any other time. But Portillo could not hear them. The door was shut in their face. But he always said that we are all equals. This made the people even angrier. They burned his house. There are burning buildings and clouds of smoke fill the central park.

The dream thus does not "refer" to decentralization. It literally decentralizes — agency, subjectivity, and blame. It is not an interpretation of an event but is itself an event, a testimony or witness, an eventual *manifestación* "that never took place as such" (Johnson 1980, 142). It thus breaks from the logic of "recounting" and performs the very inability to see or hear that so compelled protestors and lingers. To the "disjunctive syntheses" of the reconciliation process — particular agents identified and accused — it actualizes "a larger combination" in which "no concerted action by an isolable agent [is] involved" (Massumi 1992, 47–49).

That the dream occurred before the event means that this telling produces, retroactively, a foreboding, confronting skepticism but eschewing rumor. "It is *as if*," Derrida writes, "the narrative condition were the cause of the recounted thing, *as if* the narrative produced the event it is supposed to report" (1992, 122). The dream becomes both allegorical,[11] referring simply and humbly to itself, to this impossible task of retroactive warning, and performative, actualizing in the very moment of utterance what will have already occurred. "I could not tell anyone, not even my friends who participated, about my dream," Aq'ab'al laments, "could not give warning because they would not have believed me. But now, after the protests, I cannot tell them I saw it all beforehand since they will ask: 'Why didn't you warn us?'" There is nothing that can be said or heard: "The gift, like the event, as event, must remain unforeseeable, but *remain* so without keeping itself" (Derrida 1992, 122). The warning is untimely, too early and too late, verified as such, as a warning, after the fact, canceling any anticipatory force. The dream has not now been corroborated, but remains precisely as a dream, a will-have-been, intervening at the level of the virtual, something to be seen. "The dream has not yet left me," Aq'ab'al says, "and I still feel guilty."

Against the notion of a postwar Guatemala where state-sponsored violence has ended and where local voices are being empowered, the dream portends the dangers and unseen consequences of decentralization and related gestures toward peace and reconciliation. The dream concludes with a conspiracy theory, attributing the events to an unseen and unheard cryptic agency coming from very far away. "'Vamos a militizar Tecpán,' said the government, 'We are going to militarize the whole place,'" Aq'ab'al theorizes.

> The protests made this possible, to have indigenous fighting indigenous. When there is in-fighting, the government is able to come in with their armies to promote order and control. They set up agencies. They say, "We are here to make peace." Then the press says that Tecpán is violent

and the government peaceful. But the protests were prefigured from a distant place. I see the government paying people cash to loot and throw rocks. They are not gang members. I don't know who they are. It wasn't us that started the violence. The government is always trying to disrupt a movement. They make violence and then they make peace, or they promote peace and make violence. Everyone from different sides, outside the town, everyone is caught up in the excitement and is part of the event. There is a force in the air, a force we cannot see. It enters from far away.

The local political subject becomes passive, shaped by and given to this very far away agency, but not indifferent or powerless. This is perhaps only to decenter dominant formulations of blame and their reliance on the binary of intentional perpetrators and their guiltless victims. This "radically passive" (Wall 1999) subject forebodes an interhuman encounter that exists prior to social contracts, reconciliation meetings. "The interhuman," according to Levinas,

> lies in a non indifference of one to another, in a responsibility of one for another, but before the reciprocity of this responsibility, which will be inscribed in impersonal laws, comes to be superimposed on the pure altruism of this responsibility. . . . It is prior to any contract that would specify precisely the moment of reciprocity. (2000, 100)

This passivity is thus prior to the collective identity politics articulated through pan-Maya activism, which, if always contextual, multiple, and open to change, is nonetheless predicated upon certain disjunctive syntheses (E. Fischer 2001; Fischer and Brown 1996; Warren 1998). The difference emerges in the move between the promise that "we are all equals, flesh and bones" and the particular significance of "indigenous fighting indigenous," as Don Domingo noted. Between these planes there emerges that invisible line, unseen and unheard in current discourse on violence and peace in Guatemala, ethics as neither fundamentally about ethnic difference and corrupted by in-fighting nor a demand of universal equality and quickly subverted by the fact that "we are not equal in many other ways." Ethics becomes an unequal relation to others before identity. That the "indigenous men fighting indigenous men" are anonymous reveals violence aiming at a face, rendering relating impersonal: "Their faces, their identities remain hidden." In his dreams, the fabric of relation is not balanced, neither flattened nor polarized, but is "unassumability" itself (Levinas 2000), "ill preparedness," as Aq'ab'al puts it, the impossibility to assimilate or assume the Other, but also the impossibility of simply assuming and not witnessing, a rather ethnographic quandary. Aq'ab'al himself can only assume total responsibility for the violence, for the "friends that participated," saying that he still feels "guilty." "But what passes and what comes to pass," citing Derrida again, "is that the event has been created in the life of the narrator himself; it has affected the fabric of *relation* itself . . . but first of all the relation *between* the narrator and his friend" (1992, 120).

So this passivity does not mean that collective or cultural identities are betrayed or spoiled. But to take such formulations as primordial, not already split by "an alterity in me," as Levinas (1985, 98) puts it — or, as Aq'ab'al puts it, "I see the whole thing from the outside. I see it but am not participating" — is to risk reproducing violent cycles of blame and retribution. As Levinas explains in an interview, this passivity in the face of the other is "like that sentence in Dostoyevsky: '*We are all guilty of all and for all men before all, and I more than others*'" (1985, 98). The guilt is "not really mine," and the offenses are not ones "that I would have committed." It is an infinite, rather decentered guilt that renders any local allocation of blame dubious and precipitates, in the face of violence aiming at a face, the impossible but necessary process of giving warning to and taking notice of the Other. It is a guilt that occurs "because I am responsible for a total responsibility, which answers for all the others and for all in the others, even for their responsibility" (Levinas 1985, 98–99). It is the kind of guilt that admits: "There are no innocent collectivities in the present war, despite the powerful deployment of the figure of 'innocent' killed on both sides of the divide" (Das 2003, 106). It endures in the wake of attempts at democratic compromise or reconciliation, this often silent guilt that will not put a stop to the rustling that keeps one up at night, or keeps one from waking, and, restless, stirs dreams of a good night's sleep.

SIX

Beyond Victimization

The Maya of Guatemala have long been victimized. Witness the brutalities of the Spanish conquest, the imposition of colonial rule, the institutionalized discrimination of authoritarian and democratic governments alike, violence both extraordinary and quotidian. For many, Guatemala is best remembered for the civil war that made the country a poster child for human rights causes. While rebel forces blockaded roads, blew up bridges, and assassinated (*justificaron*) plantation owners and minor politicians, the U.S.-supported Guatemalan army kidnapped and tortured thousands of suspects, massacred untold numbers of civilians, and razed hundreds of villages, burning houses and fields, scattering and killing the population. Exactly how many were killed we will never know — tens of thousands at least. The U.N.-supported Historical Clarification Commission, set up after the 1996 Peace Accords, found that over 90 percent of the 42,000 human rights violations they documented were attributable to the Guatemalan military.[1] The overwhelming majority of victims were Maya Indians, leading the commission to conclude that the Guatemalan military intentionally targeted Maya populations and thus, like the Nazis in Germany, was guilty of "acts of genocide." Indeed, regardless of when, or even if, the violence ended, regardless of how various forms of human suffering have intensified in the postwar phase, the Maya peoples have been and continue to be the primary victims. They are victims of historical oppression and of a system that continues to systematically disadvantage them and limit life chances.

Yet, there is a danger in the rhetoric of victimhood. It becomes too easy to reduce the Maya to nothing more than victims, to mere reactants to larger forces. This may be necessary for political activism, but it obscures the complex realities we strive for in cultural analysis. This danger is not simply recognized by academics. Many Maya recognize various problems associated with this discourse and are seeking to remake the conditions in which they live in other ways. As recent events (such as the June 10 protests discussed in the previous two chapters) remind us, the Maya, inasmuch as we may speak about them as a group, are more than victims. They are active protagonists in their own futures. If this seems self-evident given contemporary ethnographic sensibilities, it is still too often forgotten (for all the right reasons) when analysts look for the structural causes of ongoing inequalities. For example, "neoliberal reform" frequently serves as the bogeyman in contemporary social analysis: a global, structural system that disadvantages already marginalized peoples. Yet, as we have seen throughout this book, elements of neoliberal policies can, in certain places at certain times, serve as a venue for indigenous agency.

In this chapter, we examine efforts of the Maya in Guatemala and Chiapas, Mexico, to revalue their cultural heritage and create new spaces for resistance in regional, national, and global systems of political economy. This revaluation of culture, we argue, is a collective project shaped and enacted in a moral context characterized by loss, marginalization, and victimization. This project and the values and objectives associated with it aim at creating "something better" in postwar Guatemala. But as was the case with nontraditional agriculture, this sense of "something better" goes beyond mere economic returns. Maya cultural activism as a project that is at once social, moral, and political aims to produce outcomes that are as much about ethical orientations, cultural capital, and affective desires as they are economic entitlements and procurements. This project is not just a local one. It involves the desires, goals, and sensibilities of ethnographers, development workers, and other "outside observers" as much as the Maya communities themselves. We describe a war of representation and control over representation, but one with real-world consequences that bring to the fore inherent contradictions of literary deconstruction as applied to ethnographic representation. We argue that victimization, as a category, embodies certain limit points of desire that may satiate liberal Western fantasies but that are ultimately unfulfilling as an end (although not necessarily a means) for revindication.

Genocide and Resurgence

Guatemala's genocide sought not only to stamp out the communist threat (reason enough to secure U.S. funding of the war) but to obliterate the ground on which it presumably flourished, traditional Maya communities. Yet, out of the ashes of this destruction has emerged a vibrant social movement working to revitalize Maya cultural forms, to promote Maya ethnic pride, and to create new spaces for Maya peoples in Guatemalan political, economic, and social networks.

In the early days of the movement (the mid- to late 1980s), pan-Mayanist groups were careful to keep their focus on "non-political" issues, especially linguistic conservation and folkloric cultural revival (Fischer and Brown 1996; Montejo 2005). In the context of "postwar" Guatemala, this was an incredibly effective strategy, allowing Mayanist leaders to step out of the line of fire (both literally and figuratively) between the extreme left and the extreme right (see Stoll 1993). Pan-Mayanism offered a third-way alternative that sought nonviolent, culturally-based solutions to Guatemala's ills, and its message fell on receptive ears both among Maya peoples and among international donor organizations. After growing steadily in the late 1980s, the number of Maya non-governmental organizations in Guatemala skyrocketed during the 1990s. At the turn of the century there were hundreds of Maya NGOs, with concerns ranging from language conservation to indigenous religions to politics to economics (Bastos and Camus 1993, 1995). These groups benefited from a turn in international attention during the 1990s to the issue of indigenous peoples and their rights. In 1992, in the midst of celebrations for the Columbian Quincentenary, Rigoberta Menchú, a Maya woman from Guatemala, was awarded the Nobel Peace Prize for her efforts to bring attention to the plight of Maya peoples in Guatemala during the violence (and also, certainly, to serve as a symbol for all oppressed Native

Americans — see Nelson 1999). The United Nations declared the 1990s the Decade of Indigenous Peoples. And funding bodies — mainly the United Nations, the European Union, the Scandinavian countries, and the United States — began to target their assistance to indigenous populations.

In this context, pan-Maya groups have both benefited from and been belittled by their victimization at the hands of others. Here we refer not only to their "actual" victimization — of conquest, colonialism, the violence of the 1980s — but also to their symbolic victimization. By this we mean the representational and symbolic violence that is done to Maya communities by the application of categories of victimhood, and the models of victimization that, while championing the rights of the oppressed, very often give little voice to the very same oppressed, who are seen as victims of larger structural forces that must be righted. Such representations, sympathetic as they may be, risk constituting a pornography of poverty and violence, allowing readers (and donor organizations) a vicarious experience of suffering, relief, and distress, a removed outlet for sublimated fears and desires. It plays to our hidden and overt presuppositions of superiority — "At least we aren't like that" — even when spoken in the idiom of multicultural pluralism. This "at least" is an insidious phrase, negating radical alternatives and radical empathy while seducing the speaker with its subtle self-righteousness (which is to say, that "at least" delimits a limit point in the moral project of identity politics).

Pan-Mayanist leaders stress that they are primarily working to preserve Mayan languages and culture. Because of this strategic emphasis on cultural issues, their demands fall outside of the historical political confrontations between the Guatemalan left and right, and they are not inherently antagonistic to either side. Segments of the elite sector are ready and willing to grant demands for cultural and linguistic rights, which allows them to demonstrate their progressiveness to the rest of the world in this period of increasing concern over indigenous rights. Such concessions are also timely, given that foreign assistance is being tied closely to Guatemala's human rights record.

Playing on the recent global valuation of all things indigenous, the recognition of indigenous rights as a subset of fundamental human rights, and the ideological commitment of many academics to support the empowerment of marginalized peoples, pan-Mayanists have been very successful at gaining material support for the movement from international organizations (including the United Nations, the European Union, the U.S. Agency for International Development, and numerous private foundations).

While Maya leaders and groups have been able to capitalize on their symbolic and actual victimization (currency in the U.N. and other international organizations), the diverse practice of their lived experiences belies the confining, oppositionally defined category of victimhood. They have been victims, certainly, but they are so much more than *just* victims: they are men and women, adolescents and elderly, urban and rural peoples — individuals defined by unique conjunctures of almost infinite social, cultural, and economic vectors — who are living their lives as best they see fit, balancing self-interests with social obligations. In attempting to capture such complexity while trying to avoid further symbolic violence toward Maya peoples, we must proceed beyond the language of victimization. We must not forget the horrors of the violence, and we should not turn a blind eye to exploitation and injustice (as we may variably define them through interactions with others), but pan-Maya activism points us also toward the power of subaltern agency and intentionality and to the historically particular convergences of diverse interests that can produce radical social change without intending to be revolutionary.

The Indian Problem in Guatemala

Since the earliest days of colonization, Guatemala's rulers have grappled with the so-called Indian problem (see Sam Colop 1991). Put simply, the Indian "problem," from the perspective of non-Indian (or, ladino) privileged classes, is that there are so many of them (Mayas make up about half of the Guatemalan population) and that they represent the antithesis of what a cosmopolitan society should be (they are backward and brutish, farmers and craftsmen). During the colonial and early independence period of Guatemalan history, conservative factions promoted a policy of social and geographic separation that well suited the interest of many Maya communities. The conservatives recognized inherent differences between the Indian and Spanish populations, and in trying to avoid mutual corruption their policies insulated — in theory if not always in practice — *pueblos indios* from Spanish exploitation. In contrast, liberal politicians argued that such separation thwarted the development of an educated, ethnically homogenous population that would ensure political stability and economic prosperity. John Browning (1996) cites an illustrative early-nineteenth-century speech in which the secretary of Guatemala's liberal Sociedad Económica envisions a booming economic future based on cultural assimilation of the Indian population. He predicts an initial boom in the manufacture and sale of Spanish clothing and shoes to the Indians as they abandon their native dress for more modern attire, followed by another economic expansion as Indians begin to buy European-style furniture for their houses, and so on, ad infinitum.

Today, the debate over ethnic separation or integration continues. A significant sector of Guatemala's ladino intellectual and political elite carries the liberal banner of integration. The most outspoken proponent of this view is Mario Roberto Morales, a literary scholar and fiery editorialist. Conjuring up the Mexican doctrine of *mestizaje* and José Vasconcelos's 1925 notion of *la raza cósmica*, Morales calls on ladino and Maya Guatemalans alike to take pride in their hybrid past, to embrace their *mestizaje*. In an editorial for *Siglo XXI*, he argued that there is not only a ladino hegemony, but a Maya hegemony as well, both of which imply racial and cultural purity:

> In as much as our cultural differences articulate in infinite ways — varying according to the social class, gender, and ethnicity of the individual — to emphasize differences rather than their articulations implies the adoption of multiculturalist (separatist) criteria even as our position at the center of such articulation implies the adoption of inter-culturalist (relational) criteria. . . . The polarities of Indian–ladino or Maya–mestizo meld into an infinity of mestizo identities in which the cultural emphasis sometimes tends to the ladino side and sometimes to the Indian side, depending on the existential circumstances, social class, gender, and ethnicity of the individual. So too vary the modalities of discrimination. . . . We have yet to come to terms with our existence as inter-ethnic and inter-cultural subjects. Ladinos, assuming with pride their indigenous culture, and Indians, assuming without guilt their ladino culture, and both admitting that they are culturally mestizo and that the differences give meaning to their particular mestizo-ness. (Morales 2000)

For pan-Mayanists, Morales represents a dangerous trend — the use of the rhetorical tools of postmodernism and multiculturalism to undermine the ideological bases of ethnic activism. They point out that such textual flourishes ignore the all-too-real material conditions of the Maya, the structural violence that they continue to suffer in disproportionate numbers. In 2000, the Inter-American Development Bank reported that 80 percent of the Guatemalan population lived in poverty, and that over 60 percent lived in extreme poverty (that is, on less than the $2 a day it is estimated will buy a basket of basic necessities). Tellingly, poverty rates between ethnic groups vary substantially. Whereas 66 percent of the ladino population live in poverty (45 percent in extreme poverty), over 92 percent of the Maya population live in poverty (and 81 percent in extreme poverty). Literacy rates, infant mortality rates, access to electricity and potable water — by almost all measures of social development, the Maya population is much worse off than the ladino population. The majority of Maya households in Guatemala live from subsistence farming, and they are hurt most by the country's highly unequal distribution of land. Based on the last (1979) agricultural census, 2.5 percent of Guatemalan farms control over 65 percent of the arable land, while 88 percent of farms control only 16 percent of land. The Gini index for land distribution is 0.859 (where 0 = perfect equality, 1 = perfect inequality, and anything above 0.45 is considered destabilizing), putting Guatemala in the same class as Haiti, Brazil, and Sierra Leone.

Pan-Mayanists argue that such structural inequalities must be combated through equal opportunity and ethnically targeted affirmative action programs (Cojtí Cuxil 1991; Raxche' 1992). These projects, in turn, demand a unified Maya front that can only be forged through cultural valuation and ethnic pride, not the postmodern hybridity of Morales's intercultural *mestizaje*.

Pan-Maya groups now wield a degree of political clout in Guatemala, and their accomplishments are impressive: they have promulgated legislative reforms that favor Mayan languages; a large number of their demands were recognized in the Peace Accords; and they have also developed a burgeoning body of linguistic, cultural, and political research and analysis. In 2000, one of the earliest and most eloquent proponents of pan-Mayanism, Demetrio Cojtí Cuxil, was appointed Guatemala's Vice-Minister of Education; at the same time, Olitilia Lux was appointed Minister of Culture and Sports. In 2004, Víctor Montejo, a Maya anthropologist, was named Minister of Peace; and a growing number of Mayas work within various government ministries. Yet, in 2003, only 15 (out of 113) congressional deputies self-identified as Maya. Optimistic observers point out that this represents a radical positive change in Guatemalan society over the last ten years; pessimists remind us that these are still very low absolute and relative numbers. The organization Defensoría Maya argues that, given Guatemala's demographics, fully half of all congressional deputies should be Maya (and, one would presume, also half women).

We can think of the emerging world of democratic ideals, mandates, expectations, and desires in Guatemala as a "social imaginary," which is to say "an enabling but not fully explicable symbolic matrix within which a people imagine and act as world-making collective agents" (Gaonkar 2002, 1; Warner 2002). We can also think of this emergence as neither local nor global, but as happening among diverse collectives. There is the work of pan-Maya activists, language advocates, human rights advocates, labor organizers, religious leaders, and development specialists, whose efforts converge in the desire for economic progress and democratic reform. Economic liberalization and political decentralization have become the dominant tendencies today, and diverse collectives seek to work within these movements to achieve particular goals. The ideals of guaranteed equal rights under the law regardless of racial, ethnic, cultural, and other differences, of human rights advocacy, and of multiculturalism bring Guatemala into contact with an international public made up of journalists, monitors, and development and humanitarian workers. In this context, the ethnographic project is tensely caught between two universals. There is solidarity for a particular segment of the population, the Maya; it is a solidarity grounded in the history of violence and in ongoing forms of discrimination. Then there is the nation-state, perhaps the global or universal in general, that must partly dissolve racial and cultural differences, and in many ways neglect the past, in order to guarantee equal rights and protections. It is in this tense polarity that pan-Maya activists struggle to achieve greater representation, voice, and power at the national level while also articulating a sense of belonging to the global stream of humanity.

Pan-Mayanist Messages

In the postwar context of Guatemala, pan-Mayanist groups have developed a remarkably savvy and effective political agenda, deftly employing the tools of "strategic essentialism" in pursuit of their progressive ends (see Montejo 2005). Since the early days of the Maya movement, its leaders have stressed the need to foster cultural unity among all of Guatemala's Maya peoples, as a necessary base for political and economic power and greater social equality. Presented as a nonviolent third way in the wake of the country's devastating civil war, the pan-Maya movement opened up new democratic spaces within Guatemala's political structure and garnered the support of Western governments and the United Nations. Critics have attacked Maya leaders for being self-serving opportunists, and indeed the greatest challenge facing the movement today is to solidify and unify its grassroots, rural support.

The 1996 Peace Accords (particularly the Accord on the Identity and Rights of the Maya People) established a legal framework for directly addressing a broad range of pan-Mayanist demands. Bold in its aim, scope, and language, the Accord on Identity and Rights of the Maya People is largely based on an agenda set by pan-Mayanist organization (for further detail on the 1996 Accords and their impact on Maya activism, see Warren 1998 and Brown, Fischer, and Raxche' 1998). The Accord first clarifies and strengthens rights provided for by the 1985 Guatemalan Constitution in regard to education, language, and religion. Indeed, the greatest success of the Accords has been in promoting bilingual and bicultural education through the Ministry of Education. Language and education issues play a central role in the pan-Maya movement (see England 1996; Maxwell 1996), and a number of Maya leaders now work within the Ministry of Education developing curricular materials and training teachers. Ironically, the most significant resistance to bilingual education has come from rural communities, where many Maya parents want their children to focus on learning Spanish (the traditional language of upward mobility) rather than K'iche' or Kaqchikel or Mam. But attitudes are slowly changing, as more and more Maya have come to take new pride in their native heritage: take, for example, the scores of new private and state-chartered Maya schools opening in larger towns across the country.

More radically, the Accord calls on the state to undertake legal reforms and affirmative-action programs to ensure that the Maya gain proportional representation in political offices. To believers in a unified Guatemalan-ness, this broaches the most threatening portion of pan-Mayanist demands. It plays to the notion that the pan-Mayanists are radical separatists who would like to see the downfall of the Guatemalan state. In fact, the most extreme Maya proposals have called for political autonomy for ethno-linguistic groups, who would be represented by a Maya Parliament that would form half of a federal bicameral legislature. But such language did not make it into the Peace Accords, and even the advocates of such views admit they have a slim chance of ever being considered, much less implemented, by the Guatemalan state.

The Peace Accords do call for much greater accommodation and representation of indigenous peoples and traditions within the existing legal and political framework — providing translators and native-language legal counsel to indigenous defendants, incorporating traditional legal practices of the community into the local court system, ensuring more proportionate Maya representation in the national government. In such ways, the Peace Accords outline what we may call a neoliberal approach to affirmative action: devolving power back to communities in order to allow for greater self-determination for the majority of indigenous peoples. Implementation, however, has been slow, thwarted both by the 1998 defeat of the Consulta Popular (a popular referendum to amend the Constitution in ways mandated by the Peace Accords) and the unwillingness of government officials to enact reforms (see Warren 2003). The presumed moral superiority of local governance has also been called into question, following an epidemic of lynchings in rural communities in recent years. The Peace Accords also call for some taxation authority to be devolved from the central government to municipal authorities — the notion being that indigenous peoples could then participate more directly in the governmental decision-making process. This fails to account for the fact that many rural Mayas distrust their local government officials as much as the state bureaucracy (see Chapter 4).

The greatest challenge facing the national pan-Maya movement is reconciling local concerns with the broader goal of fostering pan-Maya unity and ethnic consciousness. Maya leaders themselves acknowledge that the movement speaks only for "organized Maya" and not all Maya (Gálvez and Esquit 1997, 88–90). At the same time, Demetrio Cojtí writes that, with the exception of those who are thoroughly assimilated into ladino society, "the Maya *pueblo* is entirely Mayanist and thus anti-colonialist, just with different degrees of consciousness and forms of action" (1997, 51). He divides levels of Maya ethnic consciousness into three categories. First, there is the mostly illiterate Maya peasantry who have a fundamental (yet largely untapped) sense of themselves as part of the Maya *pueblo*, reinforced through the constant lived experience of ethnic discrimination and social marginalization. Second, there are the Maya peasants and workers incorporated into popular (i.e., class-based) organizations, whose ethnic awareness is subsumed to class consciousness. Finally, there are the educated middle- and lower-class Maya who promote pan-Maya unity through "more authentic Maya practice" in their "initiatives in the fight against colonialism" (52–52). Cojtí concludes that the pan-Maya movement seeks

> the development of a Maya consciousness in, of, and for itself and to fight for the rights of the Maya *pueblo*. Its primary obligation is logically to achieve clear and complete ethnic consciousness among all Indians, and to realize this it has to resolve the problems of communication and the diffusion of ideas encountered in a multilingual country such as Guatemala. (53)

The pan-Maya project is one that emphasizes accommodation to the economic, political, and social process of globalization. In this light, one might see pan-Maya activism as a limit point, seemingly committed to radical change while accepting the compromises inherent in working within (rather than in opposition to) the political-economic system. Critics accuse pan-Maya leaders of taking advantage of multicultural sensitivities and mandates to simply further their own careers, of having their resistance co-opted and neutralized by monetary and status rewards. The Zapatistas of Chiapas, Mexico, on the other hand, are developing a moral project that they see as equally based in traditional Maya values and social relations, but one that more radically contests state authority and global economic structures.

The Zapatistas

The Ejército Zapatista de Liberación Nacional (EZLN), in what has become a tired but fitting phrase, burst onto the world scene on January 1, 1994, their debut set to coincide with the initial implementation of the North American Free Trade Agreement (NAFTA) linking Mexico, the United States, and Canada. The Zapatistas are unique in a world filled with social movements, having neatly combined concerns with indigenous rights, the inequities of globalized capitalism, and a media savvy that is the envy of Mexico's Madison Avenue counterparts (see Marcos 2001; Stephen 2002; Russ, Hernández Castillo, and Mattiace 2003; Pitarch 2004; G. Collier 1994; Higgins 2004).

In their early days, the Zapatistas translated the language of class conflict into a discourse of identity and indigenous rights, appealing to the academic interests and leftist political sensibilities of the 1990s and the turn of the twenty-first century (see Pitarch 2004). Like the pan-Mayanists in Guatemala, the Zapatistas have self-consciously leveraged the cultural capital af forded by their Indianness to garner concessions from the Mexican state. Even more than Guatemala's pan-Mayanists, the Zapatistas have exploited the disintermediation in global communications networks to pursue their own ends. They have several websites that post news and official communiqués as well providing a secure Web mail service and providing bank transfer details for donations (see www.fzln.org.mx, www.ezln.org, and www .ezlnaldf.org). By making available to the national and international press their own perspective, the Zapatistas are not dependent on biased local or regional press coverage that might (or might not) get picked up by other media outlets. In this way, they have been skillful at reaching out directly to individuals and groups in other parts of the world, and in effectively mobilizing international interest and support they have been able to apply pressure on Mexico from both within and without.

The Zapatistas have benefited from a diminution of traditional state power in Mexico. Gary Gossen (2004) argues that they were instrumental in bringing down the government of the PRI (the Partido Revolucionario Institucional), which had run the country for most of the twentieth century until the July 2000 election of Vicente Fox of the right-moderate Partido Acción Nacional (the PAN). At the same time, the Zapatista stance cannot be reduced to merely a reflexive opposition to the Mexican state. Even the adoption of their namesake — Emiliano Zapata, a hero of the Mexican Revolution — is a self-conscious assertion that they are true patriots upholding the ideals of the Mexican Constitution. Indeed, their message goes, the Zapatistas are more patriotic than those politicians and functionaries who purport to represent the state.

The enigmatic and charismatic leader of the Zapatistas is Subcomandante Marcos, whose black ski mask and smoking pipe have taken on iconic status in Mexican popular culture. Marcos frequently issues forth his communiqués and manifestos as poetry, stylized stories, and imagined dialogues. Through all of these "fictions," Marcos is able to reveal profound truths about Mexican society and its contradictions — a complexity that social scientists are hard-pressed to capture. (This sense of truth evokes the scandal concerning Rigoberta Menchú's testimony.) Take, for example, the following imagined interrogation between Marcos and an agent of Mexico's Centro de Investigaciones y Seguridad Nacional:

> He who is speaking [Marcos] confesses that, in the company of other Mexicans, Maya Indians in their majority, they decided to honor a document that, says he who is speaking, is taught in the schools, that outlines the rights of Mexican citizens and that is called "The Political Constitution of the United States of Mexico." He who is speaking indicates that in Article 39 of this document it says that the people have the right to change their government. At this point, the investigating agent, in a fit of jealousy, orders that this subversive document be confiscated and burned without so much as looking at it, after which he continued to take the statement of the individual with the prominent nose and contaminating pipe. He who is speaking confessed that, not being able to exercise this right through peaceful or legal means, he decided, along with his accomplices (those whom the speaker refers to as "brothers"), to take up arms against the supreme government and cry "Enough Already!" to the lie that, says he who is speaking, determines our destinies.[2]

Here we clearly see that Zapatismo is not a rejection of the idea of the Mexican state, as many politicians fear, just of its current form, which is seen as a corrupted and debased version of the promise of the Mexican Revolution. This is an especially effective strategy, allowing the Zapatistas to build on rather than refute the nationalist lore of the country's founding.

Along these same line, another of Marcos's politically charged poems tries to explain the complicated feelings of nationalism and pride:

> This thing that is one's country is somewhat difficult to explain
> But it is more difficult to understand what it is to love one's country
> For example,
> They taught us that to love one's country is,
> for example,
> To salute the flag
> To rise upon hearing the National Anthem
> To get drunk as we please when the national soccer team loses
> To get drunk as we please when the national soccer team wins
> And a few other et ceteras that change little from one presidency to
>   the next . . .

And, for example,
they didn't teach us that to love one's country can be,
for example,
to whistle like one who is becoming ever more distant, but
behind that mountain there is also part of our country where nobody sees us
And where we open our hearts
(because one always opens one's heart when no one is watching)
And we tell this country,
for example,
everything we hate about it
and everything we love about it
and how it is always better to say it,
for example,
with gunshots and smiling.

And, for example,
they taught us that to love one's country is,
for example,
to wear a big sombrero
to know the names of the child heroes of Chapultepec
to shout "Viva — arriba México!"
even though Mexico is down and dead.
And other et ceteras which change little from one presidency to the next . . .

And, for example,
they did not teach us that
to love one's country
could be
for example,
to be quiet as one who dies,
but no,
for beneath this earth there is also a country
where no one hears us
and where we open our hearts
(because one always opens one's heart when no one is listening)
and, we tell our country
the short and hard history
of those who went on dying to love her
and who are no longer here to give their reasons why,
but who give them all the same without being here,

those who taught us
that one can love one's country,
for example,
with gunshots and smiling.[3]

Like the pan-Maya movement in Guatemala, the Zapatista Army of National Liberation advocates a multicultural future for Mexico, but through more militant calls for political, economic, and social reform. Pedro Pitarch (2004, 297) offers an iconoclastic interpretation that the adoption of "identity politics" as the movement's banner has thwarted the Zapatista's revolutionary potential because it implies that "the roots of injustice are found not in a poor distribution of goods and resources, but in a lack of cultural recognition." As such, the very success of Zapatista identity politics acts as a limit point in the fight for social justice. Ironically, then, the innovative ways in which both pan-Mayanists and Zapatistas articulate Maya identity to validate their claims prompt those concerned with state sovereignty and security — and non-Indian privilege — to dismiss this new Maya-ness as nothing more than the political opportunism of an already assimilated Maya elite or the product of outside agitation.[4]

Between Universals: The Local and the Global

Anthropologists have a tendency to view all culture change as a loss, similar to ecological extinction. But this is a fundamentally paternalistic point of view. Culture change is not inherently negative. Indeed, it is the one great constant of social life — that change, adoption, and hybridization combine to enrich forms of life. Victoria Bricker (2004) has recently pointed out that linguistic change itself need not imply loss; she gives an example from the Yucatec Maya, where trabàahoh (from the Spanish trabajo, used in the Maya context to mean specifically "wage labor") has been added to the vocabulary to complement hač meyah ("real work"), thus enriching (and not diminishing) the linguistic and semantic domain (see also Berkley 1998). The pan-Mayanists of Guatemala and the Zapatistas of Chiapas provide a plethora of such examples of enriching discourse through cultural fusion. Refusing to give up what makes them *them* (as least to themselves at a given moment), while also refusing to close down that discussion through a superficial promotion of cultural traits, they borrow freely from diverse ideological, cultural, and political forms available to them, creating dynamic new hybrid forms of what Gary Gossen (1999) calls "postmodern social movements."

What we commonly term "globalization" is the convergence of diverse forces acting on our lives in very different ways, depending on our life histories, our positions in grander schemes, and the resources we have available to us. There are potential economic benefits, but these can be fleeting and may lead to a mere transmogrification of previous patterns of exploitation. Exploitation, as we showed earlier, can shift from a political-economic relationship to a more localized set of existential changes. Today, people from all over the world imagine different futures for themselves (Appadurai 1996). Above all, globalization seems to be about worlds cognitively remade through global cultures and identities as well as local experiences of optimism and pessimism. The toolkit of cultural resources has vastly expanded, and this process may be liberating for some (or many, depending on how it is played out). One problem within this shifting global field of expectations and desires is that inequality has not been addressed adequately, either by technocrats, academics, or indigenous peoples. We do not have to fall back into the dated, polarizing debate between capitalism and traditionalism, or even left and right, to analyze the ways that power, wealth, health services, and life chances are distributed and contested around the world. The very complexities and ambiguities of everyday life in settings that are at once thoroughly local and imminently global push us toward richer, more concrete understandings of vexing economic, political, and cultural predicaments. It is in this way that a reframing of the language of identity politics does not replace a concern with identity politics. It is to acknowledge that the expansion of desire and expectation in the world today — highlighted in various contexts throughout this book — is not a unilateral flow. Desiring, as we have emphasized, is a social process and thus occurs *between* people and groups. An expansion of desire and expectation may be occurring on a global scale, but it is nonetheless happening *between* local worlds that are themselves diverse, traversed by competing commitments and different perspectives. Consider the desire to belong, as we have seen it mobilized in identity politics. The desire to belong is a universal aspiration, a desire to belong to a social world or a community. Yet it is never universal, in the sense that belonging will be defined and experienced differently in specific situations and, at times, may be exclusive and divisive. The question of identity politics is most effectively posed *between* these two senses of universality. Between local manifestations of belonging or exclusion and the global expansion of desire and expectation, the possibility of a broader articulation of collective belonging and participation in the global is left open for the better. This is why it is dangerous to reduce Maya experience and expression to victimization. The desire among outsiders to represent on behalf of the Maya-as-victims can ironically lead to a portrait of the Maya as thoroughly local and can reproduce a division between them and us.

Beyond Victimization

Conceptions and discourses of victimization are simultaneously empowering and disempowering. They open up global assemblages and histories of the present for ethical questioning and political framing. But they situate victims and their identities in a particular embodied, often highly localized, way. To the sensitive observer, victimization may embolden political activity. Such was the case with the 1980s Central American solidarity movement in the United States, and with the worldwide anti-globalization movement of the late 1990s and early 2000s. This is well, good, and necessary; international pressure certainly forced the Guatemalan government to scale back human rights abuses and to negotiate a settlement with the guerrillas. Victimization may also be used as moral leverage for political reform by victimized peoples, as pan-Mayanists have strategically deployed it in this age of globalized multiculturalism.

Yet, at the same time, it is too easy to reduce victims to nothing more than victimhood, thereby losing sight of the rich complexity of their motivations, expectations, and actions. Discursively reducing the Maya to victimhood lays blame for their situation on structural conditions and can actually pull us away from the existential conditions in which the experience of being a victim is social, historical, and immediate. Again, this broad framing is well, good, and necessary: Maya peoples clearly suffer from structural iniquities in Guatemalan society. And, as we have shown above, pan-Mayanist leaders are promoting creative and concrete alternatives to the present system.

Knowing where good intentions and wishful thinking can lead, we should be ever wary of our own moral positioning, always insistent on a translocal framing for projects of solidarity, ethical deliberation, or moral experience

(Rappaport 2005). Even the legalistic language of human and indigenous rights that was used in the Guatemalan struggle for social justice often essentialized and romanticized Maya peoples and communities. Such "discourses, strategies and legal frameworks which reify stereotypes of harmonious and 'traditional' indigenous communities risk further marginalizing indigenous people from national processes, and may even deny access to justice to the most disadvantaged sectors within the indigenous population" (Sieder and Witchell 2001, 202).

Victimhood is a negation of power. Thus, to understand Maya cultural activism we need to see power as a social field, and the exercise of power as a negotiation rather than a unilateral relation. The postwar setting in Guatemala has not so much denied the Maya "power" as it has created new ways for distributing material resources and political voice, producing citizens and local community leaders, and promoting feelings of national identity and multicultural ideals. One might say that it has reconfigured participation in the Guatemalan national project, participation in a common stream of humanity and citizenship. The Maya are active players in this process even if the benefits are not evenly distributed and social hierarchies and forms of wealth have been kept in place or expanded. We do not mean to suggest that the Maya — as active protagonists — should be blamed for their oppression, that their involvement justifies the conditions they live in, or that activists should cease using the language of victimhood to press for social justice. Rather, we insist that reducing the Maya to nothing more than their victimization adds symbolic insult to violent injury by denying the complexity of their humanity. Furthermore, equating ongoing suffering in the postwar phase with a waning of power or a denial of participation misses a crucial paradox, one highlighted in previous chapters: the postwar enfranchisement of the Maya and the creation of a democratic public sphere in which formerly excluded voices can be heard and demand response can become a dangerous way to justify inequalities and ongoing forms of material and symbolic violence. It can make equality, participation, and empowerment into ideological buzzwords that actually mask the persistent bases of inequality and marginalization. The current task is to think of postwar governance as happening at local and national levels, and as involving competing moral models of development. Governance in Guatemala today is at once about withdrawal and about intervention, about the wishful thinking of development and the existential failures of the state to take notice of the desperate realities at its margins. In this context, democratic processes combine with the most vicious forms of exclusion, peace processes run together with violence, and development entails shortchanges that call into question the entire enterprise.

Conclusion

The *idea* of globalization invokes strong passions, with rhetorical positions accelerating toward logical extremes as they move among the connections that are the *practice* of globalization. Given the digital medium of many global connections, it is appropriate that globalization itself be frequently represented in binary form — it is either good or bad, politicians and pundits must be either for it or against it. Believers in the power of enlightened self-interest celebrate global connections as the natural state of affairs, saved (after a fall from grace into the hands of "regulation" and "government intervention," sins considered so heinous now that the very words sound menacing) by neoliberal reforms that unleash connections between rational actors pursuing their own interests. Others see these same global connections as inherently dangerous, reinforcing inequalities built into a system of trade and empire. Despite an emphasis on connections, both of these perspectives obfuscate the nature and scope of global interdependence in our world today.

Like "desiring," "globalization" is a diffuse, collective process that, while it takes on a life greater than the sum of its parts, is nonetheless always grounded in particular practices. We have adopted an ecumenical stance and have avoided taking a moral position on "globalization" (and "desiring") in the abstract in order to capture the intricate patterns of individual and local moral values that cling to specific nodes in the global broccoli trade.

This book is our attempt to represent why the Maya farmers with whom we have worked engage in the risky, sometimes unprofitable and perhaps even irrational, enterprise of export agriculture — in short, why broccoli production is both dangerous and compelling. The specific desires (to get ahead financially, to provide for their families, to participate in the world system) that propel Maya farmers to grow and sell broccoli for export connect to distant — and perhaps more fickle — desires related to public discourse about health and culinary moralities that fuel the growing consumption of broccoli in the United States. Such concrete desires arise at the interface of large-scale political-economic structures and local social processes and cultural representations. Between Nashville grocery stores and Highland Maya farms, the connection of desires plays into political-economic structures in ways that alternately support and erode those same structures. Viewing consumers and producers within a common analytic frame speaks to ethical issues of exploitation and resistance, solidarity and competition, morality and market imperatives. Yet, in a social world in which growers have more at stake than making money, export production also speaks to other kinds of commitments and concerns. We find farmers growing broccoli and snow peas because it offers a viable local channel through which desires for the "something more" and "something better" of *algo más* are materialized. The various desires of broccoli growers emerge in a place characterized by persistent and new kinds of violence and social suffering, neoliberal political and economic reforms, and the struggles of Maya communities for participation and belonging in postwar Guatemala. Their struggles offer a useful lens into how global connectivity is articulated, registered, and contested in an emerging market setting. In the face of narratives about top-down exploitation and bottom-up resistance, we are pushed to consider why farmers stick with a practice that is not altogether beneficial.

Our ethnographic analysis of the global broccoli trade takes place between different planes of reality, roughly corresponding to the familiar divisions between base and superstructure, and between local and global. On the one hand, the broccoli trade exists as a material infrastructure, a global (or rather, translocal) set of technologies and relationships. On the other hand, the broccoli trade, at each and every point along the way, is embedded in local ideational worlds, or forms of life (M. Fischer 2003), that involve particular and embedded cultural logics and identities, moral orientations, and styles of social engagement. In some ways, these levels operate independently; for example, the Kroger produce manager in Nashville thinks not of Maya moralities of reciprocity when he orders more broccoli. Yet the translocal infrastructure of the broccoli trade has to interface with the particular styles and forms of life that are to be found at all the different points along the commodity trail.

It is between these two levels — translocal and local — that we can pose questions about ethics, politics, and power. The particular relationship between these levels in a given historical moment can be thought of as a "global assemblage" (Collier and Ong 2005). Here, the interface between technologies, ethics, and forms of life is given a particular shape. People come to think about it — the broccoli trade — as a thing, and justify or contest it on that basis. Global assemblages become hegemonic where cultural consensus develops with regard to the particular organization of the technological infrastructure. Within the local places traversed by the commodity chain, the specific translocal organization comes to seem natural, the way things are supposed to be. Here, cultural ideologies, such as the promise of "something better," become locally embedded in ways that justify larger formations. Even where there might be a divergence of interests and attitudes across locales, there can be a general consensus with regard to the global assemblage as a whole.

Our findings speak to the hegemonic quality of the global broccoli trade. Emergent forms of life, such as healthy eating among consumers or entrepreneurial farming among producers, reveal how divergent interests articulate into a general convergence of desire across locales. But our findings also speak to the inherently ambivalent and fractured quality of the global broccoli trade — indeed, of any hegemonic assemblage. The attitudes of producers speak to their dissatisfaction with the organizational infrastructure, with dimensions of trade policies and reforms, and with the demands of consumers. The attitudes of consumers speak to their anxieties about the global scope of food production, the ethical dilemmas of trade policies, and, at times, a paradoxically distant affiliation with marginal producers.

Our ethnographic examination across these two worlds pushes us toward a more ambivalent explanation of this global food system than those offered by staunch critics or apologists of free trade. Working between a translocal infrastructure and localized situations, we find that greater ethical consideration needs to be given to how infrastructures are naturalized through ideologies and practices of progress, development, and "something better." We also find, however, that greater ethnographic consideration needs to be given to how the desire for something better, evident in the practices of Maya farmers, for example, limits the kinds of large-scale social criticism to which scholars are often committed. A wholesale criticism of the capitalist infrastructure misses, in this case, the point that broccoli farmers are taking advantage of the global marketplace in their own ways, and that they are genuinely compelled by the desire for something better, and not necessarily something radically different.

Throughout, we have relied on the concept of desire as a social production in order to avoid naturalizing the economic decisions of broccoli farmers and consumers. These naturalized phenomena are typically termed "preferences," or "interests." Economic decisions happen in the stream of social experience, where what is valuable, desirable, and moral is neither natural nor neutral. Orthodox neoclassical economics rests on an assumption that, in the aggregate, humans pursue their own self-interest, defined in terms of maximizing one's utilities, given unlimited wants and finite resources. Utility maximization, in turn, rests on one's preferences, which are tautologically defined as what an individual prefers (as revealed by her allocation of resources). In such a conception, the concept of desire is often naturalized as a primordial drive to accumulate. In contrast, the work of anthropologists for over a century has shown the great variety of moral, social, and cultural values that frame and motivate economic decisions. Even within the consumerist societies of the Western world, where self-interest is most pronounced and venerated, anthropologists have shown the power of moral values, inflections of class and culture, and psychic anxieties inherent in acts of production and consumption. Thus, we contend that desires are conditioned in social fields where resources and life chances are often limited, where commitments and concerns are in large measure shared, and where global connections can be threatening or rewarding.

Desiring refers to a social process in which individuals come to expect certain outcomes and aspire for others, encounter resistance and hardship, accept certain facts of life and challenge others, find ways of making do, and engage in practical struggles. Despite claims about rationality, material production is also a dynamic and value-laden process of social production, a deeply affective process that makes individuals into certain kinds of subjects at the most basic levels of caring and commitment. In purchasing broccoli, Nashville shoppers make micro-decisions about prices and household budgets, about calories and diets; at the same time, the existential basis for their behavior is the production of desire and the ways their identities are constituted through consumption. Likewise, broccoli farmers in Highland Guatemala do not just grow broccoli. They do so for a certain reason, with specific expectations, with futures in mind and with various kinds of obstacles, risks, and challenges to contend with. This affective side is why "desiring" is a useful concept for thinking about global processes in the late capitalist world, for rather than having to think about separate existences, distinct ontological worlds, and subjective interests, we can think in terms of the *connections* between producers and consumers.

Desiring-Economies and Global Processes

Late capitalism is not simply a system for supplying commodities. It is also a system for making affects, sensations, desires, beliefs, expectations, and aspirations. Advertising, for example, is not just about conveying information about a product; it is also about inciting feelings, desires, and expectations associated with a brand or product (see Jameson 1981). But this secondary process does not simply take place in the superficial realms of cultural production and fictive capital. The manufacture of desires is not an immaterial process. It is concrete and occurs at the level of commodity production. For example, it is not simply the association of the global marketplace with ideas about abundance and opportunity that makes export agriculture compelling for poor Maya farmers. It is the very process of production itself, where a little extra cash is indeed realized — but never a lot, never enough to allow a poor farmer to stop desiring "something better." This is the grip of the desiring-economy. In the mundane process of growing broccoli, applying chemicals and fertilizer, facing the weather, and taking a product to the market, desiring takes *a certain shape*. In this case, desiring comes to fix on the promise of something better, even though the actual material returns on the product do not attest to any such shift.

Thus, it is not only broccoli that gets produced in this global connection between Maya farmers and American consumers. The felt power of "something better" — the concrete force of universal aspirations in the lives of men and women — is also relayed and transformed as it enlivens diverse practices across the food chain. Thought about in this way — the global broccoli trade as an interrelated system — it is impossible to separate the desiring of producers and consumers. Even in the mundane process of going to the grocery store, there is something deeply at stake for the consumer with healthy living and good eating in mind. Broccoli becomes a medium, a concrete tool, contributing to an overall project aimed at "something better." And these desires are not totally localized in the mind and body of the consumer. As they reflect shared concerns with health evident in the forms of public culture in the United States, they are also connected to the desiring of far-off broccoli farmers. As farmers continue to supply the market and are better able to ensure quality, as long as broccoli is available all year long in places like Nashville, the desiring of consumers will be attenuated.

Notice how the global broccoli trade — in this way of seeing things — is neither consumer- nor producer-driven. It is driven by a productive confluence of desires that motivate people in different places to grow and eat broccoli. But this confluence is not natural. The global broccoli trade is not carried out in a vacuum. It benefits consumers who want cheap food that looks attractive and is available year-round. This has opened up an opportunity for farmers living in impoverished conditions, used to migrating to work on coffee plantations and struggling to remake social worlds in the wake of decades of state-sponsored warfare. Against this backdrop, it is not difficult to see how "something better" has taken hold as a compelling field of desire for farmers. But it also appears that consumers have little if any loyalty to this particular arrangement, such that if cheaper broccoli were available elsewhere there would be a shift in the channels of production without any necessary reorientation of consumer desires. This is happening today, as Guatemala increasingly competes with farming operations throughout the Americas.

The Dangers of Desire

The concept of desire helps us think of broccoli producers and consumers *together*, connected globally. There are no doubt different things at stake, on farms in Tecpán, at the airport in Guatemala City, or at supermarkets in

Nashville. But there is also the fact of a relationship between these locations. Consumers depend on the material production of broccoli, but they also depend on, take advantage of, one might even say exploit, the expansion of the desire for "something more" that makes export agriculture so compelling for poor Maya farmers in the Guatemalan Highlands. Even the desire to correct an inequitable flow can do more harm than good. For example, it can allow consumers in the West to disavow, through claims of solidarity and care, the fact that their own consumption of cheap, year-round fresh and frozen produce actually sustains that very flow. Understanding broccoli production among Maya farmers turns out to be just as much about "our" productivity as consumers.

In the context of marginalized peoples such as the Maya of Guatemala, economic activities are usually talked about in terms of need. Somehow, desire seems superficial, with poor folks worried too much about the needs of the day to desire anything. Kate Soper (1981, 1993) effectively critiques universalist assumptions of "need," and Curtis (2004, 105) points out that "all human needs and wants are socially produced" (cf. the hierarchy of needs approach advocated by Doyal and Gough 1991). Like romantic love, it is perhaps comforting to think of desire as born of the affluent West, the Third World being far too preoccupied with survival to think about anything other than what we believe they should be thinking about. But it does not follow that because these Maya farmers are exploited and living in poverty they operate according to need alone. In fact, this presupposition dangerously manifests a binary logic pernicious in anthropological thought, in which the Maya are situated on the side of practical reason and pure need, and the West on the side of symbols (see Sahlins 1976). The growers with whom we have worked do not discuss their decision to switch to export agriculture as arising primarily out of need. Following their lead, we have avoided the language of need and the discourse of victimization that goes with it.

But shifting from a language of need to a language of desire does not elide crucial questions of power, agency, and inequality. Impoverished living conditions, histories of violence and warfare, the felt power of desperation and urgency, and emerging feelings of modernity combine in the Highlands such that desiring is not totally distinct from needing. Desiring is not a superficial process, but rather is embedded in the most basic structures of need, struggle, and survival. This is what makes desire so compelling, so difficult to turn away from, and indeed sometimes counterproductive and dangerous. "What gives our local worlds their immense power to absorb our attention," Kleinman writes, "so as to direct our action, sometimes even away from personal interests, into collective projects and thereby force conformity or pressure one to contest and resist local conditions has do with the character of danger at the core of interpersonal engagement that imparts a legitimate sense of threat to what is most at stake" (1999a, 379). The certain shape that collective desiring takes, such as the felt power of "something better," can actually become debilitating for communities on the margins of the global stream of humanity. For Maya farmers, for example, the promise of "something better" sometimes overshadows the realities of risk, lack of control, and economic shortchanges. With little control over demand, and at the mercy of the global marketplace, there is the danger that the deeper Maya farmers dig into the promise of "something better," the more compelling it can become, since it will cling, closer and closer, to basic structures of need and desperation.

As a concept, desire is often used to romanticize or celebrate the potential to shake things up, break apart exploitative systems, overturn the status quo. The sense of potential — the belief that things are really going to change — stokes the fires of desire, fueling political engagement and economic activity. But because desiring is productive and compelling, it is also limiting, dangerous, and sometimes debilitating. The social production of desire can determine shared ways of thinking and acting toward means and ends that sustain power structures, sustain political or economic inequalities, or play into rigid definitions of community and participation.

In the lives of Maya farmers the promise of *algo más* becomes compelling, becomes desirable, because it seems to orient the future away from both the violence of the past and the disappointments of the present. If farmers have turned to broccoli and other nontraditional crops as a way of getting ahead, striving for something better, it must be emphasized that better is defined not simply in economic terms (i.e., profit) but also along various cultural and moral lines. These have to do with local efforts at community organization and political mobilization, values associated with family life and moral obligations, and shifting registers of imagination, expectation, and affiliation vis-à-vis modernity at large. These farmers are struggling to belong and achieve success in the modern world, to "participate in the global stream of humanity" (Tsing 2005, 1). It is not that farmers naively accept a foreign idea of progress. Nor do they want to disregard the past and simply escape the present. Rather, their desires articulate with needs, their aspirations with desperation, and in this struggle desiring becomes a conduit for extending, contesting, and remaking collective identities and processes.

Global Connections and the Ethnographic Voice

We juxtapose the vignettes of the grocery shopper and the export farmer in the Introduction in order to get away from the antinomy of needs versus desires, the South versus the North. Our desire is to pair Pablo and Susan as a conceptual couple. We want to conceive of their worlds and their desires together, in order to confront the ethical and political questions that inevitably arise when distant practices become mutually dependent and constitutive. This work thus speaks to the ambiguities embodied in global connections, where expectations and opportunities are mediated by geographies of class, capital, and individual subjectivities. Global connections can lead to an expanded sense of human belonging across social worlds or they can effect more acute and rigid conceptions of community. The potential to actualize desire is circumscribed by living conditions, life chances, and an individual's position within the global hierarchy. The realities of how the global broccoli trade is structured — the economic and cultural mediations involved — condition how and what Maya farmers desire, as well as their abilities to respond to, control, or challenge the desires of consumers. This commodity chain, therefore, does not operate in a vacuum but is constituted by larger processes and relationships that determine flows of information, differences of wealth, and structures of power. It is not that needing and desiring are mutually exclusive spaces. These processes interface in complicated ways for Maya farmers, for whom impoverished living conditions, a history of violence and warfare, and emerging feelings of modernity combine to produce collective desires that are attenuated and reinforced by feelings of need and of "something more" or "something better." The interplay of desiring and needing for Maya farmers is thus very different from what it is that consumers feel. Consumers sometimes feel that they "need" broccoli and other fresh produce year-round, that they cannot live without it. Consumers in the United States benefit from a cheap supply of food, and Maya farmers are one part of that system. Consumers are able to live comfortable lives not only because poor Maya farmers do backbreaking labor but also because, in the experiences of those farmers, this unequal relationship is paradoxically a way to participate in the global stream of humanity.

We are broccoli consumers. As members of the American middle class we benefit from this global food system. But as anthropologists researching at the margins of the global stream of humanity, in coming to know some of the folks who grow our food, we are in a position to pose ethical and political questions that can complicate both the neoliberal naturalization and the anti-globalization renunciation of global exchange. If consumers can see their lives as directly connected to the lives of food producers, then perhaps they will be compelled to take a stake in that distant world (Thompson and Wiggins 2002). If we can see "our" desiring as interlaced with "their" desiring, we may be compelled to demand something different than the images and ideologies that justify inequalities across global food systems.

Challenges and transformations arise when we acknowledge that producers are acting within a flow of desire and not simply according to need. If "they" produce for need and "we" consume for desire, then our worlds remain not just ontologically divided but also ethically split. The formulation of an ethical question (i.e., as a consumer, should I be concerned with the living conditions of food producers in the Global South?) would come from the outside, even if the questioner already depends on the work of the producer. One asks these questions, locates problems, laments the system, and yet continues to eat broccoli, enjoying a comfortable existence and assured of a morally justified self-identity because of the consciousness one brings to the table. Miranda Joseph argues that consumption should be regarded as a form of production, the two linked across a social expanse of desire. This allows us "to read the discursive aspects of commodity production not in order to leave the realm of needs, inequality, exploitation, and oppression but rather to offer an adequate account of the social process produced therein" (1998, 30). This is what we have tried to offer in this book. It is an attempt to understand how we as broccoli consumers are connected to Maya farmers, not to indict the system because of its inequalities but to understand the social world of farmers, what matters to them, their struggles, where they are coming from and where they are going. By coming to understand this world, we achieve a more pragmatic view of the global food chain, realizing a convergence of desires around the promise of "something better." This does not diminish the fact that Maya farmers' decisions are often more consequential in material (and, one could argue, moral) terms. "An American consumer desiring broccoli for his/her stir-fry that night," one reviewer of an earlier version of this work wrote, "is quite a different experience from a Maya farmer and his/her family 'desiring' to survive, not knowing what price he or she will receive in the market for broccoli." Certainly we acknowledge that the uneven distribution of risk and reward along the broccoli commodity chain means that the desire to eat the product is not identical to the desire to grow it (a product of "disarticulated accumulation," in de Janvry's [1981] words), and we do not wish to diminish the reality of human suffering that accompanies material poverty in many Maya communities. There is much more at stake in a Maya farmer's "choice" than in a shopper's "choice" made at a Nashville supermarket. And yet we must also be aware of the representational dangers in distancing the farmer in the construction of our own political platforms, be they neoliberal or anti-globalization.

It is our hope that such a viewpoint will lead not to simplified justifications or overt denunciations of global processes but to more complicated — and so more practical and concrete — ways of operating upon, challenging, and transforming, global connections. We see this endeavor as a kind of humanism, one that is firmly grounded in political economy, aware of cultural specificity, and insistent upon the primacy of the social in human experience. Desiring — even though it might involve universal aspirations — is never universal because it is a social process, not an individual affair, occurring *between* people and not *inside* them. So even if the desire for "something better" is evident around the world today, even if there is a proliferation of "desire and expectation on a global scale" (Comaroff and Comaroff 2000, 298), such desires are never universal or uniform because they take hold *between* different social worlds. Anna Tsing puts it nicely: "Global connections give *grip* to universal aspirations. As we let go of the universal as a self-fulfilling abstract truth, we must become embroiled in specific situations" (2005, 1–2).

From our own earlier desire to tell a story about exploitation we have been pushed toward a perspective that is not reformist but rather ethnographic and pragmatic. We at first took a reactive pose to farmers' insistence that "things are better now," considering that such comments often emerged from stories about price declines or crises. This did not jibe with our understanding of the political-economic setting in which that statement becomes a powerful ideological limit point. Our sentiments were confounded as farmers continued to insist upon the promises of exporting, even after price crashes. Becoming friends with these growers — and this, we think, is one of the methodological virtues of ethnography — pushed us to wonder whether the "objective" context was already circumscribed and complicated by varying senses of what "better" means. Among growers, "better" often has less to do with economics, global or local, than with a potential future at the level of family and community. The view from afar translates the desires of growers into a language of need, putting the observer in a position of ethical authority, negating, paradoxically, the capacity of others to make their own decisions, especially where actions are seen as "risky" and less than desirable from "our" perspective. Political strategies and ethical deliberations are most effective where the practical concerns and daily predicaments of others are taken into account (Kleinman 1999a, 1999b). Political and ethical models become pragmatic when elaborated with an eye toward the quotidian structures of everyday life, limited life chances, and shared forms of compelling experience — that is, desiring — upon which projects are envisioned and built. This holds for both the distant laborer and the grocery shopper closer to home. How macro-level socioeconomic and political forces influence desires in local worlds is not a process of reflection or determination but one of refraction, convergence, and negotiation. Our findings challenge the ways in which scholarship on the food chain assumes that poor producers act according to structural determinations whereas wealthy consumers act according to their own agency and preferences. For broccoli growers, resources and life chances are limited, but not necessarily because of a lack of knowledge or a waning of affect. They are limited because the expansion of desire and expectations on a global scale converges with limited controls and an inadequate capacity to confront risks in a collective way. We were struck again and again in our interviews with Maya farmers by their understanding of the risks involved in export agriculture and their sense of the top-heavy networks through which profits ascend. But their desiring and laboring plays into the desires of others — desires to maintain economic asymmetries, desires for cheap food, and desires for aesthetic and quality foods. It is not the abstract universal — the feeling that something better might be on the horizon — that makes this global connection exploitative, but the concrete ways by which profits are added at each node of the commodity chain and, ultimately, the quality demanded, but at a low price, by the consumer. Knowing the risks and being aware of these inequalities of wealth and power do not lessen the exploitation implied.

That global flows have different effects — economic, cultural, and moral — across social worlds pushes us to identify, highlight, and become practically involved in the constitution of "good" globalizations over "bad" globalizations, for these twin processes are already at work in specific situations. The way the global broccoli trade has become enmeshed in the world of growers in Highland Guatemala, for example, reveals some effects that farmers would designate as good and others that they would see as threatening, dangerous, and unnecessary. There is localization and globalization, increased class differentiation and a reaffirmation of tradition, talk of community organizing and development and a felt loss of economic control. The global proliferation of one kind of universal aspiration — the feeling of "something better" — does not achieve a simple consensus or homogenization. Nor does it, in this case, meet broad-based opposition or resistance. What the idea of "something better" meets is a local world itself traversed and shaped by various other emergent and residual tendencies, sensibilities about the past and hesitations about the future, such that what "something better" means becomes ambivalent, variable. From the perspective of the Guatemalan Highlands, the economic exploitation — the differential in monetary returns between primary producers, secondary producers, and consumers — observed in other global processes is just as apparent. But given the other effects of this flow and the ways that producers have articulated their economic practices with socially elaborated desires for something more, the political task may not be the anti-globalization strategy of "putting the brakes" on things (Massumi 1992, 139). Political strategies within global processes often seek to bring a flow to a halt, since that flow is seen to be exploitative of producers. Yet such a restriction overlaps, ironically, with the neoliberal logic of individual needs and interests, since it starts not in the middle, not in the desiring that links producers and consumers, but at the individuated ends. Such restrictions assume something about the "best interests" of others, even those eager to engage in global processes that may or may not be economically exploitative.

The actualization of counterforces within global political economies — the creation of new sensibilities, new ways of seeing things, and shared practices — may not, at least in this case, involve providing an objective outlook (i.e., revealing the universal promise of "something better" as a fantasy). It is not so much a matter of further restricting desire as much as expanding desire around collective rather than individual objectives. This could include both *localization* strategies (shifts to local markets) and *globalization* strategies (elaborating ethical and political connections between unknowing consumers and producers). Most importantly, these strategies need to be grounded in an ethnographic stance toward universal aspirations, which involves both an affirmation of what "something better" means in specific situations and an acknowledgment of the concrete connections that exist between situations. What Maya farmers have to say is often at odds with the utopian paradigms of neoliberal economics, blanket criticisms of the world market as a system of exploitation, and celebratory models of resistance and solidarity. Anthropologists and activists alike would do well to hear their voices and heed their example.

Notes

INTRODUCTION

1. Comaroff and Comaroff (2000, 298) point to the rise of "desire and expectation on a global scale" characteristic of late capitalism; on the changing existential
dimensions of this phase, see also Appadurai (1996), Friedman (1994), Hardt and
Negri (2000), Jameson (1991), Kleinman (2006), Lash and Urry (1987), Ong (1999),
Stewart (2000), and the contributions in Ong and Collier (2005).

2. On consumption in late capitalism, see Stewart (1988), Friedman (1994, 2002),
Jameson (1998), Mankekar (1999), and Giddens (1990). In his *Contribution to the Critique of Political Economy*, Marx presciently observed that capitalist expansion feeds on
the ever-widening realm of unrequited (and unrequitable) desires, and anthropologists have uncovered how consumer desires for exotic comestibles in affluent Western societies can perversely exploit the needs of distant workers and reinforce unjust
workplace conditions abroad (Mintz 1985; Roseberry 1996; Appadurai 1986; Barndy
2002; cf. Weiss 1996). Curtis (2004) effectively critiques a common, if largely implicit, academic disdain for identity production through consumption (e.g., Giddens
1994; Baudrillard 1983, 1998). She observes that "consumer culture can at times
deliver the goods, so to speak, that the promise of pleasure, for example, might be
fulfilled" (2004, 117). See the insightful work of Garber (2002), Bell and Valentine
(1997), and Freidberg (2004) on produce marketing and consumption. Guthman
(2003) looks at the "reflexive tastes" and false dichotomies that popular discourses on
eating healthfully have produced.

3. On the promises and predicaments of utopia, see Harvey (2000) and Jameson
(2005).

4. On modernity and belonging in late-capitalist societies, see Appadurai (1996),
Knauft (2002b), Mankekar (1999), Pred and Watts (1992), and Trouillot (2003). Our
discussion of universality and modernity draws especially on the work of Tsing (2005)
and Spivak (1999), who emphasize the continued importance of universality and
modernity as ongoing and vital projects in these globalized times. Such a perspective
differs from the position taken by Habermas, for example, in emphasizing the inherent ambivalence and cultural differences that always inflect the experience of moder-

nity or the feeling of universality. This perspective also refutes the idea that modernity belongs solely to the West, that it is simply the superstructure of late capitalism, or that it is an all-powerful web of power/knowledge. Universality and modernity are seen as processes of translation and transition, meaning that they are located, ambivalent, and always in flux. To locate modernity on the side of the West or to suggest that universality is only a ruse of power and truth actually suppresses marginal claims to universality and belonging that are struggled over in out-of-the-way places around the world today (see also Fischer 1999).

5. Throughout this book, we adopt the terminology of moral experience developed by Kleinman (1999a), as well as that of social suffering found in Kleinman, Das, and Lock (1997), and of violence and trauma described by Das et al. (2001). "Social experience" refers to the felt flow of engagements in a local world. "Local world" refers to a somewhat circumscribed domain within which daily life takes place. What defines all local worlds is the fact that something is at stake, which defines "moral experience," a concept described below (Kleinman 1999a).

6. See Laqueur (1992) for a discussion of desire in early industrial capitalism. See Lingis (1985) for an overview of philosophies of libido, desire, and sexuality. Desire has achieved wide usage in philosophy and the humanities, but has not found the same analytic footing in anthropology. This may be due to our discipline's historical emphasis on the collective and the patterned over the individual or the idiosyncratic (Abu-Lughod 1991; Ortner 1989). But desire is not an individual affair. Individual desires are social outcomes and, in some measure, reflect shared feelings, commitments, and concerns. A growing number of ethnographies use the analytic of desire to understand zones of intimacy in cultural life. In these spaces, subjectivity articulates in concrete ways with enduring histories, political formations, social movements, and economic structures (Nelson 1999; Salzinger 2000; Scheper-Hughes 1992; Stewart 2000; Stoler 1995; Trouillot 2001).

7. Spivak (1987, 1999) takes issue with the vague notion of desire as deployed in French structuralism and poststructuralism. In her work, desire becomes a much more pragmatic case of socially, culturally, and historically inflected interests that define real struggles at the margins of global economies. While "interest" is not the static and universal concept that neoclassical economists assume, it is also not the case, she argues, that desire is a top-down mechanism of discipline and control. She emphasizes that desire is never determined by either tradition or global culture. Rather, desires are practical concerns staked out at the interface between the global process and the local world, such that they are always differential and never fully determined. See also Buchanan (2000), Grossberg (1992), Hardt and Negri (2000), Massumi (1992), and Rodowick (2001).

8. Fischer began collecting data on nontraditional agriculture as a tangential part of his research on Maya cultural activism in Tecpán in the 1990s. Benson and Fischer began collaborating on the current project in 2000, carrying out joint research during the summers from 2001 to 2004. During this time, we conducted in-depth inter-

views with scores of farmers — trekking to the fields and interrupting their labors to record their thoughts on nontraditional agriculture. We employed a common interview schedule, but the questions were open-ended to encourage respondents to expound on the themes they found most significant. Interviews were transcribed in the field and are the source of the direct quotes in the text.

Follow-up interviews were conducted to explore questions that arose during transcription, and five farmers became key sources of information and were repeatedly interviewed, formally and informally, throughout the research. The sample size for this qualitative data set is relatively small, but our findings are backed up by random-sample surveys of 267 households conducted in the area in 1998 and 2000 (in collaboration with Christopher Jones, Sarah Hamilton, and Linda Asturias de Barrios; see Hamilton and Fischer 2003, E. Fischer 2004).

Tracing the impact of broccoli production in Tecpán led us to consider the broader contexts in which it has flourished, from the local political environment to the commodity chain stretching to U.S. supermarkets. Thus, we rely on interviews conducted with non-farming Tecpanecos as well as ethnographic observations of new forms of violence and political activism in the town. To document the varied meanings of export agriculture at different nodes along the commodity chain, we interviewed a number of cooperative leaders, packing-plant workers, foreign exporters, and government development officials. Finally, the broccoli trail led us to conduct surveys and ethnographic observation over several months in the produce section of a Nashville, Tennessee supermarket in Fall 2002 and Spring 2003.

Many of the farmers we interviewed preferred not to be quoted by name — there is still a deep suspicion of attribution in postwar Guatemala — and so we have used pseudonyms to protect their privacy. On the other hand, development workers, government officials, and exporters were often eager to be cited and so we honor their requests as well.

9. For more background on Tecpán, see Hendrickson (1995), E. Fischer (2001), and Fischer and Hendrickson (2002). Tecpán was founded in 1524 by the conquistador Pedro de Alvarado on the site of the Kaqchikel Empire's capital of Iximche'. See Nance, Whittington, and Borg (2003) on the archaeology of Iximche', and Maxwell and Hill (2006) for Kaqchikel chronicles of life before and after the Spanish invasion. Esquit Choy (2002) and Carey (2001) present the modern history of the region from a Kaqchikel perspective. Cabbarús (1998) provides a valuable description of Tecpán and the rise of ethnic consciousness there in the 1960s and 1970s. See Annis (1987) and Little (2004) on the political economies of neighboring towns.

10. See the debate between Scheper-Hughes (1995) and D'Andrade (1995) for an example of competing attitudes toward the importance of moral models in anthropological research. Castañeda (2006) provides an insightful analysis of the terminology and practice of the ethics of anthropological moralities. See Sayer (2004) for a compelling call to rejoin moral and economic concerns in critiques of political economy.

CHAPTER I. SOMETHING BETTER

I. For a recent history of agriculture in California, including the rise of agribusiness, the centrality of farm labor, and labor organizing, see Wells (1996). For connections between the farm labor system in the United States today, the rise of agribusiness, and global processes in food production, see Thompson and Wiggins (2002).

2. See Hamm (1992), Klak (1999), McCracken (1992), and Thrupp (1995) on Guatemala's role in the global vegetable trade. See Tomlinson (1999, 125–26) for a discussion of seasonal variation and global food production. For the area around Tecpán, also see E. Fischer (2001, 2004).

3. This critique was the essence of the early-twentieth-century school of institutional economics, seen in the work of Thorstein Veblen and others, before the mathematical turn of general equilibrium theorists, including Vilfredo Pareto, gained dominance in the discipline of economics. For a sociological critique of rational-choice theory in economic decision-making, see Bourdieu (1977). For agricultural producers specifically, see, e.g., Huacuja (2001).

4. Herzfeld (2003) argues that the cultural identities that take shape among producers of commodities in the world today are not embedded in individual commodities but emerge out of relationships between commodities. The moral and cultural values associated with broccoli production, in this case, are related to other forms of licit and illicit production.

5. In April 1992, DEA officers in Miami confiscated 6.7 tons of cocaine in a shipment of frozen broccoli from Guatemala, one of the largest seizures ever (Smyth 1993). In June 1995, leaders of the Cali cartel were indicted in federal court in Miami on (among other charges) seventeen counts of importing cocaine in produce shipments from Guatemala between 1986 and 1992. A key passage of the indictment reads:

> The defendant JOSE SANTACRUZ-LONDONO, until the date of the return of this indictment, operated a Cali-based narcotics organization, which, in 1986, established and developed frozen vegetable cargo companies in Guatemala and Miami for the purpose of smuggling cocaine for the Enterprise. These companies were ultimately brought under the control of MIGUEL RODRIGUEZ-OREJUELA. Portions of quantities of cocaine transported by the RODRIGUEZ-OREJUELA faction of the CALI CARTEL into the United States were turned over to representatives of SANTACRUZ-LONDONO for distribution.

The full indictment is available online at http://www.courttv.com/archive/legaldocs/misc/cali.html.

6. For more on economic well-being and nontraditional agricultural exports in Guatemala, see Goldín and Asturias de Barrios (2001) and Goldín and Saenz de Tejada (1993). Economic well-being is clearly an important measure of development, but we must also remember that it becomes locally and personally meaningful only as a form of social experience that involves affective states, desires, and forms of suffering that are irreducible to, and not fully determined by, monetary success or failure.

7. On aesthetic standards in global food production and the impact that the anxious and expectant pursuits of consumers have on marginalized producers, see Freidburg (2004) and Bureau et al. (2002).

8. For comparison, see Mayol (1998, 101–13) on supermarkets in France; Miller (1998, 15–52) on supermarkets in London; and Freidberg (2004) on a comparison of French and British produce aesthetics.

9. Participants in Fischer's Fall 2002 graduate seminar on ethnography aided in constructing and administering the surveys; Avery Dickins, Nathan Goates, Peter Redvers-Lee, Erin Slinker, and Brent Woodfill also produced ethnographic reports that inform our analysis here.

10. As Giard observes, "With acceleration of the means of transportation . . . the monitoring of food preservation conditions, whether raw or cooked (sterilization at high temperature, pasteurization, freeze-drying, freezing and deep-freezing), the memory of the constant struggles of the peasant, wholesaler, and housewife against heat, humidity, insects, and rodents in order to preserve stored supplies (seeds, fodder, winter provisions) has become blurred within a few generations" (1998, 172; see also the other chapters in de Certeau, Giard, and Mayol 1998).

11. http://www.peta.org.

12. See Barney Broccoli and hear his music at http://www.dole5aday.com.

13. For more on broccoli nutrition, see the Broccoli Town website at http://www.broccoli.com.

14. The Environmental Working Group reports that broccoli is one of the fresh vegetables least likely to contain harmful levels of chemical residues. This may be due to its high level of naturally occurring indole-3-carbinol. *Der Spiegel* (2005, 79) reports that if broccoli were itself a pesticide, its indole-3-carbinol levels would make it too toxic to be used on food crops.

15. See E. Fischer (2004). These surveys were carried out in areas close to the Pan-American Highway and should not be considered representative of more remote areas in the municipality. Surveys were conducted by Edward Fischer, Pakal B'alam, Christopher Jones, Marvin Tecún, Ixchel Espantzay, and Paola Lux. We surveyed fifty-six households and separately interviewed both husbands and wives.

16. Median household land holdings were 15.8 cuerdas (1.8 hectares). Depending on soil quality, between 5 and 9 cuerdas of land are needed to supply subsistence needs for a family of six. In our surveys, 14.3 percent of households controlled less than 5 cuerdas of land, and 41.1 percent controlled less than 9 cuerdas.

17. In anthropological studies of global processes and political economies, imagination and desperation are often seen as incommensurable, leading to a polarized optimistic-versus-pessimistic debate. Appadurai's (1996) work on imagination shows how new forms of global thinking, even among marginalized groups, are crucial to reconfigurations of identities and senses of place; we do not have to argue the opposite — that poor people on the margins of wealth and power lack imagination — in order to emphasize the uneven expansion of political economies in the world today. Neoliberal arrangements often do not meet absolute resistance in local worlds, but

obtain a more subtle and complicated grip in entangled experiences of expectation, desperation, and desire among the members of marginal communities for whom "something better" is crucially at stake.

18. In Tecpán the 1990s witnessed a sea change in terms of access to information (Fischer and Hendrickson 2002). In the early 1990s, it was almost impossible to get a copy of one of Guatemala's national newspapers; by 2001 they were being sold out of many neighborhood stores. In the early 1990s there were just three communal telephones in town, with intermittent service; following the privatization of the state telephone company in 1998 and the scramble to sign up new customers, all but the poorest households now have phone service (and with international rates often better than those in the competitive U.S. market).

19. In his analysis of the global tuna and sushi trade, Bestor (2001) makes the point that temporal differences exist across the various nodes of activity of a given commodity chain. It is not simply that activities take place *at* different times, but rather that each node is structured, existentially, *in* different times that affect how actors envision the temporality and scale of their activity, what he calls "timescapes" (see also Sassen 2000).

20. Scott's contribution reflects a certain 1980s theoretical zeitgeist that, along with Benedict Anderson's (1983) "imagined communities" and Hobsbawm's (1983) "invented traditions," have provided enduring analytic concepts.

CHAPTER 2. DISCOURSES OF DEVELOPMENT

1. Our thinking about expectations of modernity and the confluence of rural and urban poverty, development projects, and governance has been influenced by the work of Ferguson (1999).

2. On the culture of neoliberalism and development politics, see Ferguson (1990). On the convergence of economic neoliberalism and political liberalism, see Kalb (2005). For the particular context of Guatemala and the Maya, see Nash (2001), Nelson (1999), and Warren and Jackson (2003).

3. This was part of a general trend in Latin American countries (see Kay 1989; Gwynne and Kay 1999). Elizabeth Oglesby (2004) presents a compelling analysis of neoliberal approaches to development and the construction of hegemonic discourses in the Guatemalan sugar industry's foundation, FUNDAZUCAR.

4. Thanks to Kedron Thomas for pointing this out; for more on the lives of women in the global assemblage of offshore production in North and Central America see Barndt (1999).

5. Recent ethnographic work on maquiladora production has emphasized these complexities and ambivalent moral realities. Melissa Wright (1997, 1998, 2001) emphasizes not just the power of forms of discipline, training, and domination that are part of workplace culture at maquiladoras but also how these very forms take hold in much more ambivalent and sometimes dangerous ways in the moral and emotional lives of the women who work there.

6. Cf. Carol Smith's work with petty commodity producers in Highland Guatemala in which she offers an analysis that goes beyond dependency theory (1978) while situating local producers clearly in a global context (1984).

7. Lingis (1998, 92) writes that "the land the Guatemalan Indian inhabits, the milpa he cultivates which demands the utmost of his rationality and leaves no indulgence for caprice and fantasies, are not means for him; he lives not only from them but for them, they are his dignity. The frijoles in baked-clay plates his wife lays out on the table for him and their children are not a means for the refurbishing of depleted body-cells in view of labor for ends beyond; in the repast their cares come to rest and their laborious existence finds an hour of accomplishment."

8. In this same vein, Aj Ticonel has very progressive gender policies that include the preferential hiring of producers' wives and daughters and a costly maternity-leave program. This approach converges not only with international trends in gender equity but also with extant local practices. At the same time, we must bear in mind the simultaneously confining aspect of policies built around perceived "traditional" gender roles.

9. But, as Giddens cautions, "the current phase of globalization . . . should not be confused with the preceding one, whose structures it acts increasingly to subvert. . . . Although still dominated by Western power, globalization today can no longer be spoken of only as a matter of one-way imperialism. . . . Increasingly there is no obvious 'direction' to globalization at all and its ramifications are more or less ever present" (1994, 96). Gramsci himself was writing at a time that presented theoretical and practical dilemmas much like those evident today, in which economic integration is accompanied by social and institutional Balkanization. Indeed, as Ernesto Laclau has argued, the present moment is characterized by blurrier distinctions between the state, civil society, and the economy, which only necessitates a deeper concern with hegemonic processes: "The globalization of the economy, the reduction of the functions and powers of nation-states, the proliferation of international quasi-state organizations — everything points in the direction of complex processes of decision-making which could be approached in terms of hegemonic logics" (2000, 53).

10. In this light, globalization reveals a paradoxical power dynamic: aspirant hegemonies, national or otherwise, operate at or from a distance, removed from the theater of exploitation and control, and so are potentially more insidious and yet at the same time necessarily open to subversion, if only locally, through practices that elude their distanced controlling processes and disavowed mediations. New forms of interest groups emerge, with various, often competing styles and interests, to complicate and fracture the general framework of development and economic transformation.

11. The notion of "local culture" is itself problematic in presuming that certain events are more "global" or "less situated" than others. As Terence Turner observes: "Disturbingly, the transnationalists' master trope, the binary classification of local societies and cultures as 'inertial' and lacking in dynamic capacities for resistance or change, while all agency, dynamism and effectively invincible force is ascribed to

transnational processes of the global system, repeats the form of the most ethnocentric and ideologically imperialist chronotype of all, the evolutionist vision of the dynamic, historically innovative and spatially expansive West as the bearer of global progressive change to the historically inert, spatially closed and culturally 'traditional' Others. The global system is Us; 'local communities' are Them; the myth of the historic 'break' constituted by transnationalism puts Them in the past and makes Us the bearers of history" (2002, 62). Moreover, the term "local" has recently come to serve as a kind of surrogate for more outmoded terminology like "community," "structure," and "society," while encoding similar claims to situatedness and boundedness (Gupta and Ferguson 1997a, 1997b). The notion makes particular circumscriptions regarding the spatial and temporal constitution of social interactions; that certain relations are "local" problematically views those relations through sharply territorial and unequivocally culturalist lenses. Highland Guatemala, like most other areas of the world — which also includes the West — is deeply enmeshed in transnational flows of goods and ideas in ways that are largely unique to this historical moment (E. Fischer 2001; see also Friedman 1994; Hannerz 1996; Tomlinson 1999). Yet it is worth restating, *pace* the term's trendy and novel connotations, that "globalization" is not an entirely new phenomenon, and global economic and political connections have long been a modus operandi of culture and history, especially within various colonial and postcolonial contexts (Mintz 1985; Wolf 1982).

Jonathan Friedman points to the shortcomings of the position of global cosmopolitanism. He writes that cosmopolitanism "implies the capacity to distance oneself from one's place of origin, and to occupy a higher place above a world in which indigenous, national, and migrant populations all inhabit an enriched cultural territory. This cultural difference is consumed in the form of cultural products, from cuisine to art, and is, of course, the stuff for innumerable festivals. Difference is consumed in the lives of the elites and becomes a kind of furnishing of their existences. The embodiment of the world's diversity becomes a new kind of self-representation" (2002, 37).

CHAPTER 3. ULTIMATUMS, MORAL MODELS,
AND THE LIMIT POINTS OF HEGEMONY

1. Note the similarity to recent work on "risk society" and to discourses of risk management. Ulrich Beck (1992) points to the political potential of control involved in the sorts of risks produced in late-modern societies. Both Beck and Lupton (1999) identify the existential angst that accompanies the failed promises of the security of modernity (and the prominent role of risk management that is simultaneously risk production).

2. We draw on the concept of figured worlds in Holland et al. (1998) and local worlds in Kleinman (1999b) and Kleinman, Das, and Lock (1997).

3. We define "ethical," following Kleinman (1999b), as a set of universal prescriptions and guidelines developed by an elite group, such as bioethicists and

philosophers, development specialists, economists, and so on. This is opposed to the moral mode of experience figured around what matters most to people in a local world.

4. See Fischer and Dickins (2006) for more detail. Borrowing from established methodologies (Güth, Schmittberger, and Schwarze 1982; Camerer 2003; Smith 2000; Kagel and Roth 1995), we played the Ultimatum Game based on a common protocol. The pot size for the games we conducted was 10 quetzales (approximately $1.25). This relatively small stake size is equal to the lowest day-wage for unskilled domestic or agricultural labor in rural Tecpán. Games were played with from eight to twenty individuals at a time, divided into two groups. The two groups were kept in separate rooms throughout the game, and were anonymously paired based on randomly selected numbers. The game was explained in Spanish and in Kaqchikel Mayan. Immediately before each participant played the game, investigators individually explained the rules to that player and asked him or her to respond to certain hypothetical game scenarios. During games, we worked with local assistants to act as intermediaries between the two anonymously paired players. Offer-making and the subsequent acceptance or rejection were made by players, one on one, in the presence of one of the investigators who had checked the players' understanding of the game and had given them the opportunity to ask questions. Once all offers had been accepted or rejected, and disbursed accordingly, we brought all of the players together and held a group discussion to debrief the participants and to explore their comments and observations regarding the game.

5. Hegemonies, like advertising strategies, are most effective when they habituate desires in ways that become indistinguishable from desire itself — where an image says "Image is nothing," for example, or where Coke is ironically (not) "It" (Žižek 2000a, 21–23). The form of advertising (or the abstract practice of export agriculture), not necessarily its content, appears as an end in itself. The hegemony question here shifts from the conventional (how the contingent passes as universal in the production of knowledge and the maintenance of power) to how is it that structures, practices, expectations *are* so often seen as contingent *and* always also nonetheless taken for granted. Žižek, writing on the persistent failure of ideological interpellation to capture its subject and the apparent threat that asking "Am I that name?" might pose to a political structure, insists instead that "such a self-probing attitude, far from effectively threatening the predominant ideological regime, is what ultimately makes it 'livable'" (2000b, 104). It is precisely the recognition of contingency in the ideological system that opens up a space of what Žižek calls "false disidentification," where the hailed subject senses herself to be *further*, and so putatively freer, from "the actual co-ordinates." This produces the limit point at which political energies are at once mobilized and shortchanged (102). Think of how often television viewers disavow the ideological effectiveness of the content of advertising precisely by pointing to its manipulative form — and yet witness its continued effectiveness.

6. On the conception of desire as force and flow, see Deleuze and Guattari (1983, 1987) and Massumi (2002). On the conception of power as a diffuse and impersonal

flow, see Foucault (1978, 1983). For an elaboration of the ways that processes of production and consumption shape collective desires, political commitments, and moral values, see Grossberg (1992).

Building on these works, a fluid and ethnographically situated understanding of hegemonic power becomes a way of considering the contradictory force of desires and consequences in people's everyday lives, even and especially where desires are linked tightly to systems of exploitation. "How is it," ask Comaroff and Comaroff (1991, 17), "that if all meaning were potentially open to contest, all power potentially unfixed, history keeps generating hegemonies that, for long periods, seem able to impose a degree of order and stability on the world?" It is because hegemonic processes are acts of seduction, siren calls enticing individuals to align their self-perceptions and interests with the desires of a privileged class through processes of recognition, identification, affective determination, and ideological channeling (Eagleton 1991). Hegemonic formulations are effective and insidious because they work behind the scenes, out of the purview of the common man, creating a cultural context that limits thought and action in a way that benefits the interests of a particular ruling class. In exploring how hegemonies play into and configure desires and the limits of satisfaction and consent, we are able to account for political horizons and the movement of what is generally termed agency (see Fox 1985). The conventional usage of hegemony subsumes the practical concerns and stakes of the subaltern to the ethical framing and interpretive expertise of the scholar. The concept of hegemony has been especially seductive to ethnographers, marrying an affinity for cultural explanations to a quest for moral guideposts in a landscape of postmodern relativism. It also plays into ethnographers' yearnings to re-present what Willis and Trondman (2000) call "ah ha" moments, those flashes of epiphany where Max Weber's descriptive *Verstehen* feeds into explanatory *Erklärung* to uncover what motivates individuals to willingly act in ways that are seemingly not in their own rational self-interest. The uncovering of these formations has been extremely fruitful intellectual ground, liberating and politically relevant in a way that scholarship rarely is (e.g., Anderson 1983; Hobsbawm 1983; Scott 1985, 1990).

Still, hegemony and resistance are often presented as a stark binary such that moral positioning becomes clear for ethnographers who take seriously their commitment to the usually subaltern and increasingly mobilized populations they study. Hegemonic processes are seen as structured, usually externally imposed, givens. The actions of "agents of domination" are "seen largely as a reflex of political and economic processes" (Comaroff and Comaroff 1991, 9). Moreover, the actions of those being dominated are inductively read as modes of creative resistance, even where this is not a salient motivation for those involved (Maddox 1997; cf. Scott 1990). Even in this age of decentralized power structures, the declining relevance of nation-states, and the "end of history," hegemonic systems certainly still operate in the world, even if, or perhaps precisely because, they are more seductively cosmopolitan than ever before. Certain actors are undoubtedly better positioned to exercise power and impose their desires based on certain capacities enabled by governmental and institutional structures, capacities that therefore elicit historical precedent and cultural conventions. The clarity and moral certainty of this framing remains appealing. Yet the abstractions can gloss over the complexities and internal contradictions of empirical documentation and subjective understanding.

A reflexive conception of hegemony provides a way around two key epistemological problems, one having to do with "access-to-information" and the other with the production and distribution of knowledge. Social actors, because of always-imperfect access to information, may not realize that they are being exploited, even according to terms of exploitation that they themselves define and privilege. The ethnographer might indeed be able to offer privileged insight into a social or economic predicament, at least according to certain assumptions about that situation: with privileged access to certain information, the ethnographer can speak on behalf, yet must recognize that her truth claims are themselves potentially hegemonic, even as they are presented as a critique of a perceived or taken-for-granted hegemonic process. We must ask how and under what conditions does "hegemony" become grist for theoretical mills? What historical forces enable or prompt ethnographic desires to represent or to "write on behalf"? These questions should not be taken for granted if solidarity is to shape our reading and writing and if we are to target hegemonic processes as critical ethical projects. Hegemonic processes need to be rethought in terms of competing moral models and ethical orientations as well as the ambivalence of knowledge production (M. Fischer 2004; Mignolo 2000), while also recognizing "the significance of local knowledge as the source of much of our own theorizing" (Herzfeld 2001, 94). Herzfeld's suggestion to reflexively interrogate our own theoretical insight for "what the natives might have taught us" is vital: hegemony moves from grand theory embedded in Western epistemological and ethical canons (and the accompanying universalizing moral positions) to local understandings and ethical orientations. Here, the emphasis shifts from how things ought to be based on abstract appraisal and ethical deliberation to how things are — what production and consumption mean to people — within concrete settings of everyday life. A more conventional view would lead us to label the global broccoli trade as exploitative. And this view is productive of a quest to uncover hidden consciousness. But this desire is itself an act of sublimating troublesome inconsistencies in facile formulations of "solidarity" and "resistance." Such stances are often self-defeating on their own political terms inasmuch as they negate the multivalent desires that propel the agency of subaltern agents.

It may not be altogether advisable to use "hegemony" to make binary claims — good or bad, right or wrong — no matter how seemingly overt and explicit are forms of domination and exploitation, or to "out-theorize" local explanations of why certain things happen and what they mean as a way of relaying an a priori moral and intellectual authority which is surely undeserved. There is more to be said about the expansion of capital than simply that it is inequitable. That social problems need not be framed in binary moral terms, far from ignoring processes of exploitation and domination, only affords a richer way of understanding their durability, potency, contingency, points of alteration, and other contradictory conditions through which lived realities are made and remade (see Kleinman 1999a; Ortner 1995). Against West-centered, mechanistic models, hegemonies might be dealt with through processes of cultural translation in which the ethnographer is pushed to interrogate her own desires and beliefs concerning power with local interpretations, objectives, and concerns. This would involve foregrounding those interstices in which communication becomes incomplete (cf. Bhabha 1994; Clifford 1997).

7. Limit points emerge above the flow and flux of desire as nodes of intensity and compulsion. Limit points provide "a site, a territory, a horizon" for desire (Rodowick 2001, 28). Horizons of thought and action become somewhat stabilized, social experience characterized by senses of safety, security, certainty. Stable nodes may arise through marketing channels for individual desires, but they also work at the macro level. For example, in the Doha Round of the World Trade Organization talks (advertised as the "development round" — implicitly acknowledging the inequality previous liberalizations have fostered), agriculture has been a key issue. It is estimated that opening up the U.S. and E.U. agricultural markets would be worth tens of billions in foreign assistance each year. Thus, a number of non-governmental organizations and less-developed countries (led by Brazil) are pushing for greater (if still strategically located) liberalizations. This opposition position has become focused on the limit point of agricultural liberalization (a more radical neoliberalism than the U.S. and other champions of neoliberalism can bear), such that more radical reforms (e.g., that might question the rational assumptions of neoliberal capitalism itself) do not make it to the table. Limit points function similarly in the political market as well — for example, voting based on criteria such as "electability" (voting for a candidate not because his or her stance accurately reflects one's own politics because *at least* that candidate is not as bad as the opponent).

Žižek (1989, 174) cites Lewis Carroll on this point: "'I'm so glad I don't like asparagus,' said the small girl to a sympathetic friend, 'because if I did, I should have to eat it — and I can't bear it!'" Žižek reads this as speaking to an "immanent limit" constitutive of the desiring subject that allows at least some relative sense of security or "minimum of positive consistency."

In a similar vein, Gutmann (2002) makes a powerful case that the "romance of democracy" has served as an effective limit point to political change in Mexico for most of the twentieth century (cf. Rus, Mattiace, and Hernández Castillo 2003 on Zapatista imagined utopias).

8. See Fox (1989) for a relevant discussion of Gandhian utopianism and issues of power.

9. See Kearney (1996) and Colleredo-Mansfeld (1999) for nuanced studies of the vernacular modernities worked out in the context of transnational flows.

10. We have borrowed this phrase from Jan Rus (personal communication).

CHAPTER 4. SOCIAL SUFFERING IN THE POSTWAR ERA

1. There are similarities between this framing and the analysis of contemporary political and economic struggles among Zapatistas in Chiapas, Mexico, offered by June Nash (2001). In Chiapas, the idea of autonomy, related as it is to new international political formations, has had ambivalent implications for local Maya communities. Precisely in providing a channel that could bypass the nation, the autonomy of the local community within the milieu of globalization has also meant more diffuse and insidious economic relations with distant powers. See Chapter 6 for more on the Zapatistas.

2. The ideas here stem from conversations begun at the 2002 annual meetings of the American Anthropological Association in the panel "Struggling to Put the Post in Postwar Guatemala: The Successes and Failures Six Years after the Peace Accords."

3. We borrow this phrase from Kathleen Stewart, who argues that the political uses and moral implications of nostalgia all depend on "where you are standing" (1988). Nostalgia, that is, is not always reactionary or bourgeois. It takes different forms and has different social implications. Like nostalgia, what violence means and what forms of violence matter are also a matter of perspective and cultural location. The common framing of violence as reactionary, immoral, or unethical is a situated one that depends upon, and in turn reinforces, dominant contours of vision, speech, thought. Butler (2002, 178–79) makes this point with regard to the U.S. "war on terror":

> The articulation of this hegemony takes place in part through producing a consensus on what certain terms will mean, how they can be used, and what lines of solidarity are implicitly drawn through this use. We reserve "acts of terror" for events such as the September 11 attacks on the United States, distinguishing these acts of violence from those that might be justified through foreign policy decisions or public declarations of war. On the other hand, these terrorist acts are construed as "declarations of war" by the Bush administration, which then positions the military response as a justified act of self-defense.

Butler's theorization echoes the words of one Tecpaneco who noted that the hijackers had a "very serious political critique." This man finds the violence of September 11 both compelling and disheartening — he recounts that he could not stop watching the televised coverage and yet he understands that the hijackings emerged into a global discursive field already conditioned to recognize, or "hear," as Butler puts it, only certain forms of political activity as such.

4. This discussion of the events of June 10, 2002, is a revised version of Benson 2004.

5. Over seven hundred young women and girls were murdered (many raped and ritually mutilated) in Guatemala City between 2001 and 2003, crimes Guatemalan police attribute to *delincuentes*, "roving gangs" of young people (Taussig 2003, 9).

While U.S. deportation policies do not embody an overt intention to produce those deaths and create pockets of delinquency and violence, they still cite a discursive regularity in which the representation and impression of "safety" in the center depends — as a constitutive and partitioned outside — on representations and realities of "danger" in outer zones (places, like Guatemala, outside the mainstream of economic prosperity, health care, and political stability). This "structural" argument implicates the mainstream as a culpable actor in the forms of violent life that perpetually are disavowed and unintended.

6. Words and music by Lee Greenwood; © 1984 Music Corporation of America and Songs of Polygram International, Inc.

7. On the argument that mental illness, anxiety, depression, and stress bring all sectors of society into intimately intertwined relationships, see Kleinman and Benson (2004). On anxious, enclosed, exclusive, and violent relations between self and other in definitions of political and social community, see Lingis (1994). For an account of selves and others in the global political economy, see Lingis (1997).

CHAPTER 5. JUNE 10, SEPTEMBER 11, AND THE MORAL
UNDERSTANDING OF VIOLENCE

1. Maya religious specialists (*guías espirituales*, or spiritual guides) maintain the count of days in a sacred 260-day calendar. A key part of their diagnosis and divination is the interpretation of dreams.

2. Anthropologists have laudably weighed in on the cultural politics of September 11, as seen in recent volumes of *American Anthropologist* (2002; esp. Lutz; Mattingly, Lawlor, and Jacobs-Huey; Mamdani; Abu-Lughod) and *Anthropological Quarterly* (Howell and Shryock 2003, Nader 2003, Ghosh et al. 2002).

3. See Manz (2004) and Montejo (1992). Warren (1998, 9) captures the very mundane force of this nothingness in shaping the social experience of suffering and violence in the Highlands:

> "*Por miedo*," out of fear, people stayed in their homes. Kidnappings occurred most often in outlying hamlets. . . . Some victims vanished and were never seen again; others wandered back, frightened and mistreated, after being held for several days. Some surprised mourning relatives. . . . Splintered families fled their distant villages for the municipal center and shelter from dangerous army sweeps.

4. We draw on Žižek, who points out, following Hegel, that as Being moves from the abstract to the concrete, it passes into Nothing. It is not that the two are strictly opposed. Rather, "Being reveals itself as Nothing at the very moment when we endeavor to grasp it in its pureness, as radically opposed to Nothing" (1993, 123).

5. Alan Klima (2002) makes clear this double-binding nature of the public sphere in his ethnography of meditation practices and death rituals in Thailand. Public displays of and meditations over violent imagery have been politically efficacious for Thailand's radical democratic movement. Much like the testimonies of violence in

Highland Guatemala, these religious practices garner media sympathy and international recognition, and so provide something of a buffer against recurring state-sponsored violence. But they quickly dull the cutting edge of gore and death imagery, as the mass media thrive on facile renderings of victimization and blame. The political efficacy of this death or violence aesthetic gets disseminated — the message dispersed, and yet the very history of violence that such images seek to invoke are effaced through commoditization (see also Kleinman and Kleinman 1997).

6. See Fischer (1999) for an extended discussion of essentialist and constructivist approaches to Maya identity. The approach that we adopt here is not located at the same level as these debates. We are not claiming a particular ontology of Maya identity or the unity of the Maya worldview when we refer to the shared moral orientations called "Maya communities" by anthropologists, advocates, locals, tour guides, and others. "Moral orientations" refers to practices, which necessarily turns our attention toward existence and away from essence.

7. We are drawing on Levinas's work (1989a, 1989b) on the philosophical concept of an open relation to others that precedes self-identity and promises an escape from circumscribed or reduced identities and the logic of self autonomy. See Handelman (1991) for an excellent overview.

8. The "virtual operations" of capitalism and empire are discussed at length by Žižek (2003), where "virtual" describes a force that operates on a particular situation but without actually being seen or heard, such as the "invisible" workings of the free market. The virtual is not a force yet to emerge but a force producing real effects without any explicit organization.

9. The first-person singular in this section refers to Peter Benson (for a fuller discussion, see Benson 2004).

10. On this year (2002), June 10 fell on the date 11 Aj in the traditional Maya calendar. This is an auspicious date in Kaqchikel history: on May 20, 1493, a revolt occurred at the Kaqchikel capital of Iximche', which also coincided with 11 Aj in the Maya calendar. For 110 years, 11 Aj provided an anniversary date in relation to which all entries of historical events in the native Annals of the Kaqchikels were benchmarked (Smith 2002).

11. See Ulmer (1983, 107–13) for a discussion of the relation between montage and allegory. Ulmer indicates that if "allegoresis" has long been practiced to transcend the text and refer to external, metaphorical meanings, then "narrative allegory" explores the literal, actualizes the event in the very process of narration.

CHAPTER 6. BEYOND VICTIMIZATION

1. The commission's 1999 report, *Guatemala: Memoria del Silencio*, is available at www.hrdata.aaas.org/ceh/report/. For moving accounts of the violence and its complexities, see Manz (2004) and Montejo (1992); see also Carmack (1988).

2. This comes from a communiqué from Subcomandante Marcos sent to various newspapers on February 20, 1995. The Spanish version is available at the EZLN

website's archive of communiqués (www.ezln.org/documentos/1995/19950220.es .htm).

3. This is another communiqué from Subcomandante Marcos, released to various newspapers on March 15, 1994. This translation is by Nicholas Higgins (2000), who presents a more extended discussion of this and other poems by Marcos.

4. Marcos is not Maya, which leads critics to call into question the movement's legitimacy and authenticity. Disparaged for not being Indian and accused of being gay, Marcos deftly resists such tidy categories in a very Maya fashion by stating that he is "gay in San Francisco, a black in South Africa, Asian in Europe, a Chicano in San Isidro, an anarchist in Spain, a Palestinian in Israel, an indigenous person on the streets of San Cristóbal . . . In other words, Marcos is a human being in this world. Marcos is every untolerated, oppressed, exploited minority that is resisting and saying 'Enough!'" Here, Marcos, in his own poetic way, effectively captures a widespread sentiment among Maya activists who steadfastly refuse to be pigeonholed by dehumanizing essentialisms and categories of social containment and thus refuse to be just victims.

References

Abu-Lughod, Lila. 1990. The Romance of Resistance: Tracing the Transformations of Power through Bedouin Women. *American Ethnologist* 17: 41–55.

———. 1991. Writing against Culture. In *Recapturing Anthropology: Working in the Present*, ed. Richard G. Fox, 137–62. Santa Fe: School of American Research Press.

———. 2002. Do Muslim Women Really Need Saving? Anthropological Reflections on Cultural Relativism and Its Others. *American Anthropologist* 104, no. 3: 783–90.

Althusser, Louis. 1971. *Lenin and Philosophy and Other Essays*. New York: Monthly Review Press.

Anderson, Benedict. 1983. *Imagined Communities: Reflections on the Origin and Spread of Nationalism*. London: Verso.

Appadurai, Arjun. 1996. *Modernity at Large: Cultural Dimensions of Globalization*. Minneapolis: University of Minnesota Press.

———, ed. 1986. *The Social Life of Things: Commodities in Cultural Perspective*. Cambridge: Cambridge University Press.

Arias, Arturo, ed. 2001. *The Rigoberta Menchú Controversy*. Minneapolis: University of Minnesota Press.

Asad, Talal. 1993. *Genealogies of Religion: Discipline and Reasons of Power in Christianity and Islam*. Baltimore: Johns Hopkins University Press.

AVANCSO (Asociación para el Avance de las Ciencias Sociales en Guatemala). 1994. *Apostando al futuro con los cultivos no-tradicionales de exportación: Riesgos y oportunidades en la producción de hortalizas en Patzún, Chimaltenango*. Guatemala City: AVANCSO.

Barndt, Deborah. 2002. *Tangled Routes: Women, Work, and Globalization on the Tomato Trail*. Lanham, MD: Rowman and Littlefield.

———, ed. 1999. *Women Working the NAFTA Food Chain: Women, Food, and Globalization*. Toronto: Sumach Press.

Barthes, Roland. 1972. *Mythologies*. Trans. Annette Lavers. New York: Hill and Wang.

Bastos, Santiago, and Manuela Camus. 1993. *Quebrando el silencio: Organizaciones del pueblo maya y sus demandas (1986–1992)*. Guatemala City: Facultad Latinoamericana de Ciencias Sociales (FLACSO).

———. 1995. *Abriendo caminos: Las organizaciones mayas desde el Nobel hasta el acuerdo de derechos indígenas*. Guatemala City: Facultad Latinoamericana de Ciencias Sociales (FLACSO).

Baudrillard, Jean. 1983. *Simulations (Foreign Agents)*. New York: Semiotext[e].

———. 1988. *America*. Trans. Chris Turner. London: Verso.

Beck, Ulrich. 1992. *Risk Society: Towards a New Modernity*. London: Sage Publications.

Bell, David, and Gill Valentine. 1997. *Consuming Geographies: We Are Where We Eat*. New York: Routledge.

Benson, Peter. 2004. Nothing to See Hear. *Anthropological Quarterly* 77, no. 3): 435–67.

Berkley, Anthony. 1998. Remembrance and Revitalization: The Archive of Pure Maya. Ph.D. diss., University of Chicago.

Bestor, Theodore C. 2001. Supply-Side Sushi: Commodity, Market, and the Global City. *American Anthropologist* 103, no. 1: 76–95.

Bhabha, Homi. 1994. *The Location of Culture*. London: Routledge.

Boas, Franz. 1928. *Anthropology and Modern Life*. New York: Dover.

Bourdieu, Pierre. 1977. *Outline of a Theory of Practice*. Cambridge, MA: Harvard University Press.

———. 1999. *Acts of Resistance: Against the Tyranny of the Market*. New York: The New Press.

Bourdieu, Pierre, et al. 1999. *Weight of the World: Social Suffering in Contemporary Societies*. Stanford, CA: Stanford University Press.

Bricker, Victoria. 2004. Linguistic Continuities and Discontinuities in the Maya Area. In *Pluralizing Ethnography: Comparison and Representation in Maya Cultures, Histories, and Identities*, ed. John M. Watanabe and Edward F. Fischer, 67–94. Santa Fe, NM: School of American Research Press.

Briggs, Charles L. 2001. Modernity, Cultural Reasoning, and the Institutionalization of Social Inequality: Racializing Death in a Venezuelan Cholera Epidemic. *Comparative Study of Society and History* 43, no. 4: 665–700.

Brown, R. McKenna, Edward F. Fischer, and Raxche'. 1998. Mayan Visions for a Multilingual Society: The Guatemalan Peace Accords on Indigenous Identity and Languages. *Fourth World Bulletin on Indigenous Law and Politics* 6: 28–33.

Browning, John. 1996. Un obstáculo imprescindible: El indígena en los siglos XVIII y XIX. In *Memoria del Segundo Encuentro Nacional de Historiadores*. Guatemala: Universidad del Valle.

Buchanan, Ian. 2000. *Deleuzism: A Metacommentary*. Durham, NC: Duke University Press.

Bureau, Jean-Christophe, Wayne Jones, Estelle Gozlan, and Stephan Marettee. 2002. Issues in Demand for Quality and Trade. In *Global Food Trade and Con-*

sumer Demand for Quality, ed. Barry Kissoff, Mary Bohman, and Julie A. Caswell, 3–32. New York: Kluwer Academic/Plenum Publishers.

Butler, Judith. 1997. *Excitable Speech: A Politics of the Performative*. New York: Routledge.

———. 2000. Restaging the Universal: Hegemony and the Limits of Formalism. In *Contingency, Hegemony, Universality: Contemporary Dialogues on the Left*, ed. Judith Butler, Ernesto Laclau, and Slavoj Žižek, 11–43. London: Verso.

———. 2002. Explanation and Exoneration, or What We Can Hear. *Social Text* 20, no. 3: 177–88.

Butler, Judith, Ernesto Laclau, and Slavoj Žižek, eds. 2000. *Contingency, Hegemony, Universality: Contemporary Dialogues on the Left*. London: Verso.

Camerer, Colin F. 2003. *Behavioral Game Theory: Experiments in Strategic Interaction*. Princeton, NJ: Princeton University Press.

Canclini, Néstor García. 1995. *Hybrid Cultures: Strategies for Entering and Leaving Modernity*. Foreword by Renato Rosaldo, trans. Christopher L. Chiappari and Silvia L. López. Minneapolis: University of Minnesota Press.

Cardoso, Fernando H., and Enzo Faletto. 1967. *Dependencia y desarrollo en América Latina*. Lima: Instituto de Estudios Peruanos.

Carey, David. 2001. *Our Elders Teach Us: Maya-Kaqchikel Historical Perspectives*. Tuscaloosa: University of Alabama Press.

———. n.d. A Clash of Two Worlds: Chemical Fertilizer and Maya Land in Guatemala. Unpublished ms.

Carletto, Calogero, Alain de Janvry, and Elizabeth Sadoulet. 1999. Sustainability in the Diffusion of Innovations: Smallholder Nontraditional Agro-Exports in Guatemala. *Economic Development and Cultural Change* 47, no. 2: 345–69.

Carmack, Robert, ed. 1988. *Harvest of Violence: The Maya Indians and the Guatemalan Crisis*. Norman: University of Oklahoma Press.

Carrithers, Michael. 2005. Anthropology as a Moral Science of Possibilities. *Current Anthropology* 46, no. 3: 433–56.

Castañeda, Quetzil E. 2006. Ethnography in the Forest: An Analysis of Ethics in the Morals of Anthropology. *Cultural Anthropology* 21, no. 1: 121–45.

Chakrabarty, Dipesh. 2000. *Provincializing Europe: Postcolonial Thought and Historical Difference*. Princeton, NJ: Princeton University Press.

Clifford, James. 1997. *Routes: Travel and Translation in the Late Twentieth Century*. Cambridge, MA: Harvard University Press.

Cojtí, Demetrio Cuxil. 1991. *Configuración del pensamiento político del pueblo maya*. Quetzaltenango, Guatemala: Asociación de Escritores Mayances de Guatemala.

———. 1997. *Ri maya' moloj pa Iximulew: El movimiento maya (en guatemala)*. Guatemala: Editorial Cholsamaj.

Collier, George. 1994. *Basta! Land and the Zapatista Rebellion in Chiapas*. Oakland: Food First.

Collier, Jane. 1997. *From Duty to Desire: Remaking Families in a Spanish Village*. Princeton, NJ: Princeton University Press.

Collier, Stephen J., and Aihwa Ong. 2005. Global Assemblages, Anthropological Problems. In *Global Assemblages: Technology, Politics, and Ethics as Anthropological Problems*, ed. Aihwa Ong and Stephen J. Collier, 3–21. Malden, MA: Blackwell.

Colloredo-Mansfeld, Rudi. 1999. *The Native Leisure Class: Consumption and Cultural Creativity in the Andes*. Chicago: University of Chicago Press.

Comaroff, Jean, and John Comaroff. 1991. *Of Revelation and Revolution: Christianity and Consciousness in South Africa*. Vol. 1. Chicago: University of Chicago Press.

———. 2000. Millennial Capitalism: First Thoughts on a Second Coming. *Public Culture* 12, no. 2: 291–343.

Cook, Ian. 1994. New Fruits and Vanity: Symbolic Production in the Global Food Economy. In *From Columbus to ConAgra: The Globalization of Agriculture and Foods*, ed. Alessandro Bonanno, Lawrence Busch, William H. Friedland, Lourdes Gouveia, and Enzo Mingione, 232–48. Lawrence: University Press of Kansas.

Cook, Ian, et al. 2004. Follow the Thing: Papaya. *Antipode* 36, no. 4: 642–64.

Cook, Ian, and Philip Crang. 1996. World on a Plate: Culinary Culture, Displacement and Geographical Knowledges. *Journal of Material Culture* 1: 131–53.

Crang, Philip. 1996. Displacement, Consumption and Identity. *Environment and Planning A* 28: 47–67.

Curtis, Debra. 2004. Commodities and Sexual Subjectivities: A Look at Capitalism and Its Desires. *Cultural Anthropology* 19, no. 1: 95–121.

D'Andrade, Roy. 1995. Moral Models in Anthropology. *Current Anthropology* 36, no. 3: 399–408.

Daniel, E. Valentine. 1996. *Charred Lullabies: Chapters in an Anthropography of Violence*. Princeton, NJ: Princeton University Press.

Das, Veena. 1998. Wittgenstein and Anthropology. *Annual Review of Anthropology* 27: 171–95.

———. 2003. Violence and Translation. *Anthropological Quarterly* 75, no. 1: 105–12.

Das, Veena, Arthur Kleinman, Mamphela Ramphele, and Pamela Reynolds, eds. 2000. *Violence and Subjectivity*. Berkeley: University of California Press.

de Certeau, Michel. 1984. *The Practice of Everyday Life*. Trans. Steven Rendall. Berkeley: University of California Press.

———. 1986. The Laugh of Michel Foucault. In *Heterologies: Discourse on the Other*, trans. Brian Massumi, 193–98. Minneapolis: University of Minnesota Press.

de Certeau, Michel, Luce Giard, and Pierre Mayol. 1998. *Living and Cooking*, vol. 2 of Michel de Certeau, *The Practice of Everyday Life*, new revised and augmented edition, ed. Luce Giard, trans. Timothy J. Tomasik. Minneapolis: University of Minnesota Press.

De Janvry, Alain. 1981. *The Agrarian Question and Reformism in Latin America*. Baltimore: Johns Hopkins University Press.

Delamont, Sara. 1995. *Appetites and Identities: An Introduction to the Social Anthropology of Western Europe*. New York: Routledge.

Deleuze, Gilles. 1988. *Foucault.* Trans. Seán Hand. Minneapolis: University of Minnesota Press.

———. 1995. *Negotiations, 1972–1990.* New York: Columbia University Press.

———. 1997 [1994]. Desire and Pleasure. In *Foucault and His Interlocutors,* ed. Arnold I. Davidson, trans. Daniel W. Smith, 183–92. Chicago: University of Chicago Press.

Deleuze, Gilles, and Felix Guattari. 1983. *Anti-Oedipus: Capitalism and Schizophrenia.* Minneapolis: University of Minnesota Press.

———. 1987. *A Thousand Plateaus: Capitalism and Schizophrenia.* Trans. B. Massumi. Minneapolis: University of Minnesota Press.

Derrida, Jacques. 1981. *Dissemination.* Trans. Barbara Johnson. Chicago: University of Chicago Press.

———. 1992. *Given Time: I. Counterfeit Money.* Trans. Peggy Kamuf. Chicago: University of Chicago Press.

Doyal, Len, and Ian Gough. 1991. *Theory of Human Need.* London: Palgrave.

Eagleton, Terry. 1991. *Ideology: An Introduction.* London: Verso.

England, Nora. 1996. The Role of Language Standardization in Revitalization. In *Maya Cultural Activism in Guatemala,* ed. Edward F. Fischer and R. McKenna Brown, 178–94. Austin: University of Texas Press.

Ensminger, Jean. 2004. Market Integration and Fairness: Evidence from Ultimatum, Dictator, and Public Goods Experiments in East Africa. In *Foundations of Human Sociality: Economic Experiments and Ethnographic Evidence from Fifteen Small-Scale Societies,* ed. Joseph Henrich, Robert Boyd, Samuel Bowles, Colin Camerer, Ernst Fehr, and Hebert Gintis, 356–81. Oxford: Oxford University Press.

Errington, Frederick, and Deborah Gewertz. 2004. *Yali's Question: Sugar, Culture, and History.* Chicago: University of Chicago Press.

Ferguson, James. 1990. *The Anti-Politics Machine: "Development," Depoliticization, and Bureaucratic Power in Lesotho.* Cambridge: Cambridge University Press.

———. 1999. *Expectations of Modernity: Myths and Meanings of Urban Life on the Zambian Copperbelt.* Berkeley: University of California Press.

Fischer, Edward F. 1999. Maya Identity and Cultural Logic: Rethinking Essentialism and Constructivism. *Current Anthropology* 43, no. 4: 473–99.

———. 2001. *Cultural Logics and Global Economies: Maya Identity in Thought and Practice.* Austin: University of Texas Press.

———. 2004. The Janus Face of Globalization: Economic Production and Cultural Reproduction in Highland Guatemala. In *Pluralizing Ethnography: Comparison and Representation in Maya Cultures, Histories, and Identities,* ed. John M. Watanabe and Edward F. Fischer. Santa Fe, NM: School of American Research Press.

Fischer, Edward F., and Avery Dickins. 2006. Rationality, Self-Interest, and Cultural Context: Results of Economic Experiments in Two Guatemalan Maya Communities. *Southern Anthropological Society Proceedings* 40.

Fischer, Edward F., and Carol Hendrickson. 2002. *Tecpán Guatemala: A Modern Maya Town in Local and Global Context*. Boulder, CO: Westview Press.

Fischer, Edward F., and R. McKenna Brown, eds. 1996. *Maya Cultural Activism in Guatemala*. Austin: University of Texas Press.

Fischer, Michael M. J. 2003. *Emergent Forms of Life and the Anthropological Voice*. Durham, NC: Duke University Press.

Foucault, Michel. 1978. *The History of Sexuality*, vol. 1, *An Introduction*. Trans. Robert Hurley. New York: Vintage.

———. 1983. The Subject and Power. In *Michel Foucault: Beyond Structuralism and Hermeneutics*, Hubert L. Dreyfus and Paul Rabinow, 208–26. Chicago: University of Chicago Press.

Fox, Richard G. 1989. *Gandhian Utopia: Experiments in Culture*. Boston: Beacon Press.

Frank, Andre Gunder. 1967. *Capitalism and Underdevelopment in Latin America: Historical Studies of Chile and Brazil*. New York: Monthly Review Press.

Freidberg, Susanne. 2004. *French Beans and Food Scares: Culture and Commerce in an Anxious Age*. Oxford: Oxford University Press.

Friedland, William H. 1994. The New Globalization: The Case of Fresh Produce. In *From Columbus to ConAgra: The Globalization of Agriculture and Foods*, ed. Alessandro Bonanno, Lawrence Busch, William H. Friedland, Lourdes Gouveia, and Enzo Mingione, 210–31. Lawrence: University Press of Kansas.

Friedman, Jonathan. 1994. *Cultural Identity and Global Process*. Thousand Oaks, CA.: Sage Publications.

———. 2002. Champagne Liberals and the New "Dangerous Classes": Reconfigurations of Class, Identity, and Cultural Production in the Contemporary Global System. *Social Analysis* 46, no. 2: 33–55.

Food Marketing Institute. 2002. *Trends in the United States: Consumer Attitudes and the Supermarket*. Washington, DC: Food Marketing Institute.

Fox, Richard G. 1985. *Lions of the Punjab: Culture in the Making*. Berkeley: University of California Press.

———. 1989. *Gandhian Utopia: Experiments in Culture*. Boston: Beacon Press.

Fukuyama, Francis. 1992. *The End of History and the Last Man*. New York: Free Press.

Gálvez, Víctor, and Alberto Esquit Choy. 1997. *The Mayan Movement Today: Issues of Indigenous Culture and Development in Guatemala*. Guatemala City: FLACSO-Guatemala.

Gaonkar, Dilip Parameshwar. 2002. Toward New Imaginaries: An Introduction. *Public Culture* 14, no. 1: 1–19.

Garber, Marjorie. 2002. *Quotation Marks*. New York: Routledge.

Geertz, Clifford. 1973. Deep Play: Notes on the Balinese Cockfight. In *The Interpretation of Cultures*, 412–53. New York: Basic Books.

Ghosh, Gautam, et al. 2002. Civilization, Vulnerability, and Translation: Reflections in the Aftermath of September 11th [a series of essays edited by Gautam Ghosh]. *Anthropological Quarterly* 75, no. 1: 92–203.

Giard, Luce. 1998. Plat du Jour. In *Living and Cooking*, by Michel de Certeau, Luce Giard, and Pierre Mayol, 171–98; vol. 2 of Michel de Certeau, *The Practice of Everyday Life*, new revised and augmented edition, ed. Luce Giard, trans. Timothy J. Tomasik. Minneapolis: University of Minnesota Press.

Giddens, Anthony. 1991. The *Consequences of Modernity*. Stanford, CA: Stanford University Press.

———. 1994. Living in a Post-traditional Society. In *Reflexive Modernization: Politics, Traditions, and Aesthetics in the Modern Social Order*, ed. Ulrich Beck, Anthony Giddens, and Scott Lash, 56–109. Stanford, CA: Stanford University Press.

Gilory, Paul A. 2000. *Against Race: Imagining Political Culture beyond the Color Line*. Cambridge, MA: Belknap/Harvard Press.

Goldin, Liliana R. 1996. Economic Mobility Strategies among Guatemalan Peasants: Prospects and Limits of Nontraditional Vegetable Cash Crops. *Human Organization* 55, no. 1: 99–107.

Goldin, Liliana R., and Linda Asturias de Barrios. 2001. Perceptions of the Economy in the Context of Non-traditional Agricultural Exports in the Central Highlands of Guatemala. *Culture & Agriculture* 23, no. 1: 18–31.

Goldin, Liliana R., and Eugenia Sáenz de Tejada. 1993. Uneven Development in Western Guatemala. *Ethnology* 32, no. 3: 237–51.

Gossen, Gary H. 1999. *Telling Maya Tales: Tzotzil Identities in Modern Mexico*. New York: Routledge.

———. 2004. "Everything has begun to change": Appraisals of the Mexican State in Chiapas Maya Discourse, 1980–2000. In *Pluralizing Ethnography: Comparison and Representation in Maya Cultures, Histories, and Identities*, ed. John M. Watanabe and Edward F. Fischer, 127–62. Santa Fe, NM: School of American Research Press.

Graham, Jorie. 1995. The Hiding Place. In *The Dream of the Unified Field: Selected Poems, 1974–1994*, 112–14. Hopewell, NJ: Ecco.

Gramsci, Antonio. 1971. *Selections from the Prison Notebooks of Antonio Gramsci*, ed. and trans. Quintin Hoare and Geoffrey Nowell Smith. New York: International Publishers.

Green, Linda. 2003. Notes on Maya Youth and Rural Industrialization in Guatemala. *Critique of Anthropology* 23, no. 1: 51–73.

Greenhouse, Carol J. 2005. Hegemony and Hidden Transcripts: The Discursive Arts of Neoliberal Legitimation. *American Anthropologist* 107, no. 3: 356–68.

Grossberg, Lawrence. 1992. *We Gotta Get Out of This Place: Popular Conservatism and Postmodern Culture*. New York: Routledge.

Gudeman, Stephen, and Alberto Rivera. 1990. *Conversations in Colombia: The Domestic Economy in Life and Text*. Cambridge: Cambridge University Press.

Gupta, Akhil. 1998. *Postcolonial Developments: Agriculture in the Making of Modern India*. Durham, NC: Duke University Press.

Gupta, Akhil, and James Ferguson. 1997a. Culture, Power, Place: Ethnography at the End of an Era. In *Culture, Power, Place: Explorations in Critical Anthropology*, ed. Akhil Gupta and James Ferguson, 1–32. Durham, NC: Duke University Press.

———. 1997b. Beyond Culture: Space, Identity, and the Politics of Difference. In *Culture, Power, Place: Explorations in Critical Anthropology*, ed. Akhil Gupta and James Ferguson, 33–51. Durham, NC: Duke University Press.

Güth, Wener, Rolf Schmittberger, and Bernd Schwarze. 1995. An Experimental Analysis of Ultimatum Bargaining. *Journal of Economic Behavior and Organization* 3, no. 4: 367–88.

Guthman, Julie. 2003. Fast Food/Organic Food: Reflexive Tastes and the Making of "Yuppie Chow." *Social and Cultural Geography* 4, no. 1: 45–58.

Gutmann, Matthew. 2002. *The Romance of Democracy: Compliant Defiance in Contemporary Mexico*. Berkeley: University of California Press.

Gwynne, Robert N., and Cristóbal Kay, eds. 1999. *Latin America Transformed: Globalization and Modernity*. New York: Oxford University Press.

Hall, Stuart. 1985. Signification, Representation, Ideology: Althusser and the Post-Structuralist Debates. *Critical Studies in Mass Communication* 2, no. 2: 91–114.

Hamilton, Sarah, and Edward F. Fischer. 2003. Nontraditional Agricultural Exports in Highland Guatemala: Understandings of Risk and Perceptions of Change. *Latin American Research Review* 38, no. 3: 82–110.

Hamm, Shannon Reid. 1992. The U.S. Supply of Vegetables. In *Vegetable Markets in the Western Hemisphere*, ed. Rigoberta A. López and Leo C. Polopolus, 3–19. Ames: Iowa State University Press.

Handelman, Susan A. 1991. *Fragments of Redemption: Benjamin, Scholem, and Levinas*. Bloomington: Indiana University Press.

Hannerz, Ulf. 1996. *Transnational Connections*. London: Routledge.

Haraway, Donna. 1991. *Simians, Cyborgs, and Women: The Reinvention of Nature*. London: Routledge.

Hardt, Michael, and Antonio Negri. 2000. *Empire*. Cambridge, MA: Harvard University Press.

Harvey, David. 2000. *Spaces of Hope*. Berkeley: University of California Press.

Hendrickson, Carol. 1995. *Weaving Identities: Construction of Dress and Self in a Highland Guatemala Town*. Austin: University of Texas Press.

———. 1996. Selling Guatemala: Maya Export Products in U.S. Mail-Order Catalogues. In *Cross-cultural Consumption: Global Markets, Local Realities*, ed. David Howes, 106–21. New York: Routledge.

Henrich, Joseph, Robert Boyd, Samuel Bowles, Colin F. Camerer, Ernst Fehr, Herbert Gintis, and Richard McElreath. 2004. Overview and synthesis. In *Foundations of Human Sociality: Economic Experiments and Ethnographic Evidence from Fifteen Small-Scale Societies*, ed. Joseph Henrich, Robert Boyd, Samuel Bowles, Colin Camerer, Ernst Fehr, and Hebert Gintis, 8–54. Oxford: Oxford University Press.

Herzfeld, Michael. 1997. *Cultural Intimacy: Social Poetics in the Nation-State*. New York: Routledge.

————. 2001. *Anthropology: Theoretical Practice in Culture and Society*. Malden, MA: Blackwell Publishers.

————. 2003. *The Body Impolitic: Artisans and Artifice in the Global Hierarchy of Value*. Chicago: University of Chicago Press.

Higgins, Nicholas. 2000. The Zapatista Uprising and the Poetics of Cultural Resistance. *Alternatives* 25: 359–74.

————. 2004. *Understanding the Chiapas Rebellion: Modernist Visions and the Invisible Indian*. Austin: University of Texas Press.

Hobsbawm, Eric. 1983. Introduction: Inventing Traditions. In *The Invention of Tradition*, ed. Eric Hobsbawm and Terence Ranger, 1–14. Cambridge: Cambridge University Press.

Holland, Dorothy, William S. Lachicotte Jr., Debra Skinner, and Carole Cain. 1998. *Identity and Agency in Cultural Worlds*. Cambridge, MA: Harvard University Press.

Howell, Sally, and Andrew Shryock. 2003. Cracking Down on Diaspora: Arab Detroit and America's "War on Terror." *Anthropological Quarterly* 76, no. 3: 443–62.

Huacuja, Flavia Echánove. 2001. Working under Contract for the Vegetable Agroindustry in Mexico: A Means of Survival. *Culture & Agriculture* 23, no. 3: 13–23.

Hughes, Alex, and Suzanne Reimer, eds. 2004. *Geographies of Commodity Chains*. New York: Routledge.

Immink, Maarten D. C., and Jorge A. Alarcon. 1993. Household Income, Food Availability, and Commercial Crop Production by Smallholder Farmers in the Western Highlands of Guatemala. Economic *Development and Cultural Change* 4, no. 1: 319–43.

Jameson, Fredric. 1981. *The Political Unconscious: Narrative as a Socially Symbolic Act*. Ithaca, NY: Cornell University Press.

————. 1991. *Postmodernism, or, The Cultural Logic of Late Capitalism*. Durham, NC: Duke University Press.

————. 1998. Notes on Globalization as a Philosophical Issue. In *The Cultures of Globalization*, ed. Fredric Jameson and Masao Miyoshi, 54–77. Durham, NC: Duke University Press.

————. 2005. *Archaeologies of the Future: The Desire Called Utopia and Other Science Fictions*. London: Verso.

Johnson, Barbara. 1980. The Frame of Reference: Poe, Lacan, Derrida. In *The Critical Difference*, 110–46. Baltimore: Johns Hopkins University Press.

Joseph, Miranda. 1998. The Performance of Production and Consumption. *Social Text* 54: 25–61.

————. 2002. *Against the Romance of Community*. Minneapolis: University of Minnesota Press.

Kagel, John H., and Alvin E. Roth. 1995. *The Handbook of Experimental Economics*. Princeton, NJ: Princeton University Press.

Kalb, Don. 2005. From Flows to Violence: Politics and Knowledge in the Debates on Globalization and Empire. *Anthropological Theory* 5, no. 2: 176–204.

Kalcik, Susan. 1984. Ethnic Foodways in America: Symbol and the Performance of Identity. In *Ethnic and Regional Foodways in the United States*, ed. Linda K. Brown and Kay Mussell, 37–65. Knoxville: University of Tennessee Press.

Katzen, Mollie. 1982. *The Enchanted Broccoli Forest*. Berkeley: Ten Speed Press.

Kay, Cristóbal. 1989. *Latin American Theories of Development and Underdevelopment*. London: Routledge.

Kearney. Michael. 1996. *Reconceptualizing the Peasantry: Anthropology in Global Perspective*. Boulder: Westview Press.

Klak, Thomas. 1999. Globalization, Neoliberalism, and Economic Change in Central America and the Caribbean. In *Latin America Transformed: Globalization and Modernity*, ed. Robert N. Gwynne and Cristóbal Kay, 98–126. New York: Oxford University Press.

Kleinman, Arthur. 1995. *Writing at the Margin: Discourse Between Medicine and Anthropology*. Berkeley: University of California Press.

———. 1999a. Experience and Its Moral Modes: Culture, Human Conditions, and Disorder. In *The Tanner Lectures on Human Values*, vol. 20, ed. Grethe B. Peterson. Salt Lake City: University of Utah Press.

———. 1999b. Moral Experience and Ethical Reflection: Can Ethnography Reconcile Them? A Quandary for "The New Bioethics." *Daedalus* 128, no. 4: 69–97.

———. 2006. *What Really Matters: Living a Moral Life amidst Uncertainty and Danger*. Oxford: Oxford University Press.

Kleinman, Arthur, and Peter Benson. 2004. La vida moral de los que sufren enfermedad y el fracaso existencial de la medicina. *Monografías Humanitas* 2: 17–26.

Kleinman, Arthur, and Joan Kleinman. 1991. Suffering and Its Professional Transformation: Towards an Ethnography of Interpersonal Experience. *Culture, Medicine, and Psychiatry* 15, no. 3: 275–301.

———. 1997. The Appeal of Experience; The Dismay of Images: Cultural Appropriations of Suffering in Our Times. In *Social Suffering*, ed. Arthur Kleinman, Veena Das, and Margaret Lock. Berkeley: University of California Press.

Klima, Alan. 2002. *The Funeral Casino: Meditation, Massacre, and Exchange with the Dead in Thailand*. Princeton, NJ: Princeton University Press.

Knauft, Bruce M. 2002a. *Exchanging the Past: A Rainforest World Before and After*. Chicago: University of Chicago Press.

———, ed. 2002b. *Critically Modern: Alternatives, Alterities, Anthropologies*. Bloomington: Indiana University Press.

Lacan, Jacques. 1972. *The Four Fundamental Concepts of Psycho-Analysis*. Trans. Alan Sheridan. New York: W. W. Norton.

———. 1977. *Écrits: A Selection*. Trans. Alan Sheridan. New York: W. W. Norton.

Laclau, Ernesto. 2000. Identity and Hegemony: The Role of Universality in the Constitution of Political Logics. In *Contingency, Hegemony, Universality: Contemporary Dialogues on the Left*, ed. Judith Butler, Ernesto Laclau, and Slavoj Žižek, 44–89. London: Verso.

Laqueur, Thomas. 1992. Sexual Desire and the Market Economy during the Industrial Revolution. In *Histories of Sexuality*, ed. Domna C. Stanton. Ann Arbor: University of Michigan Press.

Lash, Scott, and John Urry. 1987. *The End of Organized Capitalism*. Cambridge: Polity Press.

Latour, Bruno. 1993. *We Have Never Been Modern*. Trans. Catherine Porter. Cambridge, MA: Harvard University Press.

Levinas, Emmanuel. 1969. *Totality and Infinity*. Trans. Alphonso Lingis. Pittsburgh: Duquesne University Press.

———. 1981. *Otherwise than Being or Beyond Essence*. Trans. Alphonso Lingis. Pittsburgh: Duquesne University Press.

———. 1985. *Ethics and Infinity*. Trans. Richard A. Cohen. Pittsburgh: Duquesne University Press.

———. 1989a. There Is: Existence Without Existents. In *The Levinas Reader*, ed. Seán Hand, 29–36. Oxford: Blackwell.

———. 1989b. Time and the Other. In *The Levinas Reader*, ed. Seán Hand, 37–58. Oxford: Blackwell.

———. 2000. Useless Suffering. In *Entre Nous: Thinking-of-the-Other*, trans. Michael B. Smith and Barbara Harshav, 91–101. New York: Columbia University Press.

Lingis, Alphonso. 1985. *Libido: The French Existential Theories*. Bloomington: Indiana University Press.

———. 1994. *The Community of Those Who Have Nothing in Common*. Bloomington: University of Indiana Press.

———. 1997. Anger. In *On Jean-Luc Nancy*, ed. Darren Sheppard, Simon Sparks, and Colin Thomas, 197–215. London: Routledge.

———. 1998. *The Imperative*. Bloomington: University of Indiana Press.

Lovell, W. George. 2000. *A Beauty That Hurts: Life and Death in Guatemala*. Austin: University of Texas Press.

Lunt, Peter K., and Sonia M. Livingstone. 1992. *Mass Consumption and Personal Identity: Everyday Economic Experience*. Buckingham: Open University Press.

Lupton, Deborah. 1999. *Risk*. London: Routledge.

Lutz, Catherine. 2002. Making War at Home in the United States: Militarization and the Current Crisis. *American Anthropologist* 104, no. 3: 723–35.

Lyons, Barry J. 2005. Discipline and the Arts of Domination: Rituals of Respect in Chimborazo, Ecuador. *Cultural Anthropology* 20, no. 1: 97–127.

MacIntyre, Alasdair. 1981. *After Virtue*. South Bend, IN: University of Notre Dame Press.

Maddox, Richard. 1997. Bombs, Bikinis, and the Popes of Rock 'n' Roll: Reflections on Resistance, the Play of Subordinations, and Liberalism in Andalusi and Academia, 1983–1995. In *Culture, Power, Place: Explorations in Critical Anthropology*, ed. Akhil Gupta and James Ferguson, 277–90. Durham, NC: Duke University Press.

Mamdani, Mahmood. 2002. Good Muslim, Bad Muslim: A Political Perspective on Culture and Terrorism. *American Anthropologist* 104, no. 3: 766–75.

Mankekar, Purnima. 1999. *Screening Culture, Viewing Politics: An Ethnography of*

Television, Womanhood, and Nation in Post-Colonial India. Durham, NC: Duke University Press.

Manz, Beatriz. 2004. *Paradise in Ashes: A Guatemalan Journey of Courage, Terror, and Hope.* Berkeley: University of California Press.

Marcos, Subcomandante. 2001. *Our Word Is Our Weapon: Selected Writings, Subcomandante Insurgente Marcos.* Ed. Juana Ponce de León. New York: Seven Stories Press.

Marcus, George E. 1998. *Ethnography through Thick and Thin.* Princeton, NJ: Princeton University Press.

Massumi, Brian. 1992. *A User's Guide to Capitalism and Schizophrenia: Deviations from Deleuze and Guattari.* Cambridge, MA: MIT Press.

———. 2002. *Parables for the Virtual: Movement, Affect, Sensation.* Durham, NC: Duke University Press.

Mattingly, Cheryl, Mary Lawlor, and Lanita Jacobs-Huey. 2002. Narrating September 11: Race, Gender, and the Play of Cultural Identities. *American Anthropologist* 104, no. 3: 743–53.

Maxwell, Judith M. 1996. Prescriptive Grammar and Kaqchikel Revitalization. In *Maya Cultural Activism in Guatemala,* ed. Edward F. Fischer and R. McKenna Brown, 195–207. Austin: University of Texas Press.

Maxwell, Judith M., and Robert M. Hill. 2006. *Kaqchikel Chronicles: The Definitive Edition.* Austin: University of Texas Press.

Mayol, Pierre. 1998. The End of the Week. In *Living and Cooking,* by Michel de Certeau, Luce Giard, and Pierre Mayol, 101–13; vol. 2 of Michel de Certeau, *The Practice of Everyday Life,* new revised and augmented edition, ed. Luce Giard, trans. Timothy J. Tomasik. Minneapolis: University of Minnesota Press.

McCracken, Vicki A. 1992. The U.S. Demand for Vegetables. In *Vegetable Markets in the Western Hemisphere,* ed. Rigoberto A. López and Leo C. Polopolus, 20–43. Ames: Iowa State University Press.

Menchú, Rigoberta. 1983. *I, Rigoberta Menchú: An Indian Woman in Guatemala.* Ed. Elisabeth Burgos-Debray; trans. Ann Wright. London: Verso.

Mignolo, Walter D. 2000. *Local Histories/Global Designs: Coloniality, Subaltern Knowledges, and Border Thinking.* Princeton, NJ: Princeton University Press.

Miller, Daniel. 1995. Consumption and Commodities. *Annual Review of Anthropology* 24: 141–61.

———. 1997. *Capitalism: An Ethnographic Account.* Oxford: Berg.

———. 1998. *A Theory of Shopping.* Cambridge: Polity Press.

Mintz, Sidney. 1985. *Sweetness and Power: The Place of Sugar in Modern History.* New York: Penguin.

Mitchell, Timothy P. 2005. The Work of Economics: How a Discipline Makes its World. Yale University Program in Agrarian Studies Papers. http://www.yale.edu/agrarianstudies/papers/07workofeconomics.pdf.

Moberg, Mark. 2005. Fair Trade and Eastern Caribbean Banana Farmers: Rhetoric and Reality in the Anti-globalization Movement. *Human Organization* 64, no. 1: 4–15.

Montejo, Víctor. 1992. *Testimonio: Muerte de una comunidad indígena en Guatemala.*

Guatemala City: Editorial Universitaria, Universidad de San Carlos en Guatemala.

———. 2005. *Maya Intellectual Renaissance: Identity, Representation, and Leadership.* Austin: University of Texas Press.

Morales, Mario Roberto. Sujetos Interétnicos y Moda Posmo en Xela. *Siglo XXI,* 19 June 2000, 23.

Nader, Laura. 1997. Controlling Processes: Tracing the Dynamic Components of Power. *Current Anthropology* 38, no. 5: 711–37.

———. 2003. Iraq and Democracy. *Anthropological Quarterly* 76, no. 3: 479–83.

Nance, Roger C., Stepehen L. Whittington, and Barbara E. Borg. 2003. *Archaeology and Ethnohistory of Iximche.* Gainsville: University of Florida Press.

Nash, June. 2001. *Mayan Visions: The Quest for Autonomy in an Age of Globalization.* New York: Routledge.

Nash, June, and María Patricia Fernández Kelly, eds. 1983. *Women, Men, and the International Division of Labor.* Albany: State University of New York Press.

Nelson, Diane. 1999. *A Finger in the Wound: Body Politics in Quincentennial Guatemala.* Berkeley: University of California Press.

———. 2001. Phantom Limbs and Invisible Hands: Bodies, Prosthetics, and Late Capitalist Identifications. *Cultural Anthropology* 16, no. 1: 303–12.

Offe, Claus. 1984. *The Contradictions of the Welfare State.* London: Hutchinson.

Oglesby, Elizabeth. 2004. Corporate Citizenship? Elites, Labor, and the Geographics of Work in Guatemala. *Environment and Planning D: Society and Space* 22: 553–72.

Ong, Aihwa. 1999. *Flexible Citizenship: The Cultural Logics of Transnationality.* Durham, NC: Duke University Press.

Ong, Aihwa, and Stephen J. Collier, eds. 2005. *Global Assemblages: Technology, Politics, and Ethics as Anthropological Problems.* Malden, MA: Blackwell.

Ortner, Sherry. 1995. Resistance and the Problem of Ethnographic Refusal. *Comparative Studies in Society and History* 37, no. 1: 173–93.

———. 1989. *High Religion: A Cultural and Political History of Sherpa Buddhism.* Princeton, NJ: Princeton University Press.

Pile, Steve, and Michael Keith, eds. 1997. *Geographies of Resistance.* London: Routledge.

Pirog, Rich, Timothy Van Pelt, Kamyar Enshayan, and Ellen Cook. 2001. *Food, Fuel, and Freeways.* Ames: Leopold Center for Sustainable Agriculture, Iowa State University.

Pitarch, Pedro. 2004. The Zapatistas and the Art of Ventriloquism. *Journal of Human Rights* 3, no. 3: 291–312.

Pred, Allan, and Michael John Watts. 1992. *Reworking Modernity: Capitalisms and Symbolic Discontent.* New Brunswick, NJ: Rutgers University Press.

Rappaport, Joanne. 2005. *Intercultural Utopias: Public Intellectuals, Cultural Experimentation, and Ethnic Pluralism in Colombia.* Durham, NC: Duke University Press.

Raxche' [Demetrio Rodríguez Guaján], ed. 1992. *Cultura Maya y políticas de desar-*

rollo. Chimaltenango, Guatemala: Coordinadora Cakchiquel de Desarrollo Integral (COCADI).

Rodowick, David. 2001. *Reading the Figural, or, Philosophy after the New Media.* Durham, NC: Duke University Press.

Rosaldo, Renato. 1989. *Culture and Truth: The Remaking of Social Analysis.* Boston: Beacon.

Roseberry, William. 1996. The Rise of Yuppie Coffees and the Reimagining of Class in the United States. *American Anthropologist* 98, no. 4: 762–75.

Ruskin, John. 1862a. *Munera Pulveris: Six Essays on the Elements of Political Economy.* London: Charles E. Merril.

———. 1862b. *Unto This Last: Four Essays on the First Principles of Political Economy.* London: Smith, Elder.

Russ, Jan, Rosalva Aída Hernández Castillo, and Shannan L. Mattiace, eds. 2003. *Mayan Lives, Mayan Utopias: The Indigenous People of Chiapas and the Zapatista Rebellion.* Lanham, MD: Rowman and Littlefield.

Sahlins, Marshall. 1976. *Culture and Practical Reason.* Chicago: University of Chicago Press.

Salzinger, Leslie. 2000. Manufacturing Sexual Subjects: "Harassment," Desire, and Discipline on a Maquiladora Shopfloor. *Ethnography* 1, no. 1: 67–92.

Sam Colop, Enrique. 1991. *Jub'aqtun omay kuchum k'aslemal: Cinco siglos de encubrimiento.* Seminario Permanente de Estudios Mayas, Cuaderno 1. Guatemala City: Editorial Cholsamaj.

Sassen, Saskia. 2000. Spatialities and Temporalities of the Global: Elements for a Theorization. *Public Culture* 12, no. 1: 215–32.

Sayer, Andrew. 2004. Moral Economy. Working Paper of the Department of Sociology, Lancaster University. http://www.comp.lancs.ac.uk/sociology/papers/sayer-moral-economy.pdf.

Scheper-Hughes, Nancy. 1992. *Death without Weeping: The Violence of Everyday Life in Brazil.* Berkeley: University of California Press.

———. 1995. The Primacy of the Ethical: Propositions for a Militant Anthropology. *Current Anthropology* 36, no. 3: 409–40.

Scott, James C. 1985. *Weapons of the Weak: Everyday Forms of Peasant Resistance.* New Haven, CT: Yale University Press.

———. 1990. *Domination and the Arts of Resistance: Hidden Transcripts.* New Haven, CT: Yale University Press.

Shapiro, Michael J., and Hayward R. Alker, eds. 1995. *Challenging Boundaries: Global Flows, Territorial Identities.* Minneapolis: University of Minnesota Press.

Sieder, Rachel, and Jessica Witchell. 2001. Advancing Indigenous Claims through the Law: Reflections on the Guatemalan Peace Process. In *Culture and Rights: Anthropological Perspectives,* ed. Jane Cowan, Marie-Bénédicte Dembour, and Richard A. Wilson, 201–25. Cambridge: Cambridge University Press.

Smith, Adam. 1976 [1776]. *An Inquiry into the Nature and Causes of the Wealth of Nations.* Oxford: Clarendon Press.

Smith, Carol A. 1978. Beyond Dependency Theory: National and Regional Patterns of Underdevelopment in Guatemala. *American Ethnologist* 5: 574–617.

———. 1984. Local History in Global Context: Social and Economic Transformations in Western Guatemala. *Comparative Studies in Society and History* 26, no. 22: 193–228.

Smith, Timothy J. 2002. Skipping Years and Scribal Errors: Kaqchikel Maya Timekeeping in the Fifteenth, Sixteenth, and Seventeenth Centuries. *Ancient Mesoamerica* 13, no. 1: 65–76.

Smith, Vernon L. 1999. *Bargaining and Market Behavior: Essays in Experimental Economics*. New York: Cambridge University Press.

Smyth, Frank. 1993. A New Kingdom of Cocaine: Colombian Cartels in Guatemala. *Washington Post*, 26 December 1993.

Soper, Kate. 1981. *On Human Needs: Open and Closed Theories in Marxist Perspectives*. Bighton, UK: Harvester Press.

———. 1993. A Theory of Human Need. *New Left Review*, no. 197: 113–28.

Der Spiegel. 2005. Frust statt Lust. *Der Spiegel*, 20 June 2005: 70–82.

Spivak, Gayatri. 1974. Introduction to *Of Grammatology*, by Jacques Derrida. Baltimore: Johns Hopkins University Press.

———. 1987. Speculations on Reading Marx: After Reading Derrida. In *Poststructuralism and the Question of History*, ed. D. Attridge et al., 30–62. New York: Cambridge University Press.

———. 1999. *A Critique of Postcolonial Reason: Toward a History of the Vanishing Present*. Cambridge, MA: Harvard University Press.

Stephen, Lynn. 2002. *Zapata Lives! Histories and Cultural Politics in Southern Mexico*. Berkeley: University of California Press.

Stewart, Kathleen. 1988. Nostalgia — A Polemic. *Cultural Anthropology* 3, no. 3: 227–41.

———. 2000. Real American Dreams (Can Be Nightmares). In *Cultural Studies and Political Theory*, ed. Jodi Dean, 243–57. Ithaca, NY: Cornell University Press.

Stoler, Ann Laura. 1995. *Race and the Education of Desire: Foucault's History of Sexuality and the Colonial Order of Things*. Durham, NC: Duke University Press.

Stoll, David. 1993. *Between Two Armies in the Ixil Towns of Guatemala*. New York: Columbia University Press.

———. 1999. *Rigoberta Menchú and the Story of All Poor Guatemalans*. Boulder, CO: Westview Press.

Taussig, Michael. 1987. *Shamanism, Colonialism, and the Wild Man: A Study in Terror and Healing*. Chicago: University of Chicago Press.

———. 2003. *Law in a Lawless Land: Diary of a Limpieza*. New York: The New Press.

Thompson, Charles D., Jr., and Melinda F. Wiggins, eds. 2002. *The Human Cost of Food: Farmworkers' Lives, Labor, and Advocacy*. Austin: University of Texas Press.

Thrupp, Lori Ann, with Gilles Bergeron and William F. Waters. 1995. *Bittersweet Harvests for Global Supermarkets: Challenges in Latin America's Agricultural Export Boom*. Washington, DC: World Resources Institute.

Tomlinson, John. 1999. *Globalization and Culture*. Chicago: University of Chicago Press.

Trouillot, Michel-Rolph. 2001. The Anthropology of the State in the Age of Globalization: Close Encounters of the Deceptive Kind. *Current Anthropology* 42, no. 1: 125–38.

———. 2003. *Global Transformations: Anthropology and the Modern World*. New York: Palgrave.

Tsing, Anna. 2000a. Inside the Economy of Appearances. *Public Culture* 12, no. 1: 115–44.

———. 2000b. The Global Situation. *Cultural Anthropology* 15, no. 3: 327–60.

———. 2005. *Friction: An Ethnography of Global Connection*. Princeton, NJ: Princeton University Press.

Turner, Terence. 2002. Shifting the Frame from Nation-State to Global Market: Class and Social Consciousness in the Advanced Capitalist Countries. *Social Analysis* 46, no. 2: 56–82.

Ulmer, Gregory L. 1983. The Object of Post-Criticism. In *The Anti-Aesthetic: Essays on Postmodern Culture*, ed. Hal Foster, 93–126. New York: The New Press.

Von Braun, Joachim, David Hotchkiss, and Maarten Immink. 1989. Nontraditional Export Crops in Guatemala: Effects on Production, Income, and Nutrition. International Food Policy Research Institute Research Report 73. Washington, DC: International Food Policy Research Institute.

Wall, Thomas Carl. 1999. *Radical Passivity: Levinas, Blanchot, and Agamben*. Albany: State University of New York Press.

Wallerstein, Immanuel. 1974. *The Modern World System: Capitalist Agriculture and the Origins of the European World Economy in the Sixteenth Century*. New York: Academic Press.

Warner, Michael. 2002. Publics and Counterpublics. *Public Culture* 14, no. 1: 49–90.

Warren, Kay B. 1998. *Indigenous Movements and Their Critics: Pan-Maya Activism in Guatemala*. Princeton, NJ: Princeton University Press.

———. 2003. Voting against Indigenous Rights in Guatemala: Lessons from the 1999 Referendum. In *Indigenous Movements, Self-Representation, and the State in Latin America*, ed. Kay B. Warren and Jean E. Jackson. Austin: University of Texas Press.

Warren, Kay B., and Jean E. Jackson, eds. 2003. *Indigenous Movements, Self-Representation, and the State in Latin America*. Austin: University of Texas Press.

Watanabe, John, and Edward F. Fischer, eds. 2004. *Pluralizing Ethnography: Comparison and Representation in Maya Cultures, Histories, and Identities*. Santa Fe, NM: School of American Research Press.

Watts, Michael J. 1992. Living Under Contract: Work, Production, Politics, and the Manufacture of Discontent in a Peasant Society. In *Reworking Modernity: Capitalism and Symbolic Discontent*, ed. Allan Pred and Michael J. Watts, 65–105. New Brunswick, NJ: Rutgers University Press.

Watts, Michael J., and David Goodman. 1997. Agrarian Questions: Global Appetite, Local Metabolism: Nature, Culture, and Industry in Fin-de-Siécle Agro-Food Systems. In *Globalizing Food: Agrarian Questions and Global Restructuring*, ed. David Goodman and Michael J. Watts, 1–31. New York: Routledge.

Wells, Miriam J. 1996. *Strawberry Fields: Politics, Class, and Work in California Agriculture*. Ithaca, NY: Cornell University Press.

Weiss, Brad. 1996. Coffee Breaks and Coffee Connections: The Lived Experience of a Commodity in Tanzania and European Worlds. In *Cross-cultural Consumption: Global Markets, Local Realities*, ed. David Howes, 93–105. New York: Routledge.

Williams, Raymond. 1977. *Marxism and Literature*. Oxford: Oxford University Press.

Willis, Paul E. 1977. *Learning to Labour: How Working Class Kids Get Working Class Jobs*. London: Saxon House.

Willis, Paul, and Mats Trondman. 2000. Manifesto for Ethnography. *Ethnography* 1, no. 1: 5–16.

Wolf, Eric. 1982. *Europe and the People Without History*. Berkeley: University of California Press.

Wright, Melissa W. 1997. Crossing the Factory Frontier: Gender, Place, and Power in a Mexican Maquiladora. *Antipode* 29, no. 3: 278–302.

———. 1998. Maquiladora Mestizas and Feminist Border Politics: Revisiting Anzaldúa. *Hypatia* 13, no. 3: 114–31.

———. 2001. Desire and the Prosthetics of Supervision: A Case of Maquiladora Flexibility. *Cultural Anthropology* 16, no. 3: 354–73.

Žižek, Slavoj. 1989. *The Sublime Object of Ideology*. London: Verso.

———. 1993. *Tarrying with the Negative: Kant, Hegel, and the Critique of Ideology*. Durham, NC: Duke University Press.

———. 1999. *The Ticklish Subject: The Absent Centre of Political Ontology*. London: Verso.

———. 2000a. *The Fragile Absolute — Or, Why is the Christian Legacy Worth Fighting For?* London: Verso.

———. 2000b. Class Struggle or Postmodernism? Yes, Please! In *Contingency, Hegemony, Universality: Contemporary Dialogues on the Left*, ed. Judith Butler, Ernesto Laclau, and Slavoj Žižek, 90–235. London: Verso.

———. 2003a. *The Puppet and the Dwarf: The Perverse Core of Christianity*. Cambridge, MA: MIT Press.

———. 2003b. *Organs without Bodies: On Deleuze and Consequences*. London: Routledge.

Index

Acknowledgments

Writing this book was a collaborative endeavor through and through — a collaboration between the two authors as well as with the many people who opened their lives to us in the course of fieldwork. It was often awkward for us to ask farmers to drop their work to come speak into a tape recorder about the price of broccoli and their prospects for the future. But they did, often grateful to have a sympathetic ear. In this book we report on what they told us, trying to be true to their intentions while also placing their concerns into a broader theoretical context. Our goal is not to out-theorize the natives. Quite the contrary, we use their perspectives to critique a number of common assumptions and well-intentioned biases of social theory. We could not have written this book without their collaboration.

Special thanks for aiding our fieldwork and deepening our understanding of the social dynamics in Tecpán go to Pakal B'alam, Ixchel Carmelina Espantzay, Serapio Ordóñez, Marvin Tecún Cuxil, Paola Lux Sacabaj, and Cristóbal Cojtí. In addition, Linda Asturias de Barrios, Avery Dickins, Alberto Esquit, Sally Hamilton, Carol Hendrickson, and Christopher Jones helped formulate and execute key aspects of this research. Participants in Fischer's Fall 2001 graduate seminar on ethnography (especially Avery Dickins, Nathan Goates, Peter Redvers-Lee, Erin Slinker, and Brent Woodfill) aided data collection in Nashville.

A number of people read previous iterations of parts of this book and made helpful comments. They include Omar al-Dewachi, Ann Anagnost, Joon Choi, Demetrio Cojtí, Kingsley Garbett, Angela Garcia, Clara Han, Bill Jankowiak, Bruce Knauft, Arthur Kleinman, Víctor Montejo, Judie Maxwell, Carlota McAlister, June Nash, Diane Nelson, Nancy Postero, Joanne Rappaport, Matthew Restall, Jan Rus, Mareike Sattler, Tim Smith, Noelle Stout, Kedron Thomas, Kay Warren, James Watson, and Leon Zamosc. We also thank Chris Ahlin, Dan Cornfield, James Foster, Douglas Meeks, and the other members of the Working Group on Religion and Economy at Vanderbilt's Center for the Study of Religion and Culture for providing a critical reading of the first two chapters that pushed us to clarify and reframe our argument. Earlier versions of sections of Chapters 2 and 5 were previously published in *Anthropological Quarterly* and *Social Analysis*; thanks to the reviewers and editors for their comments. Arthur Demarest shared with us the finer points of late-night broccoli selection at Kroger. Huicho Luin drew the map of the study area, and Carol Hendrickson took the photo that introduces Part II.

Kate Wahl of Stanford University Press provided key encouragement and constructive criticism as we revised the manuscript; Kirsten Oster and Anna Eberhard Friedlander at SUP, and Laurie Palmer at Vanderbilt helped bring it all together; and Ruth Steinberg's sharp eye clarified our prose and corrected our grammar. Benson's work was supported by the Graduate Society and David Rockefeller Center for Latin American Studies at Harvard. Funding for Fischer's fieldwork came from the John D. and Catherine T. MacArthur Foundation Program on Global Security and Sustainability and the Vanderbilt University Research Council; the final stage of writing and revision was supported by the Alexander von Humboldt Foundation.